"This book is a very helpful and accessible account of the processes involved in group therapy.

Gerry's warmth and humour, as well as his therapeutic understanding and long experience of leading groups, make this book a very useful addition to the appreciation of the benefits of group therapy."

Judith Barford

"*Therapeutic Love and Heartfullness* by Gerry McNeilly is a fantastic book, essential for any psychotherapist, regardless of their foundational training, whether or not they are connected to Art Therapy. Drawing on Gerry's connection with Group Analysis, the book addresses essential concepts related to the specificities of communication and emerging phenomenology in group, individual and creative (art therapy) contexts. In an eloquent and courageous manner, Gerry McNeilly explores the therapist's affectionateness as a participating agent in the therapeutic relational process. Innovatively, he introduces the concept of Therapeutic Love and its contribution to the heartfullness of the psychotherapeutic experience, particularly in the context of artistic creation."

Ruy Carvalho, *doctor, art psychotherapist,*
founder and president, Board of the Portuguese
Society of Art Therapy (SPAT)

I0131052

Therapeutic Love and Heartfullness

This book introduces the concepts of 'therapeutic love' and 'heartfullness,' combining models of group analysis, art therapy and individual psychotherapy to present a new psychotherapeutic framework where non-erotic love is engendered and evoked within therapeutic encounters.

The heart has often been conceptualised as symbolic of sexuality and eroticism, with little meaning beyond the romantic, and therefore often removed from psychotherapeutic perspectives. Responding to this, the author calls for placing the heart as the central point of reference in therapeutic work, emphasising how it is touched during a therapeutic session. This, in turn, gives way for the therapist's own emotions and thoughts, such as empathy, identification, concern, protectiveness and laughter, to be released.

Building upon the author's 40 years of experience in practice and new developments in these models, this book 'meanders' through evolving theories and integrates them for both patients and trainees across backgrounds and cultures. Enriched with the author's personal clinical vignettes and unique influences of music, art, golf and even Ireland, this book aims to give a greater voice to the patient – and their heart – within the therapeutic space.

This book is essential reading for any counsellor, therapist or analyst and offers a new way of looking at therapeutic endeavours across methodologies in all their simplicities and complexities.

Gerry McNeilly is a trained specialist in art therapy, psychotherapy and group analysis. Following art therapy training in 1976, he was the principal art therapist at the Ingrebourne Centre and 'Full Member' of the Institute of Group Analysis from 1987. He established and directed a psychotherapy and counselling service in Bromsgrove, England and was the principal adult psychotherapist in Warwickshire from 1995 to 2011. He is an active member of the teaching body of the Portuguese Society of Art Therapy and also the originator of Group Analytic Art Therapy. Although now retired, he still undertakes some lecturing and academic involvement.

Therapeutic Love and Heartfullness

Meanderings Through Group Analysis, Group Analytic Art Therapy and Individual Therapy

Gerry McNeilly

Routledge
Taylor & Francis Group

LONDON AND NEW YORK

Designed cover image: © Valerie Armstrong

First published 2025
by Routledge
4 Park Square, Milton Park, Abingdon, Oxon OX14 4RN

and by Routledge
605 Third Avenue, New York, NY 10158

Routledge is an imprint of the Taylor & Francis Group, an informa business

© 2025 Gerry McNeilly

The right of Gerry McNeilly to be identified as author of this work
has been asserted in accordance with sections 77 and 78 of the
Copyright, Designs and Patents Act 1988.

Trademark notice: Product or corporate names may be trademarks
or registered trademarks, and are used only for identification and
explanation without intent to infringe.

British Library Cataloguing-in-Publication Data
A catalogue record for this book is available from the British Library

ISBN: 9781032882413 (hbk)
ISBN: 9781032881935 (pbk)
ISBN: 9781003536857 (ebk)

DOI: 10.4324/9781003536857

Typeset in Times New Roman
by codeMantra

Dr Malcolm Pines 1925–2021 whose brilliance, kindness and generosity of heart and spirit shone through his humility.

Your memory lives on in what you taught me and others.

Also

Patrick McGrath who left us in 2022. A dear friend and colleague. We steered the analytic waves together.

Contents

PART 2
The Gap   181

Acknowledgements

First and foremost my thanks to Keely Beresford for typing the manuscript and administrative assistance. It would not have happened without her. Valerie Armstrong for the front cover painting. Pat McAllister, Keely, Jean and Roger Beresford for image productions and support. For help and advice in their critiques: Professor Diane Waller, who kindly wrote the Foreword and contributed greatly. Judy Barford for reading the drafts and her endorsement, Dr Tom Harrison, Dr Ruy de Carvalho and the Sociedade de Arte Terapia, Dr Chris Mace, sadly deceased, who left an indelible mark on my career and development, Adam Porter for computer assistance, Dr Gavin Miller, Dr Rollin McCraty and the HeartMath Institute, California, USA and not least the many colleagues, patients and students who have advertently and inadvertently contributed to the making of this book.

Foreword from Professor Diane Waller O.B.E, Emeritus Professor of Art Psychotherapy, Goldsmiths, University of London 2023

Gerry McNeilly, dear friend and colleague for over 40 years, has provided a welcome addition to the still rather sparse literature on art therapy and group work. He opens his first chapter with the following: "Love the greatest force we have, the thing that will mend us all in the end," which gives a hint of the style of writing that we will find in the book, perhaps more philosophical and reflective than we are used to from him.

When he asked me to write a Foreword for this new book, we were all living in a pre-pandemic world, one where the term 'Brexit' was not yet a reality, where there was no war between Russia and Ukraine (though plenty of others far away from Europe) and where the current inflationary cost-of-living crisis in the UK had yet to be imagined. The UK was half-way through a long period of Conservative government. The term 'Austerity' was very familiar, especially to those of us working in the National Health and Social Services, where we experienced at first hand the impact of cuts on health and wellbeing. At this point, Gerry (wisely if like me you regret 'Brexit') had retired and moved to the Republic of Ireland and begun to craft this latest book.

Gerry, in the same way as all UK art therapists of a certain age, will have experienced the struggle, or let's say, challenge of starting his professional life as a member of an ad hoc arts provision in the NHS to becoming a registrant of a statutory regulated profession (1997) alongside 15 others that now make up the Health and Care Professions Council. In the early days of art therapy training, Gerry was taught by pioneer Edward Adamson, whose innovative practice at Netherne Psychiatric Hospital in Surrey inspired many future art therapists. Later, in common with Gerry, a group of us art therapists decided to take seriously our interest in group work that had been sparked by involvement in the therapeutic communities movement (and to some extent by the 1960s and 1970s Encounter movements in the USA) and started training as group analytic psychotherapists. We gradually brought the theories of art therapy/art psychotherapy together with those of group psychotherapy, identifying with either or both at the same time. We established our place as practitioners, workshop leaders and supervisors and later wrote some papers and books about the way we had merged these disciplines to offer a new contribution to the raft of psychological therapies available to the public and to students training as art therapists.

During the late 1970s and early 1980s, Goldsmiths art therapy students could attend a weekly verbal group at the NHS's Paddington Centre for Psychotherapy where I worked part-time. Art therapy workshops at Goldsmiths were then mainly theme-centred and some were focused on interaction through visual art processes. Gradually we sought to integrate insights from group dynamics into art therapy workshop practice and Gerry played an important role in this and in our team discussions for some years until he moved to the Midlands. Our discussions often centred around the role of the art work, the role of the therapist and the role of talking within the group process.

Gerry's move to the Midlands enabled him to practice primarily in the NHS and Social Services, with a very wide range of patients and in a multi-disciplinary team. In this context, both group and individual therapy were required. We know that group therapy is more than individual therapy in a group (or in the group analytic framework it should be) but we would claim, counter to what is often suggested, that group therapists can practise individual therapy as, following the theories of N. Elias, sociologist who worked alongside S.H. Foulkes at the Frankfurt School, we all exist and interact in a group whether actual or virtual, present or past, with known or unknown persons, and this impacts on how we live and behave in the 'here and now.' Both group psychotherapy and individual therapy offer something specific to a patient that is appropriate at different times in their lives. In Gerry's book, we are privileged to learn about how he used both in the interests of his patients. Neither individual nor group psychotherapy are 'quick fixes' and have suffered from the misconception that severe, long-standing mental health problems can be swiftly remediated. These therapies require commitment, often long term, from both therapist and patient. Fortunately, he found a centre where this important fact was understood.

The discussions about the links between image-making and talking in groups that combined art therapy with dynamic group psychotherapy continued and questions such as timing for both were re-examined through copious examples in several publications in the 1980s and 1990s. For example, Waller's *Group Interactive Art Therapy* (1992), Skaife and Huet's *Art Psychotherapy Groups* (1998) and McNeilly's *Group Analytic Art Therapy* (2006) preceded by papers in professional journals. Other colleagues had published books and papers demonstrating how Theme Centred Interaction combined with art therapy could be used in groups. Marian Liebmann's *Art Therapy for Groups* (1986) had initially explored an extensive range of themes and exercises that could be used in groups and in 2004 her 2nd edition elaborated on these and also discussed the range of models then being used in art therapy groups, elaborating on how a theme-based group could be used in a diverse range of situations in the UK and abroad. Attention was paid to issues such as class, race, culture, ability, gender – demonstrating the remarkable social-cultural changes that had occurred since the 1980s and were now being addressed, and had become central to many art therapists in their practice and publications. *Inscape Journal* of the 1990s featured many lively discussions and disagreements about the merits or otherwise of analytic and theme centred groups!

Other colleagues focused on the Studio as a group – open sessions where making art within the confines of a studio took precedence over the study of group dynamics, and where the individual was free to pursue their own art work with attention from the facilitator. However, despite this approach being consistently practised from the 1940s onwards, the first published book in the UK on Studio art therapy came only in 2022. Christopher Brown and Helen Omand edited *Contemporary Practice in Studio Art Therapy*, tracing the emergence of the Studio back to the early days of art therapy in the old psychiatric hospitals, up to the present. The large studios of Victorian psychiatric hospitals had often acted as a refuge, or an oasis in an impersonal, corridor-dominated building, where outstanding art work could be found produced by people on whom 'society' had long given up. These studios were much lamented by art therapists, who, whilst welcoming the closure of the old hospitals, regretted the inferior spaces that were usually assigned to art therapy in the substituted day centres or general hospitals. We could see how important it had been to have dedicated spaces where experimental art work could be made and left from one day or week till the next. Sometimes running art therapy groups abroad, where some of the old hospitals still existed, gave a reminder of how much more adventurous a group could be as far as image-making and interaction is concerned when a space was available, or could be converted to be used for several days, weeks or even years at a time.

In 2003, Cathy Moon published *Studio Art Therapy* and looked at the studio as a place for establishing community solidarity, somewhere where diverse populations could gather and feel supported. Here we see connexions between art therapy and community arts, and a return to art therapy's more radical roots. On a visit to Derry in Northern Ireland in 2002, and to East Belfast around the same time, I gained a very strong impression of the importance of art-making in a political context through the presence of huge, striking and disturbing murals that spoke of the 30 years of the Troubles, a tragic, traumatic time which still reverberates across that country and abroad. Gerry, as an Irishman, cannot but be affected by that history, and indeed the earlier history and culture of Ireland, and his experience carries into the way in which he runs his groups and relates to individuals.

The importance of the Open Studio model was referred to in several publications by US writers, for example, in 2022, Megan Robb in *Group Art Therapy: Practice and Research*. Robb pulled together and discussed a number of art therapy group models being currently practised, together with their theoretical perspectives. We can see that over time the movement towards integrating approaches to group art therapy has evolved and become more flexible but with practitioners possessing a deep knowledge and understanding to begin with of the models to be integrated.

Being able to develop ideas in different socio-cultural contexts has been a most valuable experience for many art therapists, including myself. For Gerry, from the 1990s, Portugal gave him the chance to work with and help in the development of training with like-minded Portuguese pioneer art therapists and group analysts. For both parties, this has been a mutually very rewarding experience. As I see it, his regular contact with Portugal enabled him to continue to explore his ideas, away from the UK and with this friendly but serious group, passionate about the development of art therapy and group analysis and eager to share ideas with others through training, meetings and conferences. I can identify with the importance of working in a very different environment, with different cultural understandings and in another language. It gives a chance to look at your practise with another lens, and to incorporate some of unfamiliar ways of doing things, and that can give a feeling of freedom. Or it can do the opposite and cause a retreat into a rigid, culture-bound way of behaving. For Gerry, he found an opportunity to 'meander' and to expand creatively on his developing theories.

In his earlier book, *Group Analytic Art Therapy*, in a section entitled 'Portuguese Papers' we find some intriguing material about Eduardo Cortesao who studied with S.H. Foulkes and was a pioneer of group analysis in Portugal.

In this section on Portugal, Gerry explores the concept of 'resonance' linking it to intuition and wisdom. Chapter 11 is entitled 'The Matrix,' the pattern and the fullness of emptiness. He describes this chapter as 'rather ambitious,' and it is, but it is where I feel he has freed himself up and given himself permission to launch out with some challenging ideas, perhaps the start of the formation of 'Heartfullness' – and hence to his current book. Gerry acknowledges the importance to the development of his ideas with Ruy Carvalho, pioneer and founder of the Portuguese Art Therapy Association. So, what was it about working there, in Lisbon, in that particular socio-cultural environment that excited him? What was it about Ruy Carvalho's and Eduardo Cortesau's contribution ... was there a sense of 'Portuguese-ness' in their thinking? What was so special about running groups in Portugal and how was this different from the UK? At that point, Gerry was still staying close to Foulkesian group analytic theory and his own development of it but over these 20 years, till the writing of his current book, he has given himself permission to 'meander' among the very powerful influences in his professional and personal journey. Portugal, it seems to me is definitely a major one.

Gerry's book gives us a rare opportunity to share in the journey of a long-standing committed, pioneer art therapist/group analytic art therapist. We go from a place where theory has dominated to a position where, without abandoning theory, indeed by incorporating useful theory, he can practise more freely. He feels secure enough to let us know that 'Heartfullness' is where he defines his work. He spells this deliberately with two 'll's to emphasize that this means the fullness of the heart, as when emotions emerge in therapy the heart is either filling or emptying. Alongside this important concept goes 'Therapeutic Love' defined as a framework containing and channelling both the patient's and therapist's world of emotions beyond established psychotherapeutic concepts and terms. The term 'Meanderings' implies a freer way of moving between the three approaches discussed in the book (group analysis, art therapy, individual therapy) moving between the past and present and in no specific time as well. To me this beautifully describes the processes that we can go through when confident enough in our framework, our theoretical base, to allow ourselves to enter the patient's world unencumbered by rights and wrong ways to relate – something that as trainees we are often hampered by.

The rigidity imposed by some aspects of psychotherapeutic training, by strict adherence to modalities, gives a coherence to practice but can also be limiting. There is creativity involved in synthesizing different but compatible modalities delivered within a strong ethical framework. Although as Gerry says, the new formulations on therapeutic love that he addresses in his book cannot be ascribed the governmental accolade of 'evidence-based practice,' he aims to show their validity. The absence of a formal recognition does not negate this. There is now increased recognition from national bodies for Research through practice and practice-based Research (see Smith and Dean) especially in the arts and this is to be welcomed as a move away from seeing the Random Control Trial and other positivist methods as the only acceptable research in the psychological therapies, including art therapy.

Thinking about the creativity evidenced in this book, in the way that Gerry has moved away from the earlier rigid adherence to the 'rules' but maintaining at all times a strict ethical code, I recalled a quote from his earlier book, still clearly applicable now:

> I thought, what do I love about group analytic art therapy and verbal group analysis? The love for one's work is extremely important. Can it be love when a group struggles through pain and suffering or negative transference towards me? I think so, as I believe that content, process and structure elements are part of a process leading people to change and a greater love of their own life. On another level, I experience being a group analyst and psychotherapist one of the most lonely and isolating experiences, and at such times, I haven't a clue as to what is content and which is process – it's just awful. To love as a therapist means a readiness to immerse oneself in the overall experience of the therapeutic endeavour.

And now in this book: The Heart is the central point of reference on which everything else is laid upon. By this I mean that increasingly in my clinical work and theoretical endeavours, key moments emerged which created physical sensations of movement in my heart, that is, being activated through empathy, sorrow and joy. At these times, language, theory and analytic interpretation were not as dominant.

How inspiring are these quotes! Thank you Gerry for this honest, indeed 'heart-warming' story. We are very fortunate to be able to share in it.

Bibliography

Brown, C and Omand, H (2022) *Contemporary Practice in Studio Art Therapy*. Routledge, Abingdon, Oxon.

Elias, N (1978) *What Is Sociology?* Columbia University Press, New York.

Foulkes, S (1975) *Group Analytic Psychotherapy: Methods and Principles*. Gordon & Breach, London.

Liebmann, M (2004) *Art Therapy for Groups: A Handbook of Themes and Exercises* (2nd Edition) Brunner-Routledge, Hove, Sussex.

McNeilly, G (1984) Group Analytic Art Therapy. In *Group Analysis*, 17, 3, 204–210.

McNeilly, G (2006) *Group Analytic Art Therapy*. Jessica Kingsley, London.

Moon, C (2003) *Studio Art Therapy*. Jessica Kingsley, London.

Robb, MA (2022) *Group Art Therapy: Practice and Research*. Routledge, London.

Skaife, S and Huet, V (1998) *Art Psychotherapy Groups*. Routledge, London.

Smith, H and Dean, R (2009) *Practice-led Research, Research-led Practice in the Creative Arts*. Edinburgh University Press, Edinburgh, Scotland.

Waller, D (2015) *Group Interactive Art Therapy: Its Use in Training and Treatment* (2nd Edition). Routledge, Hove, Sussex.

Part 1

Introduction

Previously, in my work settings, there was more concern and focus upon describing and accounting what happened in therapy through evidence based practice, formal note taking and lesser concern with the patient's narrative during therapy. I had often been pressed to move away from building my theories and practice with the dominance of joint therapeutic narrative with patients. I believed in the importance of joint narrative. This book is about the personal dimensions of therapeutic encounters.

The term 'therapeutic love' may well conjure up both curious interest on one hand while on the other, varying levels of repulsion. In respect to the former, like the process of 'falling in love' it draws the reader in. With the latter, the term may give rise to an inference of erotic/sexualised love developing in the psychotherapeutic setting. Although this does happen in clinical settings, I will not focus upon these erotic areas specifically.

Since I retired from my psychotherapeutic practice in 2011, I have been contemplating a fuller elaboration of therapeutic love. As my professional development over a 40-year period embraced art therapy, group analysis and individual psychotherapy, I felt that I wanted to explore such a concept as 'therapeutic love' as it emerged in all of these areas. Probably it is only in the past few years that I reached a point where I felt secure enough to tackle such a project as I was no longer constricted with the many psychotherapy principles and theories, which had been important to uphold in the past. In some ways I had become freer to see things in a new light.

There are particular terms which have been used in psychotherapy and allied professions: therapeutic alliance, attachment, bonding, empathy to name a few. Increasingly in my closing years of practice, the importance of the relationship between therapist and patient was given more emphasis. These perspectives/theories either shied away or made little or no reference to love in the therapeutic setting. Certainly, a great deal has been written about the patient falling in love with the analyst/therapist, and vice versa, and the dangers of this. Hence, a great proportion of the literature condemns love to the netherlands of tragedy.

I am not denying the dangers of eroticised love, as described in conventional 'transference constellations.'[1] My aim is to raise the profile of many other emotions and transactions between the patient and the therapist; within groups, which constitute a loving experience in such settings. Some of these are care and attention;

DOI: 10.4324/9781003536857-1

empathic concern; tenderness and gentleness; and the willingness to receive things from the patient with a good heart as compared to non-acceptance and interpretation. Also, the willingness to experience fully deep and difficult times in sessions without recourse to interpretations; the use of humour and the promotion of play; the place of creating warmth within the setting; personal disclosure by the therapist, and to what degree; and the process of learning from the patient.

All of the above are ingredients of 'Therapeutic Love.'

When I reflect on my psychotherapeutic trainings much rested upon respected analytic theories and their application. In reading some of my earlier notes I could see that I was reasonably efficient in what I was doing and I think that there was a great deal of benefit to my patients and groups. However, reading between the lines and thinking again, I believe that the key areas of development and change rested with one or more of the ingredients specified above. Certainly, in those earlier years, I maintained the tried and tested cerebral approach and the notion of love in the setting was an anathema to me. In one of my earlier (unpublished) papers I said: "If you want your patient to love you, you should ask for your P45!"[2] At that time I could only see love in the therapeutic setting as sexualised/eroticised. Hopefully, this new position is healthier and devoid of such earlier arrogance.

Although I will speak of existing literature in more detail, predominantly in Chapter 4, I was drawn to a small book by J.-B. Pontalis (co-author of 'The Language of Psychoanalysis'), which filled me with great hope and conviction that I am not alone in my views.

> Being fond of one's patients: a necessary condition for me. I really see how one might retort: wouldn't it be a kind of payback, a way of assuring myself that they are fond of me? Doesn't matter: I can't imagine how I could consecrate so much time, so much attention to them, devote such a large part of my life listening to them – "Being fond of one's patients: a necessary condition for them to regain their taste for life" – "Being fond of one's patients – not too much, as if the too much were evil, a destructive love for self as for other."
>
> (Pontalis, 2003, pp. 79–80)

As yet I have said nothing about the word 'Meandering' taken from the sub-heading of the book title. Some years ago a patient said to me: "I'm rambling," which is a term for talking without a great deal of thought, she felt, that she was wasting my time with meaningless utterances. As rambling is a free walk, it is also seen as a healthy hobby. To her surprise I said: "What's wrong with that, it's a good walk with your mouth." Possibly there are similarities with 'free association' as a form of rambling.

Although the following chapters will have a general direction, I shall meander through the fields of the three professions stated in the book's subtitle.

There are four major influences underpinning the book

1   Golf Parallels – The game of golf offers so much material to compare with in order to provide mental imagery. The book is about the heart and love that are

essential in golf. When playing golf, it has provided a space for me to think through, both clinical and theoretical, challenges and forget about them, that is, if my work was extremely demanding it allowed relief; pleasure in the face of professional pressure; and it became a seminar room in between shots when I played with colleagues.

2 Musical Influences – Regarding the musical references the fact of being a musician has contributed greatly, not only in the early days, when I would use it as an adjunct to the sessions and other activities, but also in how the composite elements of music are similar to therapy. One only has to think about rhythm, timing, beat (heart), volume, silence, conductor (S.H. Foulkes' term for the group analyst) and musical colour. These, and more, are present in all therapeutic endeavours.

3 Non-psychotherapeutic references in literature – I have drawn upon a wide range of non-academic literature in order to give contrast and substance to the more conventional psychotherapy literature. This is because novelists and poets often get more to the point and use language which emanates from the heart.

4 Being Irish – What do I mean by this, and why is it important? Ireland has been described as the 'land of saints and scholars.' Much of the book will revolve around the elements of creativity, soul searching and intuition. The Irish are seen globally to be adventurers and travellers. On St Patrick's day (the patron saint of Ireland), it seems that the whole world wants to be Irish. On one of my teaching trips to St Petersburg, Russia, it was during St Patrick's day celebrations and there were many thousands in the parade, much to my surprise that it was happening in Russia. Being Irish is as much a part of my professional identity as any other psychotherapeutic part in ways that I both know and do not. There are some specific points of reference in the book but is at times expressed more subtly. Of course, I am not saying being Irish is so special or different to other nationalities as these comments are abstract generalisations, which many Irish may or may not agree with.

In speaking about those recipients of psychotherapy, I have used the singular description of 'patient,' which is used in the National Health Service. The term 'client' applies to those within Social Services. I prefer the term patient as it links to the word patience (not only for the patient but myself as well). Whereas, 'client' is more related to providing a buying and selling arrangement. Therefore, I have made use of the term patient for all, apart from students and trainees.

Notes

1 A term I coined to unite transference and countertransference as a circular concept, rather than a linear one, moving from one pole to the other.
2 P45 is a tax document at the end of employment in the UK.

Chapter 1

Setting the Scene

Love the greatest force we have, the thing that will mend us all in the end.

(Fry, 2013)

The heart is the central point of reference on which everything else is laid upon. By this I mean that increasingly in my clinical work and theoretical endeavours, key moments emerged which created physical sensations of movement in my heart, that is, being activated through empathy, sorrow and joy. It is not only about being touched through shared pain, sorrow and anger, but also through warmth, joy, pleasure and humour, as some of many emotions. At these times language, theory and analytic interpretations were not as dominant. A baseline is that when such emotions are evoked it forms an actual bond between the therapist and patient which I have defined as a form of love. It is a non-erotic form of love. Regarding the main title: 'Therapeutic Love,' the simplest way of defining this is that it is a 'framework' that contains and channels both the patient and the therapist's world of emotions, moving beyond established psychotherapeutic language and methods understandings which relies more upon thinking, cognition, translating, interpreting. Defining therapeutic love as a framework is similar to describing a marriage as a framework which enables love to be one of its currencies.

I employ the term 'Heartfullness' purposefully spelt in this way as it emphasises 'fullness of the heart.' Therefore, when emotions emerge in therapy the heart is activated, either filling or emptying. The term 'Meanderings' is intended to imply a freer way of moving between the three methods (group analysis, art therapy and individual therapy) of working, as well as moving in between past and present over a 40-year period. It is also about wandering in and out of influences of one discipline to the other and aspects of integration.

Although a number of years have passed since my retirement, I know that the British National Health Service still places a strong emphasis on 'evidence-based practice' and the guiding principles are established through the 'National Institute for Clinical Excellence.' This 'Body' ensures that there are building blocks in place, which requires clinicians to provide proven, sound and safe practices. Throughout my career I have maintained these standards through my training and practice in art

DOI: 10.4324/9781003536857-2

therapy, psychotherapy and group analysis.[1] Such trainings and their developments into employment environs are governmentally evaluated and approved. Within this array of psychological interventions, psychodynamic approaches seem to have had one of the more difficult rides within the 'evidence-based practice' debates. Shorter, more symptomatically focused approaches seem to have been more readily accepted. As much of psychodynamically oriented therapy tends to be longer term arrangements (ranging between six months and five years × one to two weekly sessions), the challenges for governmental acceptance are often greater. Longer term methods are generally more suitable for complex and demanding clinical conditions. Shorter interventions do not generally explore deeper strata of the personality or deeper meanings of symptomatology. Although my newer formulations on therapeutic love and heartfullness cannot be ascribed the governmental accolade of 'evidence-based practice,' I hope to show its validity. The absence of a formal recognition does not negate this.

On reflection I have asked myself: why, for the biggest part of my professional life, could I not see as clearly as I do now, matters of the heart within the context of therapy? In the early and middle years of practice such matters were overshadowed or explored under psychodynamic auspices, such as transference and counter-transference. With this particular area, one bridging concept that emerged between my old and new theories was my formulation of a new conceptual term: 'Transference Constellations.' This moved me away from the dual construct, a 'to-ing and fro-ing,' horizontal concept. A transference constellation infers a more overall, circular set of dynamics emerging at the interface between two and/or more people. By defining it as a 'constellation' I was moving away from seeing the patient projecting unconscious, unresolved conflicts onto me and my responding in one way or another, to experiencing a less guarded and intellectual method. I think that in my constellation formulations, it allowed me a greater awareness and an increased capacity of the heart to shine through. At times, of hearing my patients' painful accounts, I was more able to feel their respective emotions not only cognitively but also physically in various parts of my body. The transference constellation bridges ideas/formulations and moved it from the horizontal interactive process onto a more expansive set of elements. This new arrangement allowed me; my patients, groups, to move beyond the psychoanalytic stance of the patient transferring and the therapist counter-transferring (McNeilly, 2006b, pp. 68–90). This has been developed in more detail in this book.

Taking an early step into the theoretical world of 'Group Analysis,' S.H. Foulkes speaks of a 'Transpersonal Network' in which he conceptualises the group, in a similar way to my views on transference constellations

The group is a matrix of interpersonal relationships, and the events which occur in it are interpersonal phenomena. These relationships and these events exist literally between two or more people; they do not occur in one person or in another, but can only come into existence through the interaction of two or more people.

(Foulkes & Anthony, 1957/1984)

Foulkes, in this instance, moves away from the dyad of transference and counter-transference in individual therapy. Also, his alluding to 'events existing literally' parallels with the physical sensations which are evoked when the heart and other bodily areas are touched, thus enabling therapeutic love to be enacted and experienced. As such this then transcends such concepts as transference and counter-transference.

I believe that this has returned me to the simple appreciation of how the heart is a moving, driving force/factor in the greatest percentage of my clinical work from the beginning. Returning to Stephen Fry's beautiful statement on the power of love, the opening quote of this chapter, it echoes Joni Mitchell's lyrics when she sings about love being both strong, healthy and a poisonous medicine (Mitchell, 1976).

Fry and Mitchell come from the worlds of drama, film and music. Bearing in mind how the heart and love are central components in these genres our psychotherapeutic fields have not benefitted from its bounty in the same way. Fry's comments (Fry, 2013) were part of a television documentary about world attitudes to homosexuality. One of the themes that he kept returning to was how loving feelings in homosexuality were not being fully recognised by many. I felt likewise that love, in its most comprehensive and rich perspectives, is not given due attention in the psychotherapy world, irrespective of any particular training school.

I think that it is safe to say that authors in the therapeutic world struggle in trying to find like-minded quotes in vast bodies of literature that will give substance to their own work. Recently I came across a paper by Neville Symington on 'Generosity of Heart.' Much of what he says parallels my own views on therapeutic love and at no point does he make links with libido or the erotic. He tells us:

Love is so easily misunderstood that I prefer to break it up into component parts and talk of generosity, gratitude and forgiveness. These types are interrelated but here I will keep my focus upon generosity. When there is no generosity a great vacuum opens and into it pour delusion, hallucination and madness.

Further he says:

Generosity – implies that the emotional attitude of one affects the emotional current in another. We flow into one another. This is what emotions are: the streams that flow between two human beings.

(Symington, 2008, pp. 489–490)

And finally, a key point which will be developed throughout this book, and is in keeping with the influence of the heart in therapy:

"Pure giving is substance against which all else is nothing. Pure giving is a synonym for generosity" – "It is possible to be receptive to pure giving. It is this and only this that moves the heart, that melts stubbornness, that dilutes the madness in whose grip we find ourselves. All the theories, all the schools of psychoanalysis or psychotherapy are dust and ashes if this purity of giving is absent."

(Symington, 2008, pp. 498–499)

There is wisdom in what Symington has brought to our attention.

In a previous publication I have written about wisdom in relation to intuition, simplicity and resonance (McNeilly, 2006b, pp. 154–158), which on further thought stems from the heart. Returning to Symington these elements are "the streams that flow between two people." I would add that it is also about more than two people.

Matters of Love

Meandering through existing psychotherapeutic literature, matters of love which enter the arena are primarily set against erotic manifestations. For example: if the patient is feeling positive and understood by the therapist, this often moves into explorations on parental similes predominantly aligned to child/adult formulations. This is in contrast to such emergent processes being aligned to the loving, tender and empathic bonds being created between the patient and therapist. When we develop dialogue and other interactions in therapy, allowing joint emotions being present 'in the moment' without only applying analytical or interpretive procedures, this demands much more from the therapist and the patient. Thus, I believe that there is a vast array of other emotional life experiences being overlooked and negated in the former of these two approaches.

Gavin Miller speaks beautifully and succinctly about the 'taboo on tenderness,' originally described by Suttie in his seminal book on 'love and hate':

Although psychoanalytic theory has changed significantly in the decades since Suttie's contribution in *The Origins of Love and Hate*, his argument still holds true, *mutatis mutandis*. The Freudian model of love as aim-inhibited sexuality has receded – Tender feeling *(which I suggest can be ascribed as a collective term for many components of my formulations of de-eroticised love)*[2] is still intellectually tabooed, yet with even less rational excuse than in Suttie's time – for there is now a significant amount of empirical research on infant development that challenges psychoanalytic reductive explanations of love.

(Miller, 2007, p. 669)

As I read these views of Miller and Suttie I recalled many films which showed a male actor in the throes of responding to his female partners open statements: 'I love you' and his mute, squirming, embarrassed responses, saying something like: 'ditto.' It was as if he was facing a firing squad or being invited to walk on hot coals. Therefore, the phrase 'I love you' seems to have been cemented as a primarily feminine principle/law to which women have access and the ability to express more readily, but inhibited in men.

Before coming across the previous papers cited, as I originally began my literature search, I found only one paper on groups called: 'Therapeutic Love' primarily focusing on the sexual/erotic (Schamess, 1999), I was pleasantly surprised to find love referred to, but primarily as passing commentary and throwaway references apart from Suttie's book (Suttie, 1988), these will be addressed in Chapter 4. Within the literature many writers would emphasise emotional constructs either as standalone theories, or in conjunction, but the notion of love was not seen as a central or unifying force/factor within therapy in the way that I envisaged it. The heart did not figure in these writings. In Chapter 4 I will expand upon this area which has given more credence to my own formulations.

Historically, I was of the impression that I had started to formulate and publish my ideas on love within therapeutic settings in the late 1980s and early 1990s, some time before the emergence of the concept of 'therapeutic love.' Then I came across an earlier unpublished paper of mine from 1976 called: 'The Four Principles,' which were care, need, help, love. This paper explored these areas as if they were pillars, considering both the physical and emotional balances within the therapeutic community where I worked as an art therapist.

A number of years later in my role as a supervisor to another leading therapeutic community I wrote a paper called the 'The Common Ground,' which focused upon four pillars of their therapeutic model. The four pillars were inherent within therapeutic communities: large groups, small groups, art groups and psychodrama – being the four pillars of that therapeutic community.[3] Since developing these ideas I am convinced that I am not alone, although others may use different language to explain things, that is, empathy, compassion, identification and mirroring. Some may deny love as a factor, feeling more at home with traditional terms like transference and counter-transference. Indeed, those truly skilled in their use of transference and counter-transference will create powerful and meaningful emotional transactions with their patients without ever considering that love and the heart is at play/involved.

What Is to Come

I presented a basic description of therapeutic love and heartfullness at the opening of this chapter. Love, as a general construct, is described or defined as a simple feeling, with no need or wish to state anything further than, 'I feel it.' For others there is an elaboration of the elements that constitute it. Then again, a description is not necessarily the same as a definition. In general, a description aims at painting a picture of love and how it is experienced and expressed. On the other hand, a definition is built upon such premises but with the added intention of crystallising, capturing and providing a clear-cut meaning. In a previous unpublished paper, I attempted the task of describing and defining therapeutic love and heartfullness in more detail:

> Therapeutic love became crystalised through the development of physical sensations. What emerged with increasing regularity in my clinical work had been a movement towards 'physically feeling' such things i.e., my heart sinking in my chest; deep despair located in my heart area, which at the time, no other words compared with my 'heart threatening to break'. These emotions emerged when

disturbing, painful traumatic experiences were being shared by my patients in individual and group therapy. At these times I could literally feel and picture/imagine the patient's life scenes. My long held discipline in these early, and later years of holding back the tears while not dissolving into a total wreck held firm. Yet I was crumbling inside, with an odd tear brushed aside. On the other end of the spectrum when points of great joy and happiness were shared, I also had physical experiences of my heart pulsating; missing a beat; being larger in my body i.e., when I was happy and close to being at one with the patient/group.

Hopefully this illustrates that in such scenarios the heart came into play, which allowed me to experience more fully 'being within the moment.' At such times my conventional long held theoretical, practical thinking was pressing me to act interpretively, increasingly these were held in abeyance. When such events occurred, I believe that it was the deep regions of the heart that stirred which in turn led me to theoretical and interpretive interventions when required.

In closing this first chapter here is an extract from a session with a patient in individual therapy in the closing stages of her therapy. Hopefully this gives a flavour of what is intended to come in the remaining text:

> For some weeks we had been focussing upon her not giving herself enough time to 'be in the moment'. During the past week she had changed this, giving herself more time to be in the enjoyable moments. This is especially difficult as before becoming ill she had been a successful Barrister. Her life was built on giving to others. Her severe physical/psychological illness had held her in painful negative moments in contrast to current fulfilling moments. At one point, I asked her if she had contemplated or dealt with such things in her previous therapy which had been based upon a 'mindfulness' approach, she responded:
> "Mindfulness helped me address what I was thinking and changing my thoughts. This therapy has touched my heart!"
> I said: "Well, therefore it's heartfullness as compared to mindfulness."
> To which she smiled and agreed.

This small simple vignette I believe shows one aspect of therapeutic love and heartfullness, which became an ever present element, coming in many covert and overt forms throughout my work. Another way of looking at therapeutic love and heartfullness is, 'that which runs through,' it is similar to the blood and the bloodstream being driven by the heart. I came across a beautiful book called: "Heart (a Personal Journey Through its Myths and Meanings)." In her section on Hindu/Upanishads Godwin tells us:

> However, when a man is in deep, dreamless sleep, and is not aware of anything at all, this is what happens. There are seventy two thousand veins that run from the heart to the pericardium. He slips out of the heart through these veins and rests within the pericardium. He rests there oblivious to everything…
>
> (Godwin, 2001, p. 48)

Meandering through this quote possibly we can stretch our imagination. Layer upon layer of the therapeutic journey, like the 72,000 veins, will have developed until this point. Transpose this to my views on therapeutic love and heartfullness that if the heart is given prominence as the driving force the elements of therapeutic love emerge like the 72,000 veins – well maybe not that many!

A central point of note which is important to keep in mind is the impact such a book will have on patients, both in its writing and its reading. In many psychotherapy publications, as well as some of my previous publications, an emphasis has been on a more distant and objective stance, whereas this book in centred more upon the personal explorations of both my patients and myself. Thinking along the lines of expositions on transference and counter-transference, how much thought is given to the patient when the writer is intent on illustrating or proving the points? What must it feel like for the patient to see, in print, potentially complex exchanges/ interactions between them and their therapist? They may have, after many years, moved on to another stage in their life and do not want to be reminded, particularly if the material is very revealing and also, possibly for the first time, have a view of their therapist's world. What impact will such a publication have on the patient's family and friends? For others it may be a positive experience and the patient is reminded of the loving and caring therapeutic process. For some it was personal, for the therapist it was theoretical – that is if he/she had upheld a distant, analytic stance. Even with the patient giving permission for the publication to proceed there may be little space/opportunity to redress the matter. The therapist will have gone to great lengths to maintain the patient's anonymity but the patient may have little difficulty in recognising themselves through the theoretical purposefully misleading maze created to guard anonymity. As one reads this book, it is probable that somewhere in the world, a therapist's heart is touched as they facilitate their patient in helping them to voice their deepest emotions, while at the same time choking back their own emotions in the struggle to frame the patient's experience within the theory of their choice. This book is about being touched in so many ways.

A Practical Point of Note

Due to copyright restrictions, it has not been possible to produce some quotes from fiction and film, although they have been altered in order to convey their relevance to my formulations.

Notes

1 For details on my professional developments in my book *Group Analytic Art Therapy* (McNeilly, 2006b, pp. 13–39).
2 My inclusion in brackets.
3 Although large and small groups were universal within therapeutic communities, there were other pillars relevant to each particular one, that is, social, creative and work groups.

Chapter 2

Three Models and One Synthesis

Three Models – One Synthesis

The Light Has Stolen My Words.

I had hand written the first draft of this chapter many months ago and set it aside by a window. I had not realised the destructive consequences in that when I picked it up again I discovered that the light had faded the first page, returning it to being a blank sheet. I tried to rescue it, but to no avail. The faded pen indentations were unsalvageable, so I started anew.

This is relevant to the concepts of synthesis, grafting and integration in theoretical perspectives and clinical practices. When brought together each model will have differing impressions which hold firm or are modified by other impressions. As such, new structures are created. Particular elements will hold while others fade, losing import and validity, like my written words disappearing through the power of light. In a way this shows the power of reflection within therapeutic ventures, which shine a light on the lives of our patients, resulting in neurotic and other symptoms fading and disappearing, creating new life formations. In this context as I developed each separate model, much of it unplanned, synchronous aspects and synthesis ran through these developments.

The word synthesis is defined:

> "The process of combining objects or ideas into a complex whole" – "The unification of one concept with another not contained in it."
>
> (Collins, Millennium Edition)

The word 'integrate' has similar properties:

> To make or be made into a whole; incorporate or be incorporated.
>
> (Collins, Millennium Edition)

With these words in mind, it is at times difficult to see where one thing (model) starts and ends. Thus, the process of various elements existing in their own right

DOI: 10.4324/9781003536857-3

and moving along to incorporate others, to creating a new element, may be difficult to see. Then, when we see the end part of a developmental process a new beginning emerges. When we see a point of horizon in the sea, that if we travel to that point a new horizon emerges in the distance until we reach land. Until this point, the concept of horizon is both a fixed line that is always there and moves continuously.

We turn our attention now to the three areas I have travelled along. Each had its own challenges, having to be reached for its own particular purposes but had to develop through continual synthesis and integration. The three models are:

1   Art Therapy
2   Group Analysis
3   Individual Psychodynamic Psychotherapy

So! Where does each of these start and finish? What is unique to each? These are just some questions worth considering. It is not my intention to provide clear cut answers to such questions but hopefully in the light of the developing text some level of clarification will emerge. Many practitioners and theoreticians keep firmly within the tramlines of their own boundaries and much of the literature is enriched by the firmness of their stance. As I progressed through my different trainings and varying work settings it was natural, almost organic, that a great deal of movement developed within these three models. Of course, each training had to be acquired first. In musical terminology, improvisation is developed from basic rudiments. This analogy is apt in that I had to acquire my theoretical/practice rudiments before I could expand my improvisation. With the developing synthesis, there had to be an interplay between acquisition and development. This spanned a whole range of areas:

What was learned from teachers and patients?
Interpersonal relationships with work colleagues.
Opening up of new theoretical developments.
What worked and what didn't.
Life outside the consulting room.

In a similar way as my earlier comments about not answering questions directly, in an organised response, each of the points raised above will emerge throughout the book.

Chronologically my art therapy training came first in the mid-1970s and gradually moved into my group analytic and individual psychodynamic training. I did not complete my formal group analytic training until the late 1980s. In both my art therapy and later verbal psychotherapy training perspectives, the interplay between individuals and groups developed simultaneously. The following quote shines a light on this:

Progress in all the sciences during the last decades has led to the same independent and concerted conclusion; that the old juxtaposition of an inside and outside world, constitution and environment, individual and society, phantasy and reality, body and mind and so on, are untenable. They can at no stage be separated from each other, except by artificial isolation.

(Foulkes & Anthony, 1957/1984)

Therefore, for me, there has never been a conflicting dichotomy between the individual and the group; it is more a question of points of focus at different times.

Coincidence and Synchronicity

Even as far back as my leaving school at 15 with no academic qualifications I can now see the relevance of apparently chance occurrences and development. There were many short-term employments: factories, breweries, motorway construction, furniture shops, hairdressers, among many others. Looking back on this nothing was planned. A chance coincidence materialised when my first art therapy post was advertised I was in transit on holiday, in Germany, when the post was vacant. It all added up to a rich tapestry woven by coincidence, synchronicity and synthesis.

As I have defined synthesis let us also consider synchronicity and coincidence. One definition of co-incidence is:

"Coincide: to occur or exist simultaneously" – "coincidence a chance occurrence of events remarkable either for being simultaneous or for apparently being connected."

(Collins, Millennium Edition)

Whereas synchronicity is:

The occurrence of events at the same time, which appear to be related but have no obvious connection.

(Compact Oxford English Dictionary, 2008)

There have been times within therapeutic sessions when I attempted to clarify how various events coming together at the same time may have had meaning, that is, a patient who spoke of taking his wife out for dinner only to bump into an old girlfriend at the restaurant. His immediate response when I questioned the potential meaning of the 'chance encounter': "it's only a coincidence," he responded. The emphasis was on 'only.' This seemed to relegate the event to a meaningless accident. A hidden question/statement from him seemed to be: "it's irrelevant, why waste our time talking about an accidental meeting?" the word coincidence may have lost some of its meaning which is about the deeper seated meaning of things coming together at the least expected times. Bearing these points in mind, why is it that one therapeutic model/approach takes hold at a particular time/moment? I will return to these questions when I speak more directly about each model of therapy but first, some meanderings on world issues.

By taking account of the following areas these help us to contextualise the impact of life events upon the therapeutic processes. What, if any, was the coincidence of

'Brexit' being voted upon in its aim for sovereignty and a few months later Donald Trump's 'Make America Great Again' successful election? Trump and UK Prime Minister Boris Johnson were being humorously twinned. Why at the beginning of 2018 was the world in a state of anxiety as to either Trump or Kim Jong Un pressing the 'Red Button'? The synchronistic seeds seemed to be sown, at least as far as the West was concerned, but in 2021 it was not known what succeeded or failed; however, the 'red button' was not pressed. Why at this time in 2021 on 7/8th January, at the behest of an 'unhinged' President Trump (Nancy Pelosi's own language), Pelosi wrote to the military requesting non-compliance should President Trump attempt any further crisis following the attempted coup on the US Capitol Building. Once again, the greatest fear of nuclear annihilation was activated. Why in 2018 did the Armenian 'Purple/Velvet' revolution proceed and succeed so peacefully without a bullet being fired? The 'people's leader,' Nikol Pashinyan, who was soon to become Prime Minister, spoke movingly of love as a changing factor in the revolution (Pashinyan, 2018). These are major world movements and questions to which I have no answer. By expanding on these world issues, particularly the timing of events, it shows the power of synchronicity and synthesis, which is of the utmost importance when exploring events in the therapeutic environments.

On a much lesser dimension, why do particular therapeutic practices occur at times in our history, raise our awareness and become established or not? They often have a shelf life with some having longevity whereas others fall by the wayside as being suspect; not accredited by one political/Managerial Board or another; are dogged by cases of tragedy or misfortune and then assigned to histories therapeutic dustbins, that is, the decline and fall of therapeutic communities in Britain. Some of the following have been in vogue at one time or another during the 20th century. In no particular order these are: Encounter Groups; Psychodrama; Behaviour Therapy; Person Centred Counselling; Transactional Analysis; Cognitive Therapy; Family Therapy, as some examples. Some are still central parts of treatment programmes worldwide while others cling on desperately and some may no longer exist. For example, the last place where I worked was a psychotherapy department in the British National Health Service. From 1990, when it was a thriving outpatient service, there was a permanent staff of six full-time qualified psychotherapists and a rotating group of approximately 20 trainees and honorary therapists. In 2019 only one qualified therapist remained with a few honorary therapists. Possibly by 2025 it may no longer exist. Psychodynamic psychotherapy in the British National Health Service may be renewed if it embraces the principles of therapeutic love and lessens its reliance on major, apparently rigid, psychoanalytic theory and methodology. At present I believe that individual and group therapy still holds firm and is tailored to a wide range of clientele worldwide.

'Mindfulness' is being adapted to a whole range of existing therapeutic approaches, that is, mindfulness art therapy, neuroscience. In the closing years before my retirement in 2011, it was gaining in popularity. I attended a talk given by the Dali Lama in Derry, Northern Ireland in 2017, who spoke favourably about neuroscience in relation to Buddhism. Considering these wide diverse approaches and movements in time and space, what is it about a particular model, method, theory, approach, that grabs attention? Like Jung's 'collective unconscious' are there invisible national/world forces which allows some to shine through, or not, at particular times, as did the beginnings of the therapeutic community movement in response to treating war wounded soldiers during and post the Second World War. As a dominant message of love that emerged during Armenia's Purple Revolution, possibly compassion and kindness (as evoked by Princes William and Harry's messages who had been promoting mindfulness, compassion and kindness within the media) have allowed mindfulness to be at the forefront of current popularity. So, in meandering back from our world events to therapeutic sessions, this raises our awareness of our interactions with our patients. There will be ever changing scenarios in respect to what is encountered: the timing of events inside and outside; the coming together or moving apart; the acquisition of new insight and change; and the part synchronicity and synthesis plays on the road to the therapy's conclusion. This is as much the therapist's journey as the patient's.

Art Therapy

In retrospect, the creation and development growth of synthesis rests upon more than one thing coming together and joining up. My first encounter with art therapy was during my nurse training at a large psychiatric hospital in England. A new art therapy department had been created in the hospital and my role was to escort patients to and from this department. While in attendance I was expected to participate in the art activities, which at the beginning, I was somewhat wary of. Increasingly this department opened me up to something new, speaking to my artistic and musical side. This seemed to be a counterbalance to the Victorian Institutional environment of the hospital. The seeds of change were being sown. Inadvertently this was breaking down my nursing mentality but as I was still in the middle stages of nurse training, I had to complete this before starting my art therapy training. The art therapy world was coming to me, opening up the potential for synthesis with my nursing development. In the publication I referred to earlier I expanded upon how I progressed from these nursing roots. In that publication, particularly the 'Transitions' chapter (McNeilly, 2006b, pp. 91–102), it illustrates how I moved along from my nursing route to my art therapy and group analytic positions. Therefore, in the new light of examining synthesis these chronological points, that is, the developing sequence, Musician → Nurse → Art Therapist → Therapeutic Community Therapist → Psychotherapist → Group Analyst → Educator, had pivotal points that, as a whole, have led to a more comprehensive professional synthesis and integration. When new points of clinical practice and/or theory emerged, these were 'pivots of encounter,' questioning what was already in place and how the new element could be integrated or discarded. For example, during my art therapy training at a college in England, a number of training/experiential groups formed part of the training. The groups using art making as the dominant technique/method provided a space to create concrete images and time to share the process with the student group. These groups were, on the whole, fulfilling and nurturing. On the other hand, there were primarily verbal groups which were led by analysts from the 'Tavistock Institute of Human Relations' in London, which adhered to W.R. Bion's methods (Bion, 1961). In this modality, the leader of the group, eight times out of ten, said nothing during the 90 minutes of the session. As the session reached the closing minutes, the analyst would give an interpretation which was formulated on Bion's three 'Basic Assumptions': 'fight/flight,' 'pairing' and 'dependency,' either singly or in combination. Sometimes the analyst left the room at the close of the session without saying anything. Generally speaking these groups were negative experiences, unearthing destructive and potentially psychotic ramifications (the whole student body seemed to be united in this opinion).[1] In keeping with my current theories on therapeutic love and heartfullness, one could say that the college art groups scored highly with the pivots of care, support, empathy, humour, compassion, creation of motivation and insight. The Bion model's pivots were more like spikes that potentially became daggers. Therapeutic love and heartfullness were, on the whole non-existent, except for what we, the student group, gave one another to enable us to survive.

My first encounter in the role of being an art therapist came when I was still a student art therapist. As part of my training I had to spend periods of time on work placements. It was to the Henderson Therapeutic Community, in southern England, that I was sent for one of my placements. This was one of the original socio-therapeutic communities in England for people with personality disorders. Although there should have been a qualified art therapist in situ unfortunately he had left as I arrived. This was a baptism of fire – a forced grafting as compared to a gradual synthesis between qualified and student art therapists. I was perceived as more qualified than I was, although I was supervised by other senior psychotherapy staff in order to make up for the absent qualified art therapist. I have written in more detail about this in my last book (McNeilly, 2006b, pp. 40–44) on the therapeutic community. Therefore, I only want to focus on a couple of points in respect to synthesis. Technically at that stage in my development I had little to bring to the table after my first six months in college. However, what I had was my enthusiasm and willingness to try out some of the things I'd learnt at college. Nothing had equipped me to work with this patient group, people with personality disorders of varying complexities, severities as well as being elevated to the height that staff and patients were putting me. A little bit of grandiosity was attaching itself to me. A central point of reference was that the overall structure of the therapeutic community was built upon a range of therapeutic approaches, activities and group methods, which potentially created a synthesis being achieved on various levels. As well as getting to grips with a whole range of group approaches and theory the road through understanding and honing 'communication' was arduous.

Communication

Although S.H. Foulkes was not a central point of reference at the time, the following quote encapsulates what I experienced then.

Group-analytic theory and practice has almost from its beginning paid special attention to the communication process and has considered it of central importance – communication can be verbal and non-verbal, conscious and unconscious – the present writer has earlier stressed the process of translation that is the raising of communication from the inarticulate and autistic expression by the symptom to the recognition of underlying conflict and problems which can be conveyed, shared and discussed in everyday language (in the group) – principally everything happening is considered in its communicational aspect.

(Foulkes, 1964, pp. 68–69)

Further to this Foulkes speaks more colourfully when he tells us about the 'symptom mumbling secretly':

The language of the symptom, although already a form of communication, is autistic. It mumbles to itself secretly,[2] hoping to be overheard.

(Foulkes, 1964, pp. 259–260)

The power of communication is in the heart of it all. This is built upon synthesis and in turn synthesis drives and improves, or not, accordingly. I have written elsewhere about synthesis in the comparison between silence in primarily verbal groups and the blank page in both individual and group art therapy settings (McNeilly, 2006b). For brevities sake here, this draws attention to those therapists who wait silently (primarily at the start of sessions but also throughout) for the patient to speak. Often it is as if they are 'in waiting' for the work to begin with the first verbal utterances, even though they see value and meanings in the pre-emptive silence. In the art therapy settings, more so in individual art therapy, both parties are 'in waiting' for the first marks to be made as in verbal therapy. With both therapies, the process of synthesis is at play: from silence in verbal therapy when the beginning action is mobilised through speech. In the art therapy arrangement, the blank page is altered with the first marks. Statistically one wonders how much relief is experienced by therapists and patients when the spell is broken through such actions, setting in motion a mechanism of communication and synthesis to develop. Following the break in silence or first marks on the page, the silence will either be explored or be deemed as an awkward prelude to getting down to the business of dialogue. Few verbal therapists may think during the silence from an artistic perspective: this is like a blank canvas, rich in its empty potential with the patient and me preparing to paint with our words. If this is the case the possibility of a synthesis between the artistic/creative and verbal language is present. However, this does not detract from the fact that such silences, be it reverie or mounting tension of the 'said' and 'unsaid'; formed and partly formed 'word pictures' are waiting to emerge or erupt. I think that what is created in language, when it comes, brings varying levels of potential synthesis through the therapeutic relationship created between therapist and patient. Likewise, the art therapist working with individuals or groups approaches the blank sheet/page in a similar way as the verbal therapist's accommodation of the initial silence. In contrast to this, across the broad spectrum of art therapists, the blank page may simply be a material thing that the therapist brings, like their brushes, paints, etc. as tools, which equip the patient to get started in making their artwork. With the more psychotherapeutically oriented practitioners, the period of waiting between the page being placed in front of the patient and the first marks being made may also be similar to the primarily verbal therapist, that is, both therapist and patient see it as an awkward obstacle; a period of reverie; a defence against making the concrete image. It is almost as if the therapy has not started until the first marks are made. Like the silence in primarily verbal therapy, those art therapists who incorporate the dynamics of the initial and 'in process' silences, grasp the nature of these silences as being on par with the blank page waiting to be transposed into concrete imagery.

In my development of individual psychotherapy, group analysis and group analytic art therapy I was able to bring these two elements together: silence and the blank page. When I conducted primarily verbal groups, I envisaged that at points of silence individuals, groups and myself were engaged internally with existing and new mental pictures until such times as the silent spell was broken, that is, language or the first marks on the blank page in art groups. By expanding such formulations, this created a synthesis between language and art as a currency of communication.

In solely verbal psychotherapy and psychoanalysis, there are variances on the concepts of the 'blank or opaque screen' role of the therapist, which gives rise to the notion of a passive waiting game. This fits nicely with the general definition of 'being patient,' as in 'to have patience.' For me this blank/opaque concept does not exist, as the art therapy empty page is already being formed at the point it is brought into play, just as the 'silence is already creating' and is a receptacle for what is to be created with language and dialogue, not forgetting the whole array of non-verbal communication. I could not imagine an art therapist who is not psychotherapeutically oriented considering a richness of thought and imagery as they waited patiently, or impatiently, for their patients to make their first marks and 'then' their patient is 'doing art therapy' (a phrase I heard from some structural/thematic art therapists).

Returning to the matter of communication I thought further upon the correlations between art making and language within the therapeutic environs I worked in. Simply I questioned: "what is it that makes up language and art?" clearly, on one level they are miles apart in that verbal language is spoken through the mouth and is communicated to whoever listens and is confirmed, or not, by the listeners response, that is, comprehension and understanding. It is concreted through the written word or other ways, that is, electronic recording and publication. The creation of art is concrete and, as well as its potential conversion into communicable meaning, it is tactile. One cannot touch a word but words can touch.

Then I began to question primarily verbal psychotherapy and art therapy, what could be learned from both which could be integrated, while at the same time holding onto each separate identity? There was one obvious parallel:

Language before and during construction is as follows: Letters → Words → Sentences → Paragraphs → Stories → Books → Dialogue.

Punctuation Symbols: full stops/period, commas, colons, semi-colons, question marks, exclamation marks, brackets, etc.

Art: Dots → Line → Form → Images → Symbols → Structured End Products including paintings, drawings, sculptures and films.

Along with this, there are physical/tactile elements: touch, smell, taste, sight, colour creation. On reflection the points I raised could warrant a lot more in-depth exploration in order to understand the various strands that make up communication. Hopefully this has presented an introduction to such matters. My breakdown of language and art into its communicable properties is somewhat crude, but the complexities of the areas raised in the previous few paragraphs – such as synthesis, silence, blank pages, speech, the first words that break silence and art marks that impregnate the silent/empty page; therapist and patient's relief when this occurs, as some points of interest, are woven together in forming human relatedness.

Words within language may evoke colour associations just as musicians may equate music emotions with colour. Music has similar developments and properties in which some follow the 'written score' while others follow by listening and playing by ear and improvisation. I believe that by breaking down language and pictorial art forms into their component parts we can see that which is common to all. Therefore, by being able to cross refer the structure of each therapeutic practice, with its component parts, has helped me to establish a methodology which draws from each model.

Method Application

The Individual Dominance

A When sitting with an individual patient in verbal therapy the dominant interaction generally is, what is said and not said. However, as things unfold in the session I, as well as the patient presumably, will have fleeting pictures/images which continuously evolve through the life of the therapy. Equally we two would not be functioning in a vacuum as the patient's life groups outside, as well as associations with my life groups outside, will play a part. At such times I can draw on my work as a group analyst, that is, particular struggles emerging in this current individual's presentation and how this mirrors an external group and how it was understood and dealt with in that setting. This could either be in regard to a previous intervention in a group and how I adapted it to this individual patient; how two or more group members expressed similar aspects as the current individual; or a particular group dynamic/concern developed which echoed this individual setting. In this setting, here and now, there are just two of us whereas in the group there are eight. So! The potential for multiple triggers in mobilising the interactions comes into effect, rendering the transition from silent, internal imagery to be formed and expressed verbally. In the group format, it can move in many ways, which is different to linear interactions solely between therapist and patient in individual therapy. Hence, individual therapy is augmented with group dimensions.

The Group Dominance

B   When sitting with a group functioning mainly through verbal dialogue, in keeping with Foulkes' group analysis, the individual is as much a concern as the whole group. Equally, as with individual therapy, my experiences from the individual arrangement will filter through. For example, one may see how interactions in a group can mirror the experiences of individual therapy patients struggles with their own groups outside, be it family, friends or strangers. My own artistic/creative side, which is more easily utilised in art therapy, emerges at times in primarily verbal group analysis. This can allow for a greater comprehension of symbolism when it is pictorially imagined with the primarily verbal group setting. In discussion with some of my group analyst colleagues without an art/creative background, that is, those with prior medical psychiatric qualifications, they had difficulty in imagining/visualising beyond the spoken word/dialogue. For example, when I discussed an event in one of my groups with a colleague, he thought a member of my group was struggling Oedipally with me through penis envy, using intellectual/theoretical terms to frame this in the group context. He could not fathom it when I told him that I said to the patient: "you're afraid that your penis will pierce your heart." At the time I had an inner pictorial image of his penis like an arrow aimed at a target. This was about the patient being afraid to have a sexual relationship with his friend, potentially destroying their love as friends.

The Art Therapy Dominance

C   When involved in art therapy, be it individual or group, my work within primarily verbal psychotherapy would filter through. In the art therapy setting, the aim is to create a method geared more at facilitating the creation of concrete imagery. With specific reference to groups, this involved integrating a whole body of group analytic theory, among others, and making it my own, as well as developing new theory and practice. As stated earlier, it was also about establishing the uniqueness of each individual's creations in the presence of others in the group. In a similar way in individual art therapy, at various times the specific imagery may well resonate to what occurred with other individuals and groups and would be available to use if thought appropriate. Thus, the concrete imagery, along with the dialogue between the patient and me, could be influenced by the rich material in store from the other methods.

Following the completion of my group analytic training, I ventured through various professional roles. The integrative dimensions and synthesis have been more

Table 2.1 Group Session/ Therapists Processing Thoughts

Content of Session (Column A)	Therapist Commentary (Column B)
There was an initial silence of five minutes followed by Carmel, who has just joined the group (the others have been in attendance for between one and five years) asking me a number of questions: "What's the purpose of the group?" and "Are people supposed to feel comfortable?" (within an uncomfortable silence), there were other questions which were difficult to follow. Margaret said to Carmel, "I'll give you five pounds if you get a straight answer from Gerry!" I wondered if they thought I gave them crooked answers.	As stated earlier that even within such a short silence each person will be thinking and formulating their internal pictures on many levels. Silences often feel longer than they are, and depending on each person their views on how long a silence has lasted may well be different for someone with conflicting feelings/thoughts, five minutes of group silence can feel like a lifetime.
I spent about five minutes not saying anything and I was thinking hard as Carmel continued what felt like a barrage of further questions. She was forcing me to respond and I didn't want to leave her with the view that I simply wasn't willing to answer questions while also conveying my need to have space to think about the questions.	I had my own imagery of things, i.e., roadways going on straight lines – motorways or crooked mountain roads. Here I was thrown into a dual position in drawing from my experience of individual therapy in my initial responses to seeing that Carmel was an individual trying to grasp her first experience of psychotherapy while I was trying to process this within the group.
At this point my stomach begins to audibly rumble. Clare laughingly says: "Your stomach says more than you do!" Me: "Well maybe my stomach speaks for me when I can't think what to say!" they laugh about this. This seemed to herald a shift of focus from me and Margaret responded to Carmel by speaking movingly about her own development from a similar first group experience to Carmel's, i.e., what she initially expected (my giving answers and direction) and what she has gained through exploring things within the group and finding answers that way, thus changing her life outside. Her early experiences of wanting clarity, direction, feelings of comfort, loss of vagueness and ambivalence from me was replaced by unexpected things from the whole group, including me.	This brings in at least two further dimensions. The first moves us onto the psychosomatic symbolism and brings in how the communication is converted into a physical expression (my rumbling stomach). The second is how the group feels free to use me in a humorous way which invariably displays the warmth of their feelings towards me, and each other. In the face of demands from Carmel, the person with prior expectations that I would fulfil the 'all seeing' analyst, I show that I don't have the sought-after answers.

(Continued)

Table 2.1 (Continued)

Content of Session (Column A)	Therapist Commentary (Column B)
They then turned their focus back to me joking about how they see me. Margaret said she had tried to explain/describe me to her friends/family outside. She felt that I was almost impossible to fathom but she had told them about me being a musician and playing in bands. Clare said to me: "I can see you playing trumpet!" I then expand a little on this part of my life.	In Margaret's warm and moving account of her therapy experience, almost as a way of teaching, or reassuring Carmel, this shows an integration of individual demands/processes into the group analytic development. Sadly, this dynamic presence is not available in an individual psychotherapy arrangement where there is no actual other patient in the presence of a therapist with another patient saying: "be patient, it will work out in the end. Answers will come one way or another."
This brought a great deal of hilarity and laughter, from Carmel primarily. Carmel: "I didn't expect to laugh in this sort of group", she was a little hesitant here. Clare to me: "Do you mind us talking about you?" Me: "No it's fine!", Carmel: "I'll give up", when I didn't respond immediately to another question. Me to Carmel: "you don't need to give up because that will stop something that you are needing to speak about!"	Through this sequence the freedom of the group to fantasise about me allows a playful atmosphere to develop. This I believe provides a fertile soil for humour, warmth and play to be integrated. This is in comparison to the position in which the group analyst takes a more serious interpretive position, which may conceptualise such dynamic processes as defences or avoidant. Such an approach may inhibit the free expression of humour, play and warmth, and may foment fear and infantilisation, i.e., 'don't back chat your father.' What also happened in this process was that the door was being opened up to Carmel, as the new member, to start integrating with the group, i.e., her later comment: "I'll give up!" almost as if she has fallen in line (synthesis) with the others.

There was a shift of gear and the others (Anthea, Samantha, Rosie) began to speak about other professionals, i.e., psychiatrists, nurses, social workers, who had not kept boundaries with them and how my maintaining a distance, although warm, was helpful.

Margaret: "the psychiatrist treating my mother for severe anorexia is totally enmeshed with her. Both of them are getting worse!" They all bring accounts of medical general practitioners, crisis teams, inpatient treatments, recalling the generally negative experiences at the hands of these people. Then the professionals either lost their own discipline or were distant and emotionally unavailable. The mood and dialogue with the group takes a shift as Clare, in a rather manic way, spoke about a lump growing on her leg and being afraid that it was cancer. She humorously deals with this fear. "Gerry if you were a doctor, you could look at my leg!"

Me: "You (and the rest of you) were talking a few minutes ago about the importance of me keeping my distance and having boundaries."

She laughed in response. In the closing part of the session there was a free-flowing set of associations about me. Margaret: "I can see Gerry sitting in a darkened room with loads of books but only one piece of cheese in the fridge!" Anthea: "I see Gerry at home with the lights low, a glass of wine and listening to music." As the session was finishing and people were leaving the room Margaret spoke about her leg going dead which echoed Clare's comments.

After their fantasizing about me the playful interchanges moves them back to more serious issues. Concern for me; minding them talking about me like this; that I would not look after myself if only with a small piece of cheese; my intellectual endeavours required to look after them and my other patients. Hopefully here there is a visual stimulation which allows us to imagine how if this group had been conducted as an art therapy one, that such imagery would have been created, i.e., cheese in the fridge; dark rooms in large houses; books/library; £5 note; rumbling stomach; roads of direction.

In the closing part of the session, as I said, they had moved into more serious matters, such as Clare's fear surrounding cancer and the impact of Margaret's mother's longstanding anorexia. They had played with me, pushing the limits and had been reassured that this was not a threat to either mine or their boundaries.

organic as stated earlier. They seemed to grow in their own way, often from an intuitive spark or fleeting 'throw away' ideas. Many times I did not know how something came about.

The foregoing has been intended to provide a snapshot of a number of points within the methodology and how they interrelate. Hopefully it provides a window for the reader to see through both the 'stand alone' elements of each model and how, over time, levels and degrees of synthesis evolved. All three became an integral part of my inner world, which were drawn from accordingly. One of the problems in using the word 'method' is that it tends to draw the reader into thinking that what is being proposed is a prescriptive technique akin to a practical work handbook. It is not! However, therapeutic practitioners will hopefully take and adapt what I offer in their own ways.

In closing let me present an illustration taken from a long standing primarily verbal group, which brings into focus references to pictorial symbolism as well as how warmth and humour played a part in therapeutic love and heartfullness as I have defined it. The group had been in existence for a number of years, meeting once a week with a 'slow open' membership.[3] In keeping with group analytic methodology, no direction was given at the start of the session. It is presented as a table in order to simplify its presentation in conjunction with parallel technical and theoretical elements. Hopefully it shows the relative areas where synthesis of the three models is evidenced. I suggest that column A is read separately before moving to B, which is a breakdown of the key developments in the session (Table 2.1).

Conclusive Commentary

With regard to the table above, hopefully particular key points in the session will have been clear. After reading the session and cross referencing, there should be a gradual conceptualisation of the intricate processes within this session. This should give an impression of the workings of group analysis and the group analyst's involvement and technique. However, not all group analysts are the same and this will also show my idiosyncratic approach.

The purpose of this chapter has been about providing an initial perspective of the three Therapeutic Models origins and developmental processes. With each of the following chapters, these areas will be developed in greater detail, particularly for the remainder of 'Part 1.'

Notes

1 I was unable to locate Bion's directive but I believe that he did not see his theory being used as a therapeutic framework, but as a theoretical study of groups.
2 My translation of 'secretly' = silence in verbal therapy, blank page in art therapy.
3 Patients join and leave in their own time, staying between one and five years. New members join as spaces become available.

Chapter 3

Specifics in Therapeutic Love and Heartfullness

To put love into words implies being able to find the appropriate words, which may be both difficult to locate and express in equal measure. It is safe to say that feelings of love are both specific and non-specific accordingly. Specifically, it can be love for another, one's country, an occupation, a group or fellowship or a sport or hobby. Non-specifically a whole range of emotions come into play in trying to describe/define the specificity of the experience. In order to be specific about something, it is necessary to focus in greater detail on the subject in question. This entails clarifying particular characteristics and properties. On its simplest level within psychotherapy, this is primarily the persons involved – patient, therapist and group. This is the same for all therapeutic ventures but unlike psychodynamic frameworks which rely upon analytic/interpretive principles, heartfullness and therapeutic love moves us in a different direction. Whereas a general perspective of love in psychoanalysis/psychotherapy addresses this (primarily) within the sexual/erotic dimensions. Therapeutic love encompasses a whole range of experiences not aligned to the erotic/libidinal dimensions.

In the psychotherapeutic literature that I researched, the heart is seldom referred to. Therefore, the heart, both in its physical and emotional sense, is specific to 'therapeutic love.' It is the primary organ as compared to the sexual organs and the brain, which is often analogous to the mind. Returning to the theme of meandering, I recently had some passing thoughts which, on further reflection, develop the physical/psychological dimensions. Medical doctors are often seen with their stethoscope draped around their neck like a necklace. They seem to forget that it is there, as if it is a part of them. The passing thoughts were that of the 'gunslinger' in the old cowboy movies who is always ready for the ambush. The doctor is ready and prepared for the car accident or the heart attack. In this line of thought, the stethoscope is parallel with the gun, but the purpose is to save life through direct contact with the patient's heart, not a tool of death: the gun. The first point of action once the stethoscope jumps into action, both routinely and in emergencies, is to

DOI: 10.4324/9781003536857-4

tend to the heart through feeling the pulse and listening with the stethoscope. What could be more of a simple poignant psychotherapy equivalent:

Feeling and listening.

Many years ago, two student doctors attended my clinic for the first time to observe my assessments of new patients. They had their stethoscopes around their necks. I rather mischievously asked them: "what will you be doing with your scopes during the assessment?" Being somewhat 'green' (innocent, inexperienced) they felt embarrassed and did not know what to do with their scopes. I was trying to make a point that psychotherapeutic assessments were different to a medical or psychiatric assessment. In retrospect I regret this 'trying to be smart' with my stamp of authority against junior doctors, even though my intentions were good. They did see that I was teasing them and they took it in good humour. If at the time I had been seeing the heart as a driving force I may have made use of the contrast between the actual stethoscope in general medicine and a 'scope' in psychotherapy, whatever that would have been, I think there would have been a greater synthesis.

Historically, psychoanalysis and psychotherapy have laid a central authority in the realms of conscious and unconscious processes, relying on such specific components as dreams, unconscious actions, defences, sublimation and acting out as evidence of lifelong conflicts between conscious and unconscious developments. Unlike general medicine, which has a concrete relationship with the heart, psychotherapy cannot provide physical proof in the same way. We believe in this invisible force that emerges in the ways stated, but we have no physical proof/evidence, as far as I am aware. Although I believe in the unconscious and the various mechanisms stated above, it was not until I formulated my ideas regarding heartfullness and therapeutic love that things made more sense. Psychotherapists who adhere primarily to a method of examining mental processes which revolve around conscious/unconscious, brain functioning and mindfulness do not have an equivalent tool to the doctor's stethoscope. The concepts of therapeutic love I now see as a tentative link with the stethoscope. By this, I mean that clarity emerged within many therapeutic sessions when I was touched, something touched me, and I had varying physical sensations in my body, predominantly in my heart (thoracic) area. My psychological 'pulse' kicked in. Irvin Yalom makes similar observations to my views:

Before the invention of the stethoscope, a physician listened to the sounds of life with an ear pressed against the patient's rib cage. Imagine two minds pressed tight together and, like paramecia exchanging micronuclei, directly transferring thought images: that would be union nonpareil.

(Yalom, 1989, p. 180)

Recently I made contact with a research institute called 'HeartMath' in California. They have been moving along similar lines to myself, although they are primarily approaching the interconnectedness between the heart and the emotions more from the physiological perspective. Nevertheless, we seem to be in tune with one another. The main difference is that the power of the heart as the driving engine came to me spontaneously at the purely emotional field: 'HeartMath' seemed to be exploring the physiological changes in the heart which led to emotions:

> New research shows the human heart is much more than an affective pump that sustains life. Our research suggests the heart also is an access point to a source of wisdom and suggest intelligence that we can call upon to live our lives with more balance, greater creativity and enhanced intuitive capacities. The heart has been considered the source of emotion, courage and wisdom for centuries.
>
> (McCarty, 2015, p. 1)

In a similar vein to my own search their enquiries moved them to question:

> Early on in our research we asked, among other questions, why people experience the feeling or sensation of love and other regenerative emotions as well as heartache in the physical area of the heart.
>
> (McCarty, 2015, p. 1)

Even though they are approaching their subject from a different one than my own, there is a great deal of mirroring. 'HeartMath' provides a specific physiological frameworks with the heart as its core.

When, in therapeutic sessions, I was experiencing emotional pain, grief, sorrow, loss, happiness, pride, pleasure with the patient or group, it was not my brain or mind that was touched (as far as I know) but my heart. The brain kicked in afterwards, or synchronistically. Of course, in not being medically trained, such professionals in these disciplines may feel/think that what I feel at such times is a 'sympathetic nervous response/message' being transferred from my brain to my heart, thus creating rhythmic fluctuations. If this is the case where does the evocation of tears come from, be it sad or happy tears?

With my formulation the emphasis is upon fullness of the heart, considering how the heart can be full to overflowing or stretched/expanded; whether to the points of 'breaking' or 'joyous rapture.' Such 'states of being' created tangible points of closeness between me and those whom I worked with. One may also question when the opposite needs consideration in highly powerful emotive states when the heart feels diminished, as say in heartbreak or intense chronic grief in which emptiness reigns. This may also be paradoxical in that when such emotions are evoked in heartbreak following loss or death, the heart is equally full of sorrow, bursting with everything that goes with it. The word 'heartless' does not seem to fit when the heart is emptying or diminished as 'heartless' denotes someone having little thought or compassion for another. During therapeutic sessions when my heart was touched, which was leading me down into deep areas of pain and suffering that as my heart filled up through experiencing the fullness of the patient's/group's stories,

I also felt a movement towards emptiness. My caution in approaching this 'further dimension,' and with a great hesitancy is: are we approaching access to the 'soul'? When this thought came to me first I had an anxious, almost frightened reaction. I caught my breath, feeling that I was onto something but did not want to go beyond these initial thoughts. Possibly it will become clearer with time and finding the courage to pursue this line of enquiry. In his novel, 'The Anatomy School,' Bernard MacLaverty echoes some of these thoughts. One of the book's characters, Martin, ruminates:

> He picked up the slide and looked at it under the microscope. – Networks of blue nuclei. If only you could stain thoughts. The sum total of all thoughts of a lifetime – that would be the soul. He was looking at some poor bastard's soul.
>
> (MacLaverty, 2001, p. 239)

Referring to Collins Dictionary, a great deal more has been written about the heart in relation to various emotions. There are 40 emotive equations, with only two anatomical/psychological equations. It states:

> Organ considered as the seat of the emotions, especially love, 'heart and soul, absolutely; completely'.
>
> (Collins, Millennium Edition)

A Brief Meandering into Love and Hate

I think that it is safe to assume that when speaking about love and hate in conjunction this has been primarily concerned with romantic, passionate and sexual relationships that are either very fulfilling when all is well with the world, while on the other hand the love has turned sour and destruction rages. This primarily concerns a couple but can also expand to three or more. There are also larger forms of love to be considered as in love for one's neighbour or country, or hate for another country's nationality in the case of bigotry and racism. These latter dimensions are not primarily concerned with sexuality or eroticism? However, hate in regard to another race or religion can be manifested through sexual assaults on members of the hated race. Love can also be expressed on a larger scale through such things as active engagement with countries experiencing crisis, i.e., caring for refugees, missionary work and helping people who have suffered through natural disasters. However, the 'therapeutic love' that I am purporting is not so different to the expression of love for one's fellow man with the ingredients of care, empathy, compassion, respect, risk and belief in the individual or group. In these formations of love, eroticism does not play a part, although sometimes eroticism can break through and possibly this creates a channel for hate to be enabled. How often has a platonic friendship been damaged or destroyed once it crosses over to romantic and erotic expression? It would be understandable for a critic to attack my purposeful avoidance of hate but to my way of thinking this would divert us from defining/ extrapolating 'therapeutic love' as being predominantly non erotic. Certainly, the heart comes into play in both therapeutic love and romantic passionate love, but it is activated by those powerful emotions and connections which I have stated earlier.

Throughout my career that when I presented lectures at various training establishments or congresses, I let the participants hear a recorded song or piece of music. A very gifted singer/composer, Declan O'Rourke, has written some beautiful songs which captures the essence of my own findings. From his CD, 'A Big Bad Beautiful World' the following lyrics from his song 'A SONG OF LOVE AND HATE' illustrate this:

> Have you ever noticed how some words get stuck together
> Even though they're opposed forever?
> Fire and water…Dark and bright…
> Summer, winter… Day and night
> Never ever, … Now and then
> Worse and better… Thick and thin…
> Well could it be that 'love and hate' come together hand in hand?
> And has this been our fate since the universe began?
> Us and them in an ageless dance
> Could we split them up if we had the chance?
>   (©Declan O'Rourke, Album: *Big Bad Beautiful World*, 2007)

The absence of the music does not do justice to the song and needs to be heard.

Ian D Suttie's seminal work on the 'Origin of Love and Hate' is much to be admired and I felt I could not proceed further without paying tribute to that great work. Much can be learned from this book and it is tempting to stay longer than a few points of reference. In the closing comments on Suttie's book, Sheila Kitzinger states:

> The 'Origins of Love and Hate' has long had an underground reputation within psychoanalysis. It is one of the most passionate arguments for a therapeutic practice based on the physicians love for the deeply deprived patient. – A more optimistic vision than that of traditional Freudian psychology.
>   (Kitzinger, 1988, back cover of book)

This was echoed in Sandor Lorand's commentary on Ferenczi's approach who:

> Emphasises the "humanness" of the analyst, giving "love" to the patient and so forth.
>   Ferenczi experimented with adjusting the atmosphere of the analytic situation to the patient's needs. He believed that the analyst must give love to these

very difficult patients in order to help them resolve their pathological difficulties by reaching their pre-traumatic experiences.

(Alexander, Einstein, Grotjan, & Eds, 1966, p. 23)

Hopefully similarities with my own stance can be seen. Irving Yalom, in his account of a closure of therapy session says:

> That was a transforming hour. Our time of intimacy – call it love, call it love making – was redemptive. In that one hour, Elva moved from a position of for-sakenness to one of trust. She came alive and was persuaded, once more, of her capacity for intimacy.
> I think it was the best hour of therapy I ever gave.

(Yalom, 1989, p. 151)

In Suttie's own words:

> I consider that love of mother [the patient/therapist relationship – my insertion] is primal in so far as it is the first formed and directed emotional relationship. Hate, I regard not as a primal independent instinct, but as a development or intensification of separation anxiety which in turn is roused by a threat against love. It is the maximal ultimate appeal in the child's power – the most difficult for the adult to ignore. Its purpose is not death seeking or death dealing, but the preservation of the self from the isolation which is death, and the restoration of a love relationship.

(Suttie, 1988, p. 31)

Further Suttie says:

> "I find reason to believe that primal love (and its obverse, anger), while it sub-serves self-preservation by maintaining the natural relationship to the mother, is something more than the sum total of organic needs and gratifications."
> "I believe the love-bond to the infant mind has the quality of tenderness from the beginning. It is not a sexual desire degenitalized (goal-inhibited) by repression as Freud would have it."

(Suttie, 1988, p. 31)

These views resonate with my own in my attempts to dispel a singular view of love and hate being solely tied in opposition. As far as I understand, Suttie sees hate as a secondary development when the primacy of love is disturbed. If we exchange the words child/mother to patient/therapist and see therapy as basically a loving arrangement resting on tenderness, hate will find it hard to gain a foothold. If we sexualise it, that is, relying on transference/countertransference and other psychodynamic frameworks, this may raise hate when the transactions become frustrated. Possibly we can see hate as a yearning for love.

Moving away from such meaningful thoughts as developed by Suttie, we can begin to develop a wider, universal perspective of love. The following illustrations are my more playful meanderings.

The Kiss

The kiss is a specific gesture that conveys various intentions of love. Can one speak of love, in whatever form/context without considering the kiss? Certainly, when it comes to intimate lovers establishing erotic connection, the kiss is often the initial stages of later genital sharing. Thus, the lover's bodies are embraced/joined.

So, in pulling back from such erotic manifestations, the kiss in the realms of affections, platonic or otherwise, may also involve an embrace between friends and colleagues. In most cases, this is from the lips to the cheek, or the fashionable 'air kiss,' never touching in one or two movements from side to side. The lips are off bounds in these kissing gestures, apart from parents to children when a short gentle peck comes into play.

So, we turn now to psychotherapy. In my earlier years of teaching in Portugal I struggled with students and the Portuguese who kissed cheek to cheek right from the first meeting. Sometimes it was cheek touching cheek; at others it was lips to cheek. In Portugal, it is not uncommon for the therapists and patients to meet and part with an embrace or kiss on their cheeks.

In keeping with my own career and the British (possibly the USA) interactions between therapists and patients these range from no physical contact at any time; an initial handshake and one on finishing therapy, a measured embrace at the end of therapy. I always offered my hand on introduction and was happy with an embrace with a peck on the cheek at the close of therapy, or a handshake if that was more appropriate and/or comfortable. The length of such an embrace would be dictated by the patient but seldom was it more than a minute or two, never longer than this.

If, as I have suggested, there is such a thing as therapeutic love how can a love be present without some form of a kiss? As I said at different points throughout the book that when particular emotions form a bond, which at times feels physical, this is not so different to being kissed, but within the platonic range. Of course, when erotic transferences take hold this is a different 'kettle of fish' and demands a different type of attention. As shown in particular clinical illustrations throughout the book, as the heart took over between me and the patient or the group, it was as if an embrace had been created and at each stage of what was to emerge, a 'symbolic kiss' would be felt through the developing process. This would entail feelings of connection, leading to the patient/group feeling held, understood, in harmony and those feelings of sharing deep emotions as a 'soothing symbolic kiss' or a 'happy kiss' marking change on the positive end of the spectrum.

Looking at things from a more abstract position the following formulations emerged as a result of my free-floating thoughts around the kiss, as I saw shared kisses occurring in the local restaurant where I was having a meal.

1 A man was waiting and a woman came in with a very bubbly joyous presentation. She came over enthusiastically to the man and a joyous kiss occurred, with one initial deep kiss moving to gentle smaller kisses.
2 Another couple met and they hesitantly embraced and kissed gently for a few seconds. This seemed to be an intrepid encounter with not a lot of conversation ensuing. I imagined they were meeting for the first time or they were a couple who were struggling with something.
3 A couple were already having a meal and there was a gentle serious atmosphere surrounding them. As they ate, they spoke quietly with flashes of laughter and humour. When they finished their meal at one point they embraced and kissed. It was a deep, lingering, oblivious to their surroundings kiss, lasting a few minutes. It seemed to be tender and sensitive and if they felt erotic they did not show it.

So, can a parallel be drawn between these three scenarios, which are differently specific, and therapeutic love? With the first one: in therapy there is the scenario when patients enter the first meeting in an ebullient way to their surroundings. They bubble over with keenness, wanting to get down to business as quickly as possible, as well as it being a way to disguise or offset/deal with their fears about starting therapy. Therapists may readily ascribe to these patients the titles of 'manic,' 'pre-mature disclosures,' 'superficial keenness,' 'borderline search for immediate intimacy/gratification.' In discussions with colleagues over the years, they predicted a potential rush into erotic transference with such patients, which raised their uncertainties and anxieties. Looking at this from a therapeutic love perspective, that if the patient is given rein to come in this way without too much restriction and censorship, this promotes the health seeking components of the over enthusiasm, dispelling the idea that the patient is attempting seduction. Therefore, empathically listening helps in processing the painful, difficult components which feels like an open wound which is often disguised by the presenting excited verbiage. Instead of seeing this in pathological terms this is the beginning of searching for what's 'right,' not 'wrong,' with the patient. Such an approach in accepting the more boisterous initial introduction, driven by the patient, can then feel like little, soothing symbolic kisses which then leads to a calmer foundation waiting to be built upon.

With respect to the second example one may see a number of parallels. With this couple one can imagine either a first date or a couple coming together to discuss some problems over a meal and the initial kiss was a courteous but a 'closely distant' gesture. One only has to think about the countless first meetings between a therapist and a patient. The therapist is in his consulting room and the patient walks through the doorway and there is a tentative handshake, or if not, the therapist gestures with hand to 'the chair' for the patient. This is like the type of kiss shared by this couple. I would suggest that many psychodynamic therapists uphold this type of symbolic kiss. In therapeutic love terms with my first encounter I reach out to shake the wary patient's hand, along with:

Hello, I'm Gerry McNeilly, how would you like me to address you? Which chair would you like? How can I help?

All such comments of introduction combine as a symbolic platonic kiss. I, as a therapist, have to embrace this new relationship, not as someone therapising the patient and the patient receiving, but as a couple tasked with creating something new out of the old.

With our third illustration, that although I did not know the reality of their relationship it felt to be more than a new pairing. They were either a couple clearly in love or in the early stages of romance, or a couple who had weathered storms before having a fulfilling night together. The parallel here is that of a fulfilling joint therapeutic experience which has varying levels of closeness, intimacy, being oblivious to the surroundings while considering life's magnitude (Table 3.1). Transposing this overall group of three separate couples to both single therapeutic sessions and later periods of therapy, a tripartite framework can be seen, that is.

In therapeutic loving terms I am postulating a radically different arrangement. As with Illustration 3, an equivalence is there from the start as a more unified experience and is formed through the heart's dominance. From the beginning, as with this couple cited, although the therapist is maintaining levels of distance, when certain things emerge which activates the heart (in both therapist and patient) it establishes a fuller involvement with one another. That deep lingering kiss of the couple (3) is not so different to those times during and at the end of therapy, when deep feelings were shared and had brought oblivious tender moments.

Table 3.1 Parallels and Contrasts in the Personal and Therapeutic Kiss.

A The dialogue at the start of the initial assessments and early therapy weeks/months.	All of the couple's first point of contact in the restaurant. This leads onto:
B The distance between patient and therapist lessens as the therapeutic meal develops.	The meal in the restaurant over two or three courses will be an adjunct to whatever each couple processes in their dialogue.
C Therapeutic fulfilments and achievements, which were initiated with starting symbolic kisses, will be reached and metabolised; the outcome of the overall therapy.	The culmination of the three couples' total dining experience and what ensued following their meal. Of course, some dining experiences do not get beyond the first introductory stages, as does first therapy assessments.

Loving Power of the Word

Generally speaking, specific words will have particular meanings but are open to a whole range of interpretations. Within particular settings there may be a general agreement to the meaning of a word with variables in its usage, that is, the word 'dis-information' seems to be a new version of 'lying.' In some instances there is little or no 'wriggle room' as to what a word means. Considering the Irish Political position, when the 'Good Friday Agreement' on peace (10th April 1998) was negotiated, there was a great stumbling block on whether the paramilitaries would 'stop' or 'cease' the armed struggle. The argument about one word lasted a considerable time. Words like 'stop' and 'go' are not really open to interpretation, although 'hot' and 'cold' can be seen likewise, but they include variations with sliding scales.

The world of psychological therapies, on the whole, create their theories and practice upon words and language among other contributing factors. I recall the many times at the start of group sessions waiting for late-comers. There was a discomfort in the silence and then someone says:

Have we 'started' yet?
And I responded: "We 'started' five minutes ago."

For the questioner the 'start' is when everyone is there and linked to speaking. For the group analyst and some of the others in the group the 'start' is the time originally stated. Much has been written about key words and emotional descriptions of such words, that is, empathy, compassion, gratitude, among many. In another sense these are not singular words but a type of label that both encompasses and expands an experience, both freeing and capturing human thought and emotion. For example, 'love' can be seen as a promotion of openness and 'wellbeing' whereas 'hate' can be viewed as closing or killing something off and is 'not wellbeing.'

My intention from this point is to address specific words through the prism of 'therapeutic love and heartfullness.' The word 'attachment' has been central to many psychotherapies theories such as Bowlby, who sets it in conjunction with 'loss.' Thinking about attachment, the word 'affection' came to mind as this is a necessary ingredient in the creation of attachment. There is then a chain of associations to other words, that is, attachment leads to 'bonding,' which leads to 'integration' to 'internalisation' and so the chain gets greater and greater. Although the acknowledged psychotherapeutic (primarily psychodynamic) schools make use of these states, that within clinical practice methods exist in promoting such chains. There is also a dominance in maintaining therapeutic distance, that is, opaque screen; non-self-disclosure of therapist; maintaining the frame; don't give guidance, the list goes on. Upholding such principles in many cases is appropriate but this can inadvertently undermine what is being sought for in the first place, that is, attachment. Historically, I adhered to this way of thinking and practicing. With moving into 'therapeutic love' as a working model I increasingly saw the importance in using such chains. If the patient, group or I felt 'affection' then it was accepted and shown in a warm and caring way. This then would help to foment 'attachment' and strengthen the 'bond,' which adds further to potential integration, internalisation, with a greater chance of change and dealing more healthily with 'loss' at the end of therapy. The following words are grouped together because of similar properties. The illustrations are taken from my work within individual therapies. I shall explore the group perspective later in this book.

Compassion. Empathy. Sympathy

Although each word is attributed with its own specific meaning, there is an inter-relatedness. To be able to identify with others allows life to be blown into such words or leaves them stony cold. A brief definition will help us as a starting point.

Compassion: a feeling of distress and pity for the suffering or misfortune of another often including the desire to alleviate it.
Empathy: the power of understanding and imaginatively entering into another's feelings.
Sympathy: the Collins dictionary is more expansive here, but briefly:

1   The sharing of another's emotions, especially of sorrow or anguish; pity; compassion.
2   An affinity or harmony, usually of feelings of interests, between persons or things: to be in sympathy with someone.

(Collins, Millennium Edition)

These definitions clearly show, I believe, how each interrelates and overlaps. A simple guideline that I have postulated is that compassion shows an ability and willingness to be open; empathy allows me to enter into a particular position, bringing a part of myself to the table; sympathy allows these principles to be present but I can maintain a certain distance, thus allowing the other person their own unique experience while knowing I am with them and not being seen as an intruder. The following illustrations I think clarifies these areas, while showing the movement towards a therapeutic love perspective.

Claire, who is in the closing stages of therapy comes into her session complaining in her usual way about work pressures and physical ailments. This was between two and three years into her therapy and had been a recurring pattern, with nothing new emerging. At the time my focus had been upon my countertransference irritation. Here I was feeling that we were at an impasse and we could go on indefinitely and I could not mobilise her to further productive change. She was adept at avoidance and resistance. The therapy had become blindly dependent. She had reached a stage where different crises emerged each week which seemed to be the currency of the membership of therapy. Even when she was clearly distressed, I was becoming more impervious and immune to her pain. Thus, the struggle was: Is it time to stop her therapy or do I look more to my own countertransference? With my comments and interpretive interventions this took more of an objective, at times critical, confrontations – all that a disciplined psychotherapist should do (tongue in cheek). There was not much compassion, empathy or sympathy coming from me. However, things took a better turn and eventually we moved into looking at things that had changed for her.

I had been keeping quite strongly to what I had been taught in my training but in retrospect I see the seeds of therapeutic love being sown in those earlier years. In the closing sessions with Claire, I was becoming freer and taking more risks in my own technical approach. In a later session she was contemplating selling her house in order to have money to send her son to a private school. This decision was loaded with many elements. Instead of using the challenging approach from earlier I stepped in and spelt out the areas which I felt would be harmful to her and I began to feel her underlying distress. I was fluctuating between empathy and compassion and I was concerned that she would go through with this major decision, rendering herself homeless.

As things progressed to the closure of her therapy, I had to question what it was generally that got between us. Granted, she struggled to move beyond her own narcissistic proclivities which at times left me cold. I didn't doubt that she was genuine when she spoke of her painful life experiences. A number of my other patients had similar experiences as Claire and I could share more emotively with them. She was able to acknowledge her anger towards me when she felt I couldn't sympathise with her, which was justified. In retrospect that although her therapy ended in a moderately resolved way it is possible that her malignant personality along with my trying to firmly establish a specifically precise, 'by the book' psychodynamic approach, this inhibited therapeutic love to develop.

Alison, a young woman had been in therapy for 9–12 months. One of the things that stays in my memory is that during the winter months she dressed from head to toe in black and in the summer, white. This relatively controlled dress reflected much about her life. Emotionally she was almost frozen/rigid. Central to this is her feeling trapped by her parents with their own considerable problems.

As we were in the last 15 minutes of a session I had reached the point where I was getting through to her, but at other times she withdrew from me into silence and avoided eye contact. I asked her:

Do you remember the first time we met?

Alison was somewhat taken aback:

"I don't know what you mean?!" She smiled here.

At the time we had been speaking about how she internalised others actions, as she did with her parents, making these her own. I reminded her that I had to cancel her first meeting with me at the last minute and when I did see her later, she felt free to be angry with me. I was not defensive and I told her that I had been in the wrong, even though the reason for cancelling seemed justified on my part. It made more sense in that she had initially been assessed by my colleague who discharged her for a failed appointment for which she said that she was not at fault, as she did not receive his appointment letter. She sat waiting for a year until I was due to see her. Lightning struck twice when I had to cancel our first meeting and her angry outburst in our first actual meeting.

In this current session she recalled how she felt she had been let down so badly by my colleague as she had been at death's door. She began to cry at the end of our session, feeling that I had been genuine in my apologies to her and I felt very close to her at this point. We did not want to end and we sat in a peaceful silence for five minutes over time.

This seems similar to the points stated earlier when Irvin Yalom tells us of the intimate, loving end to his session with Betty, stated earlier. What emerged in my session with Alison was a strong sympathy with her in having been overlooked, she had felt forgotten but yet she suffered silently in pain. By my accepting, unequivocally, that I was wrong stopped her taking the blame. It was as if I had opened myself up to her and we both felt close to one another, hence the difficulty in stopping the session. Previously when we focused on the particular things that had gone wrong in her life, I had felt my heart being touched which was also happening now as she had sat silently crying with me. What could be more intimate or as compassionate as this? We both gained from this.

Some Further Theoretical Points

I have been struck by how often I have come across the word 'heart' being spoken about in the psychotherapeutic 'literature.' Many eminent analytic writers sprinkle their work with the word yet do not make it a part of relevant references in their papers, books index. To me compassion, empathy and sympathy are meaningless without acknowledging the heart. Returning to Yalom's writing, which I do with relish, the following quote illustrates this:

> The very heart of psychotherapy is a caring, deeply human meeting between two people, one (generally, but not always, the patient) more troubled than the other. Therapists have a dual role: they must both observe and participate in the lives of their patients. As observer, one must be sufficiently objective to provide necessary rudimentary guidance. As participant, one enters into the life of the patient and is affected and sometimes changed by the encounter.
>
> (Yalom, 1989, p. 13)

Bearing these thoughts in mind I wonder if Yalom would agree with my concepts of therapeutic love and heartfullness.

As a way of moving into my next focus of exploration, care and gratitude, I was drawn to Brian Thornes comments in relation to Person Centred Counselling, thus linking empathy to care:

> The task of empathic understanding can be accomplished only by people who are secure enough in their own identity to move into another's world without the fear of being overwhelmed by it. Once there, therapists have to move around with extreme delicacy and with utter absence of judgement.
>
> (Thorne, 1990a, p. 120)

Care and Gratitude

The great golfer Arnold Palmer was tearful in a television documentary I saw some years ago. He spoke of being touched by the spectators' joy and appreciation, and equally how much he owed them. Thinking about Palmer's comments one may assume that the galleries show him admiration, adulation and gratitude for his abilities. Indeed, it seems that Palmer was well liked in the world of golf. Another take on this could be that golf as a discipline, was given to Palmer and other great golfers to be taken care of, and they have to be 'careful' in how they do this. Palmer's debt shows a collective sense of gratitude, thus care and gratitude are bedfellows.

Returning to the matter of 'specifics' one may venture that the duel between care and gratitude is specific across the board throughout the greater percentage of caring professions. Both the patient and the therapist/doctor need to be valued, that is, being a good patient and being a good therapist. In the earlier years of my career, I invested a great deal into my training, evaluating myself through my sincerity, analytic understanding, developing a disciplined method of practice. To do this I felt I needed to care for my patients/students, and bask in others gratitude, that I was doing a good job, whether through intuitive/intellectual insights or riding to the rescue in difficult periods of crisis. Of course, the counterpoint was that a great range of feelings emerged when I got things wrong or failed in one way or another. At such times gratitude and care did not go hand in hand. The following illustration shows this.

When I worked in the therapeutic community in the 1970s/1980s I was also involved in applying psychodramatic activities to a large community group. One technique is the 'Blind Snake' where the person at the head of the snake leads the group, that all apart from the leader, have their eyes closed, around the building as a form of dance. This is one method aimed at building trust. I tried to encourage one man to take up this role. Here I thought I was doing well up to this point in my leadership. The man got up, overturned his chair and ran out of the room. Another group member, his friend, shouted at me:

Don't you know he has cataracts!

It was difficult to pull things back from the brink.

I was struck by Georg Groddeck's comments, which echoed learning and gratitude from the patient:

> The patient helps the doctor make his unconscious conscious. This is why I believe that the doctor should be grateful to his patient. The patient is the doctor's teacher. Only from the patient will the doctor be able to learn psychotherapy.
> (Groddeck, 1977/1988, p. 221)

Bearing these points in mind, I recall the first session of Suzie's therapy, which was in keeping with many other such new beginnings in therapy. Groddeck's dictum on being taught by the patient was in evidence. I said (as she contemplated continuing therapy with me) unlike her teachers much of what would be happening was about her teaching me how to be with her, in her expectations that I would be the professional and provide solutions for her, just as her teachers had done in the past.

For many patients entering psychotherapy, the initial assessment and early sessions will be extremely daunting, filled with fear, uncertainty, hope and potential resolution. As therapists we put great store on silence and its usage. For Suzie this was evident. Thinking about it the silence brought almost immediate feelings of persecution, being punished. For me it was setting the scene for her to embrace the freedom of speech. Should I expect gratitude by putting her in this uncomfortable silence? She did not feel cared for as I did not 'care' for her like teachers had done in the past. With a degree of regret, I recall the many contacts with patients in periods of long, too long, silences (some for the whole session), which I deployed as a therapy technique. While I would silently meander through my thoughts on meaning and beautiful interpretations, the patient would fidget, freeze or squirm. Sometimes it paid positive dividends and much of value emerged. In retrospect this was not very caring, not worthy of gratitude. Maybe I was grateful that the patient tolerated me and did not walk out in anger, sometimes they did. Possibly a period of between five and ten minutes can be of value but when it goes beyond this it may become problematic and counterproductive. I also recall a technique being taught while training of the value of sitting in the room for the appointed 50 minutes for individual patients or 90 minutes for group sessions when the patient(s) do not arrive with the adage 'keeping the patient in mind.' My first impressions of this phrase were that I had the opportunity to devote wholly a 'giving' to the absent patient. Here I could devote myself to a silent expedition into the abyss of absence and piece together what had gone before, in solitude, the patient and potential reasons for absence. Sanctimonious or what? I do not recall any of my patients ever knowing that I had been present for their absent sessions. I did this for some time and then caught myself on: ridiculous, pretentious. 'Therapeutic love' gains nothing from pretentions. I have become somewhat side-tracked, moving away from Suzie, so let us return. This feeling of persecution was in play when Suzie felt I was putting feelings into her by making her experience the silence. My response was:

> I cannot put feelings into you, they were already there waiting to be activated.

This may also be disingenuous and a denial of the influence and silent power that I have. To frame such processes within a therapeutic love perspective calls for the creation of shorter periods of silence being tolerated. When the therapist breaks the silence, this can be seen as a loving gesture to mobilise the patient from their internal battle. Then the patient may well have a sense of gratitude to the therapist and ultimately feel cared for. However, there are many times when longer silences are necessary and the patient does not feel grateful, or cared for if their reverie is disturbed.

For Suzie, on reflection, that although my adherence to psychodynamic methodology held firm, I was also able to introduce interventions which steered her through silences that I now see as therapeutic love formulations, that is, unlike her response to her school teachers, she was teaching me; she was justified in being angry with me as I had been in the wrong at times.

Overall Reflections

Reflecting back on the structure of this chapter, the emphasis has been upon what it is that makes up a specific aspect of 'therapeutic love and heartfullness.' In order to fulfil such a venture, it has been necessary to consider how things (emotions, thoughts, therapist/patient, physical dimensions, etc.) converge on a number of different levels, at the junctions between patients and therapists and the multifaceted spaces within therapy groups which converge and will be the focus later.

Evelyn Underhill tells us:

> By the word *heart*, of course we here mean not merely 'the seat of the affections', 'the organ of tender emotion', and the like: but rather the 'inner most' sanctuary of personal being, the deep root of its love and will, the very source of its energy and life.
>
> (Underhill, 1911/1948, pp. 71–72)

The above quote encapsulates the following illustration.

I had been meeting with Selena for about two years and we were in the later stages of therapy as she was in the process of moving to another country. I was seeing her in the early part of my career, some 30 years ago, and at that time I was using more conventional psychodynamic formulations and methods. However, what was central was that we liked one another and our relationship was strong. The following extract from one session identifies the heart as the driving force. We had been speaking about her dilemma about being stronger on her own and her need for people, partner, which seemed to diminish her strength. I had responded that the stronger people became the more they recognised 'Others' as part of that strength, but not as a method making up for feelings of vulnerability; she felt I was right. This then brought to the fore her feelings for me:

> I know I need to come to you for reassurance when I feel I'm losing strength. I could come forever but I know I can't, but part of me wants to. When I'm feeling good I don't have problems to bring.

Generally, she had been feeling a lot better which prompted her to want to know how I deal with my life problems.

> I replied: "In a similar way as you. I question my own strengths and vulnerabilities in my own therapy and supervision, and with friends."
> Selena: "I admire you and how you're able to sit through things with me and your other patients."

At times of distress she feels too much for me when she gets into anger and rage with me. She feels I do not help her make sense but feels grateful when I sometimes close our session with interpretations/interventions that calm her and helps her make sense. Also, my being available at times of crisis and quick response in between sessions brings her security. At the close of the session, she located a central conflict which may well be universal to the dilemmas/conflicts of love when she said:

> I'm afraid of how much I depend on you.

It seemed to me that she feared the curative potential of our 'therapeutic love' based on a deep level of care (when I also felt close to her) warmth, strength, in contrast to the threat of erotic love, or indeed the statement 'I want to come to you forever,' which is impossible. Such a position as Selena's has been common with many other people who have been in therapy with me, individually or in groups. I would surmise that such sentiments go 'across the board' for other therapists and patients. With the complex arrangements engendered in psychotherapy, there will be a sweeping array of commonalities while at the same time reaching conclusions/ formulations specific to each person's individual and unique experiences. With the following chapter I trust that the expansion of theoretical perspectives will aid us in this exploration.

Chapter 4

'Meandering Through the Literature'

An alternative title of the book could have been; 'The Mutterings of a Madman.' This title came to mind when reading the opening to Paul Tabori's book, 'The Natural Science of Stupidity in 1959,' in which Richard Armour's introduction says:

> Some are born stupid, some achieve stupidity and some have stupidity thrust upon them. But most are stupid not because of what has been done to them by either their ancestors or their contemporaries. It is their own hard won accomplishment. They have made fools of themselves, indeed, some perfectionists have made perfect fools of themselves. Of course they would be the last to know, and one almost hates to tell them, for ignorance of stupidity is bliss.
>
> (Tabori, 1959, p. vii)

The questions therefore beg to be answered. Am I a stupid fool to have come up with the duel concept of heartfullness and therapeutic love? Surely the notion that the heart is placed above the supreme dominance of the brain, as well as the less clear conception of the mind/mindfulness, has ventured into the realms of madness. However, in raising these questions within a chapter which focuses on 'the literature' turns our attention to other writers/theorists who have trodden upon this territory. There may be a view that if one supplies copious theoretical references from renowned professionals in the 'field' this is tantamount to verification of new literature, and dare I say it, proof. It is not my intention to prove anything in my publication but merely to elaborate on my convictions on the subject which in the end is – 'close to my heart.'

This chapter is not intended to be a critical evaluation/review of psychotherapy/psychoanalytic literature. What I found was the result of meandering through books and papers, mostly before 2005. Views of the 'heart' and 'therapeutic love' were extremely limited. Most of the more meaningful accounts of love that I found by accident were in fictional literature and music. My love of Irish literature is central to this. However, the greater percentage of this presentation will be drawn from psychotherapeutic literature.

Over 100 years ago, in 1914, Alexander Irvine from Antrim, Northern Ireland, wrote a book about his life, dominated by his reflections on his mother and growing

DOI: 10.4324/9781003536857-5

up in poverty: 'My lady of the Chimney Corner.' Although religion plays a part in his writing it is not as relevant as love, which blossomed in extreme poverty. During a conversation with his mother, while discussing thoughts about a neighbour, on love and religion, his mother says:

> No, dear, Willie (neighbour) sees only half the world. There's love in it, that's bigger than colour of ribbon or creed of Church. We've proven that, Jamie (Alexander Irvine – author) haven't we? "But what have ye decided? That love is bigger than religion." That two things are sure. One is love of God. He loves all his children and gets huffed at none. The other is that the love we have for each other is of the same warp and woof as his for us, love is enough Jamie.
>
> (Irvine, 1914, p. 26)[1]

Meandering forward to a century later another writer from Northern Ireland in his fictional 'The Poets Wives' says, in speaking about one of the central figures in the novel

> "she made herself believe that love was always stronger than words, and it was the force of her love alone that caused him now to form silently about her" and to: "Catch him on the soft hook of her love".
>
> (Park, 2014, pp. 216–217)

Later in the book:

> But what were words now without love? She tried to tell herself that words alone had no special claim over life, that it was the heart that spoke truest always, but even in the same moment her conviction faltered because she knew that throughout her life she had believed that words were holy things that should be reverenced.
>
> (Park, 2014, p. 273)

Hopefully these two references, 100 years apart, show the richness of our Irish literature.

Moving on to psychotherapeutic literature, I had enumerated in previous Chapters 1 and 2 the various elements that make up the complexities of 'heartfullness' and 'therapeutic love,' such as empathy, care and compassion. Each of the following writers takes up different strands and perspectives. Thorne turns to 'care'

> In short, a person who is cared for begins to feel at a deep level that perhaps she is after all worth caring for.
>
> (Thorne, 1990b, p. 118)

In considering love within psychoanalytic perspectives in relation to depression, Bergman, referring to Edith Jacobson, says

Jacobson pointed out that depressives try to recover their lost ability to love through the magic love they hope to receive from their love objects. They tend to establish an immediate intense rapport, or none. They often feel better without any apparent intrapsychic reasons. The mere hope that analysis will cure them is sufficient to bring improvement in their feelings, they tend to make heavy demands on their analysts.

(Kohon, 1999, p. 377)

Irvin D. Yalom in his Existential Psychotherapy book makes some interesting points. He refers to Carlos Sequin and describes the therapist/patient relationship as a special form of love:

psychotherapeutic eros is indestructible or as 'Carl Rodgers put it, "nonconditional." Other forms of love can be eroded.' – "Another aspect of psychotherapeutic eros is that it implies a genuine caring for the person of the patient. – he (therapist) should have an authentic feeling of love for the particular individual who is before him, who is *this* man and not another, who is not a 'sick man', but rather a man." The therapists *Raison d'être* is to be midwife to the birth of the patients yet unlived life.

(Yalom, 1980, p. 408)

These comments seem to echo my own formulations of 'therapeutic love.' However, I think that by using 'eros' as part of the title, it still holds on to the potential twinning with erotic, eroticism, etc. In another of Yalom's books, 'Staring at the Sun,' he speaks of the power of empathy

Empathy is the most powerful tool we have in our efforts to connect with other people. It is the glue of human connectedness and permits us to feel, at a deep level, what someone else is feeling.

(Yalom, 2011, p. 123)

In an earlier chapter I spoke of the times when I disclosed things about myself, which is an element within therapeutic love, either verbally or emotionally. Yalom, in the same book tells us:

Therapists should reveal themselves, - Therapist self-disclosure is a complex and contested area. Few suggestions I make to therapists are as unsettling as my urging them to reveal more of themselves. It sets their teeth on edge. It evokes the spectre of a patient invading their personal life. I do not mean that therapists should reveal themselves indiscriminately: to begin with they should reveal only when the revelation will be of value to the patient.

(Yalom, 2011, p. 241)

Taking a leap back in time to Evelyn Underhill's book 'Mysticism,' first published in 1911, she speaks beautifully about love throughout her book. Her definition, which echoes my views, states succinctly how love can be viewed mystically. She says

> Mysticism – is essentially a movement of the heart, seeking to transcend the limitations of the individual stand point and to surrender itself to ultimate reality; for no personal gain, to satisfy no transcendental curiosity; to obtain no other – worldly joys, but purely from an instinct of love. By the word *heart*, of course we here mean not merely "the seat of the affections", "the organ of tender emotions" and the like: but rather the inmost sanctuary of personal being, the deep root of its love and will, the very source of its energy and life. – We see – the two eternal passions of the self, the desire of love and the desire of knowledge: severally representing the hunger of heart and intellect for ultimate truth.
>
> (Underhill, 1911/1948, pp. 71–72)

I couldn't have put it better myself.

Returning to more recent years R.D. Laing in his book 'The Divided Self,' he embraces the subject of love in relation to schizophrenia. Although this is a field in which I have miniscule experience, my work with 'dissociative identity disorders' has parallels. He speaks of love and understanding:

> I think it is clear that by understanding I do not mean a purely intellectual process. For understanding one might say love. But no word has been more prostituted. What is necessary, though not enough, is a capacity to know how the patient is experiencing himself and the world, including oneself. If one cannot understand him, one is hardly in the position to begin to 'love' him in any effective way.
>
> (Laing, 1965, p. 34)

Laing later shows the complexity of love distortion within schizoid individuals

> If there is anything the schizoid individual is likely to believe in, it is his own destructiveness. He is unable to believe that he can fill his own emptiness without reducing what is there to nothing. He regards his own love and that of others as being as destructive as hate. To be loved threatens his self; but his love is equally dangerous to anyone else.
>
> (Laing, 1965, p. 165)

Bearing these points in mind I think that Laing's views can be applied across the board to other psychological conditions. He also shows how difficult it is to show and apply therapeutic love with this, schizoid/schizophrenia, group of people. Also, in his highlighting the paradox of love being experienced as destructive as hate shows that both emotional states do not necessarily need to be placed in opposition. One final point Laing makes is important, and I think does not only apply to schizophrenia. He says

The main agent in uniting the patient, in allowing the pieces to come together and cohere, is the physicians love, a love that recognizes the patients total being and accepts it, with no strings attached.

(Laing, 1965, p. 165)

With regard to sympathy, kindness and generosity, William McDougal makes some interesting comments. Although he does not use the word love in the following, this is as much a statement of love as I have purported. He says:

What I am concerned to show is that generosity and kindness are distinct qualities, which though commonly combined in the personality, are not necessarily combined. Either may be possessed and displayed in action in the absence of the other. – the word "generosity", is commonly used in a loose and confused manner, namely sympathy. In common usage a man is said to display sympathy when he shows compassion or pity, when he responds to the signs of suffering in another creature with efforts to relieve and comfort it.

(McDougal, 1927, p. 142)

McDougal develops these points by looking at the various meanings of such words, how they differ or correlate. Although he mentions kindness, he does not expand upon it.

In his chapter 'Human Nature,' from the same publication McDougal makes similar comments as Underhill regarding the heart as stated earlier

There is another side to the mind which, though it functions always in closest relation with the intellectual factors, is broadly distinguishable; this other side we may call broadly the emotional or volitional side, the "heart" in distinction from "the head." It is this other side with which we are more particularly concerned in discussing conduct and character; and we must endeavour to form a picture of the raw materials, the inborn features, factors or constituents, of this part of the total personality.

(McDougal, 1927, p. 10)

I believe that this is what I am doing in this book. Thinking about Underhill and McDougal's comments possibly the heart may have been given more credence in the early 20th century.

My impression is that the heart, as a central driving force, is present to a greater amount within mythology and fairy stories. Estes, in her book: 'Women Who Run with the Wolves' draws attention to the place of the heart in Hindu religion

The psychological and physiological centre is the heart. In Hindu *Tantras*, which are instructions from the Gods to humans, the heart is the Anáhata chakra, the nerve centre that encompasses feeling for another human, feeling for oneself, feeling for the earth, and feeling for God. It is the heart that enables us to love as a child loves: fully, without reservation, and with no hull of sarcasm, or protectionism.

(Estes, 1992, p. 159)

She refers to the myth of the 'skeleton woman,' who was brought up from the sea by a fisherman

When Skeleton woman uses the fisherman's heart, she uses the central motor of the entire psyche, the only thing that really matters, the only thing of creating pure and innocent feeling. They say it is the mind that thinks and creates. This story says otherwise, that it is the heart that thinks and calls the molecules, atoms, feelings, yearnings, and whatever else need be, into one place to create the matter that fulfils Skeleton Woman's creation.

(Estes, 1992, p. 159)

This view, that it is the heart, and not the mind that is the most important driving force in life, is the hub of my own contentions – the heart of the book.

In our meandering searches into the heart and therapeutic love, we find empathy as a primary ingredient. Heinz Kohut is a central figure in the field of 'Self Psychology.' Alan M. Siegal in his work on Kohut says

He (Kohut) turns first to his original delineation of empathy as a definer of the psychological field (1959) and restates his earlier thesis that just as the external world is studied through the extrospective instruments employed by various sciences, so the internal world is studied by the psychological observer through the instruments of empathy – the analyst immerses him or herself in the perception of the patients experience and then reflects upon the nature of that experience. – Kohut emphasizes that empathy is the means by which the psychological observer gathers information about the inner world of human experience. Empathy is a data – gathering instrument.

(Siegal, 1996, pp. 186–187)

Although I am in agreement with most of this, phrases about the analyst being a 'psychological observer,' a 'collector of data' and a 'data collection instrument' do not sit comfortably with my thesis. If the heart is a driving force of empathy, this makes it more an instrument of inclusion between two or more parties.

Staying a little longer with Kohut we can see the inclusive nature of Kohut's theories. Joseph D. Lichtenberg says

"Experience does teach us", Kohut (1971) wrote, "That many of those who choose a career in which the empathic preoccupation with others forms the centre of the professional activity are persons who have suffered traumas (of tolerable proportions) in early phases of empathy development" (Kohut, pp. 279–280) – Much of our ability to establish a fit with a particular patient depends on the fluidity with which we can gain access to our feelings and our reactions. Success in applying the empathic mode of perception in the moment-to-moment exchanges of the therapeutic hour often requires that we quickly recognize when we are having difficulty in maintaining an empathic stance.

(Goldberg, 1990, pp. 30–31)

Two of the other elements of heartfullness and therapeutic love are 'tenderness' and 'intimacy,' on one level tenderness is connected to gentleness, and intimacy cannot be achieved without either of these two. In David Smail's book, he refers to Freud on this matter:

> Freud did us no great service, perhaps, in suggesting that the origins of intimacy and tenderness is to be found in sexuality, but this view still holds sway despite the arguments which have been levelled against it forcefully and cogently by several influential psychologists and psychiatrists since Freuds time. "The appeal of Freud's view can in part be understood in the opportunities it presents in objectifying the otherwise subjective, and in some ways abstract concept (faculty, experience) of love".

(Smail, 1984, p. 56)

Smail goes on to elaborate the complexities of love as a subjective experience but I wondered that with such clarity on his side he missed commenting on the heart:

> Love is both our salvation and our greatest danger: he or she who loves reciprocally and without defences takes the most terrifying risk of annihilation. Love confirms you as a satisfactory object, but its withdrawal may destroy you. Whether or not you are loved is likely to depend on your behaving in accordance with your lovers' needs and expectations. Lovers must watch each other warily, fake, dissemble, and be ready at a moment's notice to defend themselves.

(Smail, 1984, p. 162)

Although I am in agreement generally with these comments, it seems to weigh heavily on the catastrophic potential of love, which indeed many of our patients come to us with. Smail does balance the books when he says

> Love is not to be sneezed at. In a society in which we have all become objects, it is the best and most fulfilling mode in which to conduct our relations with each other. Love and happiness go hand-in-hand. Love protects us from the sheer brutal savagery otherwise so apparent in our social intercourse. Love is our emotional currency, without which we cannot, it seems, exist.

(Smail, 1984, p. 163)

Regarding references to the art therapy literature, I initially could find very little that considered love or the heart individually or in groups. Here I am speaking primarily about the British arena. However, there were a few papers about group analytic art therapy in the Group Analysis journal but not about love in any form. The American literature was also very sparse but I found some joy in a few books considering loving factors: in art groups and individual therapy: Bruce Moons 'Art-Based Group Therapy' (Moon, n.d.); Vaculik & Nash's 'Integrative Arts Psychotherapy' (Vaculik & Nash, 2022) and Webber's 'Breakthrough Moments in Arts-Based Psychotherapy' (Webber, 2017), which is very impressive.

I am thankful to one of the 'Readers' of my book for reminding me of a paper by Caroline Case in 1990, she speaks about 'Heart Forms – The Image as a Mediator.' It is difficult to draw close parallels with my own findings as her paper is about her work with children. Nevertheless, some of our views resonate together. Her paper is specifically about individual art therapy. The following extracts from her paper illustrate our associations. I was touched by her account which is similar to mine and Yalom's earlier comments on the stethoscope, on touching and listening. At the start of her session with a boy of nine:

> On the way (to the therapy room) he clutched at his chest saying "My heart is black, it hurts, a pain. Once in the therapy room he continued "It's black, it hurts, a pain, I can't do anything." He sat with his head in his hands.[2] I went to him and knelt down beside him, put my ear to his chest and said, "I can hear it beating." He paused for a second, looked up, then jumped up all smiles and asked if I had his folder, which he began to look through.
>
> (Case, 1990, pp. 20–26)

This was very touching in its tangibleness. There is much in this paper which addresses mediation and the significance of the heart within the art therapeutic venture. In keeping with my views she says:

> When the heart is in trouble, when it is 'black' – the pain, it is mental isolation that is being expressed in some way, a loneliness at the core of being. To listen to the heart felt important in this instance because the heart is symbolic of the life principle.
>
> (Case, 1990, p. 20)

I agree that it is symbolic but it is also a concrete and physical source of emotions.

The Broken Heart

How does one mend a broken heart? There are stories of people dying from a broken heart, lifelong partners dying within hours/days of one another. Many hold the acuteness of the initial fracture while creating new loves, yet the first break remains in one form or another. Love breaks, love heals. At the time of writing this chapter I heard on the news that day about a man, living locally, who dropped dead at his wife's funeral. Possibly he died of grief. In much of general language, the concept of coincidence is seen as accidental, almost meaningless concurring events, that is, 'it's only a coincidence, forget about it.' Yet for me, there are specific meanings in apparent chance coincidences, echoing such concepts as synchronicity. I have already alluded to this in Chapter 2. Broken hearts need repairing.

The concept of reparation is central to Kleinian theory. Although I see reparation just as central to making and breaking love, I have moved away from the very primitive frame of reference which Klein advocates. Hanna Segal refers to this

> The reparative drives bring about a further step in integration. Love is brought more sharply into conflict with hate, and it is active both in controlling destructiveness and in repairing and restoring damage done. It is the wish and the capacity for restoration of the good object, internal and external, that is the basis of the ego's capacity to maintain love and relationships through conflicts and difficulties.
>
> (Segal, 1964, p. 92)

In my attempts to understand Melanie Klein's views on love, of which there are many conveyed with great gravitas, I thought about the nursery rhyme Humpty Dumpty who fell off the wall breaking into pieces. 'All the king's horses and all the king's men couldn't put humpty back together again.' By this I mean that the language of love had been broken into many pieces and in trying to put them together, the task is too great because there are too many pieces, multiplying with each attempt. In trying to grasp Klein's complex object/part-object theories, this, to me, was aimed more at breaking things down as compared to mending. At the thought of 'object relating', it is as if my mind blanked, and I withdraw. I block off. Objects are structures with particular forms and shapes ie a house, tree, coin, toothbrush and hard to relate to in human emotional equations. Could we relinquish object and replace it with heart or love and possibly both: 'Love and Heart Relating'?

Another early psychoanalytic writer, Otto Rank, drew attention to the split within sexuality, by which I'm assuming is physical eroticism and love. In Otto Rank's words

> We can only refer in this connection to one aspect of this perhaps most important of all human phenomena, the significance of which psychoanalysis missed in its identification of sexuality and love. There is just the contrast between sexuality and love that often enough causes love to resist sexuality and fly before it, just as under certain conditions sexuality can be a flight from love.
>
> (Rank, 1960, p. 274)

These thoughts are echoed later by J.A. Hadfield

> Freud, for instance, regards those components of love such as friendship and admiration as sexual, but 'aim restricted', that is to say bereft of their sexual aim of reproduction. He confuses love with sex; indeed he says in one place that sex is

all that we mean by the word love, and makes them synonymous. This is contrary to biological fact as well as contrary to experience of the *feeling* involved.

(Hadfield, 1962, p. 202)

Neville Symington in more recent years conveys similar views;

When Freud turns to love he candidly admits that he is unwilling to consider it as a component drive of libido. Instead he wants to see it as an expression of the *whole sexual current* and it seems to me to be one of the cases what one might call a basic belief does not fit his model, which still has a physiological basis.

(Symington, 1986, pp. 122–123)

Recalling my earlier comments on the similarities/difference between empathy and sympathy I postulated earlier in how, unlike sympathy, empathy employed a deeper personal identification. Harry Guntrip writes about Brierley's process theory and personal theory and expounded psychoanalysis

Therapy and research both aim at understanding the patient, but understanding a patient is more than intellectual apprehension; it is empathy, thinking and feeling *rapport* with the patient. *Empathic understanding* is akin to identification and produces personology, which he regards as 'subjective theory.'

(Guntrip, 1982, p. 142)

Throughout this book I have elaborated upon the area of dependence and interdependence and how this fits into the concepts of the heart, heartfullness and therapeutic love. In his chapter, from the same book, Guntrip draws our attention to such connections

"Dependence is, in fact, an ineradicable element in human nature, and the whole development of love and the affections arises out of our needs for one another." – "without the acceptance of that measure of dependence that lies at the heart of all human needs for relationships, one becomes incapable of love, friendship, marriage or any truly human co-operative activity."

(Guntrip, 1982, p. 383)

The main purpose of this chapter has been to present a wide spectrum of other writers in the 'field.' Throughout the book I attempt to convey the ways that love complexities are manifested. One manifestation is that of 'giving' and 'taking' love. When love is manifested as a direct stirring of the heart, giving and taking is redundant as 'IT' just happens, coming from a: 'pool of who knows where.' Eric Fromm speaks of the type of character who has a 'receptive orientation'

"In the receptive orientation a person feels the source of all good" to be outside, and he believes that the only way to get what he wants – be it something material, be it affection, love, knowledge, pleasure – is to receive it from that outside source. In this orientation the problem of love is almost exclusively that of "being loved" and not that of loving. – "They are exceedingly sensitive to any withdrawal or rebuff they experience on the part of the loved one."

(Fromm, 1949, p. 62)

Later Fromm speaks of superficiality which could easily apply, in my view, to his earlier comments on the receptive orientation, but this may also apply across the board:

The superficial character of human relationships leads many to believe that they can find depth and intensity of feeling in individual love. But love for one person and love for one's neighbour are indivisible; in any given culture, love relationships are only a more intense expression of the relatedness to man prevalent in that culture.

(Fromm, 1949, p. 75)

I think that there will be little disagreement that love is powerful. However, power comes in many forms, some active, some passive, some simmering, etc. From Rollo Mays book 'Power and Innocence,' he says

The allegory of love conquering power reveals an archetype of human experience that speaks to us all in diverse ways. We can understand again what Buber means when he writes in the same poem:

I do not know what would remain to us
Were love not transfixed power.
And power not straying love

We are the creatures of whose love is continually straying into power and whose power is occasionally transfigured by love.

(May, 1972, p. 251)

In contrast to the above, when we initially think of compassion this first appears as a somewhat benevolent concept, a gentle, tender approach to the, primarily, suffering of other, a giving over of one's heart and a silent absorption of that area of suffering into the 'compassionee' (my made up word). Looking at it in these terms one can see the power in compassion, the power to heal. This leads us onto May's views on compassion.

Compassion is the name of that form of love which is based on our understanding of each other. Compassion is the awareness that we are all in the same boat and that we all shall either sink or swim together. *Compassion arises from recognition of community.*

(May, 1972, p. 251)

Anthony Storr tells us

> I do not believe that it matters to which school the therapist belongs, nor which beliefs or theories he holds, if he himself is capable of this attitude of objective love.
>
> (Storr, 1960, p. 134)

With this in mind, a number of psychotherapists and psychoanalysts came together to present their own developmental stories in 'Odyssey in Psychotherapy.' I was drawn to these as, in a way, this book is my own odyssey. Judith V. Jordan tells us

> "The therapist's humility and respect for the wisdom and the struggles of the patient are essential for the development of mutual empathy and change."[3] – "I believe that humility and compassion are essential to real connection and a real healing, in both therapist and patient." – "Students and other therapists often search for universal techniques or answers. The best I can provide is a philosophy, an attitude of respect and mutuality, guidelines, a set of beliefs and values about what helps people grow."
>
> (Jordan, 2000, pp. 164–165)

Returning to the world of fiction, Liam Browne tells us:

> Sorrow was like love, the hub towards which everything radiated. And grieving was like being in love, its effortless centrality, so that out of the most unpromising facts and situations of everyday life you developed the ability to contrive connections to the lost or loved one.
>
> (Browne, 2006, p. 72)

In my earlier publications along with this book, I have drawn parallels between my love of golf and psychotherapy. I would like to finish with a piece from Andrew Grieg's Preferred Lies – a journey to the heart of golf:

> Somebody asked him, as a Scottish golfer, his idea of a great shot. Without hesitation he replied, 'Ben Hogan said, "A great golf shot starts in the hands and finishes in my heart" I wouldnae argue wi that' (Scottish dialect).
>
> (Grieg, 2007, p. 175)

Possibly it can also be the other way around, starting in the heart.

Notes

1 Written in the Antrim dialect.
2 This is reflective of my opening to my later chapter on Individual Therapy.
3 From my own perusals I found little written about humility in therapeutic literature.

Chapter 5

Reflections and Art Therapy Perspectives

What good is too much book learning anyway, it only corrupts the heart.

(Halam, 2005, p. 81)

The above line is taken from an interesting children's book when one of the characters is questioning the value of book learning. This appealed to me as I reflect upon my career, particularly those times when so much language, words, theories clouded the power of the heart. Further, that in looking at the following reflections, primarily through the prism of art therapy within this evolution, the heart will hopefully shed previous 'corruptive' attitudes in keeping with Halam's question on 'book learning.'

I became aware of a possible unconscious link with a paper I wrote for an address to the 'Greek Association of Classical Psychoanalysis' in 2015, which was called 'The Lost and Stolen Heart.' When I focussed upon the heart being stolen, this did not imply a purposeful theft but an indication that the range of analytic/dynamic theories and methods were, in effect, stealing the heart dominance as the driving force between psychoanalysts and those in their care. I can still see the doubting but friendly looks and discussions with 'dyed in the wool' psychoanalysts who certainly needed some convincing to take me seriously. In contrast to psychoanalysis, the introduction of 'actual' colour and concrete imagery – through painting, drawing and sculpting – in art psychotherapeutic models we can see that the therapeutic field opens up exponentially. With the psychoanalytic/psychodynamic therapist, patient/group arrangements, functioning through verbal dialogue, emotional colour is reliant primarily on verbal capacities. Language will encompass a wide range of emotional colour interspersed with other non-verbal and silent expressions, but not 'actual' colour and 'concrete' symbolism in pictorial imagery.

In verbal therapies how often are alarm bells triggered when patients speak of overpowering blackness or white isolation and hopelessness? There is little room for manoeuvre in art therapy when such concrete pictures are created. The individual art psychodynamic approach and group analytic art therapy development moved me away from other art therapy thinking and technique. On the whole this had been prescriptive, that is, particular things to say and do within the therapy

DOI: 10.4324/9781003536857-6

sessions; collective meanings for colour and symbols. Much of this had been handed down through psychiatry and early affiliations with this professional group which rested upon psychopathology.

Much has changed in art therapies evolution. I cannot claim a comprehensive knowledge of art therapy as a profession/practitioner since 1995. Since then my involvement in this field dwindled, moving me more actively into verbal therapies. However, I did continue through with academic teaching and writing, and I did have 20 years under my belt as an art therapist, conducting between five and eight art groups a week as well as trainee and student groups here and abroad.

The title of this chapter focuses upon 'reflections.' I do not intend to develop detailed lines of enquiry into art therapy per se. I will leave that to well informed practitioners more able to undertake such a task. For example, Susan Hogan's brilliant book on the History of Art Therapy is a treasure trove of information (Hogan, 2001). However, it takes us up to the mid-1990s and there is little written on art therapy groups in her book. Chris Wood contributes a further helpful text which brings together many key and important parts of art therapies moving into the 21st century in: Navigating Art Therapy (Wood, 2011). This chapter is not confined to art therapy in its strictest sense, but integrated with other factors. For me, the art therapy rudiments from my early years evolved into a tri-partite formulation and cross influencer with group analysis, group analytic art therapy and individual primarily verbal psychotherapy. Although individual art therapy occurred, it had been at a minimal level.

Meandering

From this point my subtitle of the book comes into play: 'Meandering.' This is a movement through particular and fleeting accounts/illustrations of art therapy scenarios, which are linked with group analysis and particular settings. I want to raise an extremely important point. What I offer is 'my' approach, which may appear idiosyncratic at times. In no way is it intended to convey a 'specific technique and method.' However, I hope that what I offer will stimulate the reader in their own developments. Throughout this evolution, there has always been the chicken-egg conundrum in that it is hard to see what theoretical and practical element came first. For instance, I have written about the evolution of different art group titles which culminated in my present title of 'group analytic art therapy' which progressed from the initial 'non directive art therapy' (McNeilly, 1983/1984, pp. 211–219).

With time immemorial humans have developed greater and more sophisticated desires and ways to communicate. A very simple assumption is that the greatest part of this has rested upon individuals and groups making their marks, either through thought or action. The initial marks have to be made. An image of a 'threshold' comes to mind in that with each point/mark of change through words and deeds, the courage to go over thresholds is crucial for developing Society and health. These processes I suggest cannot emerge and develop for individuals and groups without at least three ingredients: uniqueness, intuition and spontaneity, which may entail going out of one's comfort zone. Consequently, art therapy and other disciplines require such ingredients. Therefore, each art therapeutic model will be built upon particular structures/methods which are felt to deliver access to the patient and are driven by, such ingredients. Each will have particular guidelines, words, instructions, suggestions, motivating techniques created in order to help the patient/group to make marks which are unique to that setting. Therefore, the therapeutic thresholds are continually challenged.

As stated earlier, I went through a gambit of titles over many years until I came to 'group analytic art therapy,' I said at the start of each new venture into the method:

> I would like you to use the materials (paper, paint, crayons, pens, clay etc.) in the room to express whatever you want or not. Approximately half way through we will come together to discuss things.

This creates an opportunity for people to make concrete images and then move into a circle in order to have space to discuss things once the pictures are made. Group members are not duty bound to speak or to have made an image. This overall set of directives is what defines 'group analytic art therapy.'

In a way this request also ensures the uniqueness of the individual in a group analysis format where each concrete image is shaped, and remains concretely intact throughout the session, which had a guiding directive at the beginning of sessions. For those patients entering primarily verbal group analytic groups their separate individuality can at times be threatened with individuals getting lost in the group identity when the group activity and dialogue surrounds them. Unlike this format, the art group productions remain static within the dialogue. In the primarily verbal group, people are stationary, sitting in a circle of chairs. Individuals separate identities through a collective group prism are evidenced with verbal and mental pictures of their specific events and group developments. Dialogue floats around on the winds of change. All of these aspects will be part of the group analytic group but when concrete marks are made in the group analytic art group format, there can be a greater sense of presence 'in the moment,' having a different type of power which is encompassing.

Previously I wrote about my early development in my art therapy training and the various hurdles and obstacles on the way (McNeilly, 2006b, pp. 17–19). Quite early I had to experience and process the impact and influence of early well-known art therapists. Edward Adamson was one of our major art therapists along with Adrian Hill, Rita Simon, Diana Haliday and others disturbed the status quo, and in no small measure (along with many others who followed in their footsteps), in the large psychiatric, mental handicap (old terminology) hospitals and Institutes. As I was taught and learnt from these important people, many questions that were 'daring to disturb' moved within me. Not least of these was the paucity of art group theories and understandings. This was followed by my movement into group analysis and beginning to create complex structures which moved away from these older teachings. Although, at the time, some of this came across as negative, that is, being seen to be solely critical of established art therapy practices, I believe it has moved more into the constructive disturbance spectrum. These art therapy pioneers were not so different, as a whole, to the Greek psychoanalysts I spoke of earlier. As Hogan says:

> Most art therapy pioneers – were resolutely opposed to the idea of the therapist furnishing interpretations of the clients art work, although there were a few interesting and notable exceptions.
>
> (Hogan, 2001, p. 23)

Although at this point the principles of group analysis were unknown to me I intuitively valued the range of contributions, not just painting and drawing, with or without verbal interpretation. One teaching activity was that of us lying down on the floor and listening to a piece of music, at times with relaxation exercises. Following this music we made concrete images, followed by some group discussion on individual accounts of the experience. It was the first time I'd heard Tubular Bells by Mike Oldfield (1973) which was played as I/we lay on the floor, relaxing and allowing the music to wash over us, it had a powerful impact. I later used this method both at the Henderson Therapeutic Community on my student placement and later at the Ingrebourne Centre in my first professional art therapy position. Unlike the student groups, in both these settings, with the personality disorder clientele it evoked so much more extreme responses. Although many found the exercise, for want of a better word conducive, a number responded negatively as it brought up too much too quickly. Returning to the college focus, this activity was within a wide range of other therapeutic activities: individual and group painting, sculpting, drawing, music ventures, personal studio space for private creations.

In my later role as tutor/lecturer at Goldsmith's College and other Universities I made use of media beyond 2D painting drawing, etc., which began to form part of the developing tools of my trade. For example, I regularly facilitated an art therapy student groups, separate two yearly intakes for the duration of the training over a ten-year period. An early starting point was that the group would start with a brief discussion on how they wanted to use the two hours: did they want to have a theme/idea, work separately, make a group painting/sculpture or speak or not speak during the concrete image-making. By this point I was now well and truly working from a group analytic perspective but as I was not conducting it in the same way as a clinical group (which was built upon deeper treatment/psychotherapeutic exploration) this allowed for a freer, playful, adventurous structure and atmosphere. Sadly, I was unable to secure permission to include photos of the Goldsmith's group sculptures. However, Figure 5.1 shows a group sculpt from Portuguese students who created such structures during training events which I convened. As such, the finished sculpt emerged from both specific theoretical components of the pertinent curriculum and each member's personal associations.

Following along this line of thought there were many art groups when the members would make a decision about creating something as one collective image. It was also possible on these occasions for one or more to do their own piece and then bring it to the closing collective dialogue or stay separate (see Figure 5.2). The

Figure 5.1 The picture shows an art therapy group sculpture made by Portuguese art therapy students. A colourful tri-partite painting of a blue sail boat going towards a blue and white lighthouse and the land beyond.

Figure 5.2 The painting by the same Portuguese group as the previous image is a colourfully vibrant set of 13 separate rectangular paintings that have been attached to one another on a joint large circular painting. The interplay/integration looks like a wheel.

collective wish seemed to occur more with student/trainee art therapist groups as compared to groups in treatment.

In this collective structure, the students worked separately and then joined them up. As can be seen from these illustrations, they show the interplay between individual and group perspectives.

Over the years, in such groups the points I am raising were recurring with regularity. There were similar, and at times difficult, experiences, as occurred in patient groups which had to be worked with 'as if' members were regressing to patient-like states. On very rare occasions did trainees have to move into therapeutic treatment as things opened up, although it was a requirement for students to be in separate individual therapy as part of their training. Even though these were not therapeutic treatment groups, they still brought forth life experiences and challenges which were not so different. I think also that by providing a group analytic model this gave space for the therapeutic loving framework to develop as it provided a format akin to the constituent elements which I have proposed occurs in patient groups. Group sculpts were a key element in my work in the therapeutic community.

Therapy and Academia Say Hello

In a similar way to most therapeutic professions, art therapists establish a continuum from an initial graduate in the arts and other professions, that is, psychology, nursing, social work, to their post graduate art therapy training in Britain. Following this they, probably the majority, hold that position throughout their career whereas others develop new, more advanced professions, that is, psychotherapy. It is then incumbent on us to not only develop good therapeutic environs but also advance techniques and theories. Once again, one may be expected or personally driven to create new theories, or at least make existing milieus stronger and relevant to change. There are excellent art therapists who have not felt the need to go beyond their initial standing.

In previous publications I have detailed a number of my practice and theoretical developments within different settings (McNeilly, 2006b). With each of these settings much could be written about these alone. Certainly, as I made my first tentative steps into the complex structure of therapeutic communities for severe personality disorders, although I had the basic art therapy rudiments, I had no art therapy mentor or figurehead to guide me. I had to make it up as I went along. This possibly contributed to how my early papers and publications carried elements of attacking or at least criticising the status quo. Much of what I was saying and publishing was like 'groping in the dark.'

Alongside these areas I became involved in our National art therapy organisation – British Association of Art Therapists. This brought into relief the importance of art therapy being recognised governmentally with established employment rights, salaries and professional scales in similar keeping to our medical peers. In some ways art therapists had to move away from 'accepting their lot' and into the political battles for professional recognition by the 'State.' As will be seen in a later chapter my ability and flexibility to consider matters 'outside the consulting room' has its roots in these early political days. I recall being the only one going 'on strike' at the Ingrebourne Centre Therapeutic Community when the patients manned the picket line with me at the time of the dispute.

These comments pre-empt my reflections upon the general transitions in this evolution. As one may see, that in the process of becoming a solid practising art therapist, at that time, involved such extra-curricular movement. The British Art Therapy Association had its Annual General Meeting which developed a particular structure. Usually, in the early years, this occurred in London so some members would have to travel long distances from the four provinces (England, Scotland, Wales and Ireland) and some from outside, that is, Guernsey, Outer Hebrides, a long way for a day's meeting. As time progressed, the structure and function of this event became somewhat fixed with:

1 Business meeting with the years review;
2 State of play with the 'Associations Trade Union.' As stated earlier, this was during the years of governmental bodies negotiations;
3 Academic, case study presentations – this usually took up the afternoon;
4 Social event in the evening – this gave delegates the opportunity to catch up with one another, old friendships were re-established. I recall many of these with fondness.

Reflecting upon these events I have many mixed thoughts and emotions, but they were certainly key points in my own development. In contrast to the Association's togetherness in the face of governmental battles I recall many arguments about approach: art therapy v. arts therapies; conflicting differences and values of the different art therapy training schools; the struggle between those strongly linked to the political 'Union' and those against; the variations between art therapists working for the National Health Service, Education, Private Practice.

Regarding the regular slot on the days programme for the Union representative's account/update, I felt that it originally had a place but was gradually becoming irrelevant in such a setting, when there was so little time for other things to be dealt with. I thought the time given to clinical/theoretical matters was too short and as there was no other academic space for the Association, I formulated a proposal for an Annual Theoretical Conference.[1] Up until this point, the main way of presenting at the AGM was primarily built upon the 'Case Conference' model, which, as far as I'm aware, was another hand down from psychiatry. I intended such a conference to be built upon new theory where 'Case' accounts were secondary.

The 'Theoretical Approaches to Art Therapy Congress' began in 1993 as a yearly international event which I think was the springboard for a whole range of new ideas and clinicians to come forward providing a healthy forum for the profession of art therapy. It became bi-annual for a period of time.

Theory in Three Dimensions

By the time of our third congress, I was well into my work as a qualified group analyst and was now working in Social Services, so I was beginning to develop new ideas. I was forwarding a range of group analytic elements into art therapy. I was attempting to bring a new three-dimensional (3D) concreteness to existing art therapy theory, particularly the well-trodden theories on the 'triangular relationship' in art therapy. Many had written about this from their own perspectives but no-one, as far as I knew at the time, had viewed it from a 3D perspective. It was either a horizontal expression, that is, a three-way interaction across a table with the patient, therapist, image; or vertical exploration of the same three elements with each being at different points of the triangle. To my way of thinking much of what I had read by those authors did not convey the fuller bodied transactions in the triangle literature.

For my presentation I was helped by a colleague, Fran Short, who made the models which I had created on paper which progressed through from the given flat triangle ▲ to a range of triangular structures such as a four-sided pyramid; to circular drum shapes with intertwining triangular movement denoting groups. This has been covered extensively in my last book with black and white illustrations (McNeilly, 2006b, pp. 122–152). There was a large group of delegates and I had displayed the colourful sculptures as illustrated in the above publication. In this current publication, it would be too complicated to exhibit so I refer the reader to the original source. It was also following a period when one of my work situations had ended painfully which prompted me to use the opening song: 'Don't Give Up' (Gabriel, 1986) as a starting point before speaking, as I was holding past failure beside hoped for success in the lectures text. This is developed in more detail in my chapter on failure.[2] I was also considering giving up art therapy in all its forms. I am sure that this resonates with many caring professionals. Such phrases as: 'getting the last bit from the tank (petrol equation),' 'running on empty' and 'getting burnt out' seem quite apt. If we are driving a car and the petrol gauge is on empty, we function on what little remains hoping that we will make it to the next garage, avoiding disaster. So, it is with the many points in one's career that we are reaching the end of our tether, and then something occurs which sparks us back to renewed life. As all of these factors whirled around, the images of an entwined dying swan singing and a phoenix rising out of the ashes were battling it out within a surrounding circle of stones representing groups, became the dominant themes of the presentation.

I had thought I would only touch briefly upon that event in 1993 but I can now see that it was a crucial crossroads in many ways. This was a far cry from a time as a student/early qualified art therapist when a patient in individual art therapy was at a loss as to what to paint and was undecided. I said: "paint your indecision" which seemed to help but I think I was being 'ego-smart' while grappling with the early days of giving themes to follow as a specific technique. Recalling it here it makes sense of the title of the keynote address which I started this chapter with: 'The Deep End of Group Analytic Art Therapy – A Swan Song.'[3]

On another occasion my late colleague, Dr Chris Mace, had given me a couple of seconds to give him a title for my lecture, which was planned to be given to our junior doctors in psychiatric training some years ago, to which I said "being thrown in at the deep end." In that individual art therapy session, some 40 years ago, was I doing to the patient what my colleague was doing to me? Did these suggestive acts short circuit thought and, recalling the earlier points on contamination, contaminated the creative flow? As with these last two illustrations, one sees a shift in both perspective and technique from the structural theme giving to the spontaneous evocation of responding to being put on the spot. One could say that the former was a somewhat naïve event and the latter a more sophisticated response which led to greater theoretical development. To become sophisticated may convey a message of being in a greater, wiser, superior position but possibly sophistication owes more of an allegiance to simplicity.

Creative Vignette

As I dip into my memory bank and my notes I can see many times when I struggled with developments. At one time I relied upon directive methods, which in one-way simplified matters, and gave credence to me being an art therapist helping a patient or a group. On the other hand, I believe that a sophistication emerged through my group analytic studies and application to art groups. Not that it was greater or more superior but the various simple layers emerged through time and much of this was based on simple foundations. Very few of these sophisticated developments were planned. In keeping with how the heart has become a key element for me, it has been this that has opened the symbolic locks and stuck doors.

Confusion – Fusion

The following illustration comes from 1985, as I was completing my own group analytic training, which I believe holds its relevance today. As with the majority of psychotherapy training, graduating students are expected to complete both a theoretical and a clinical thesis in order to be qualified. I decided on the whisk of a moment that I had been confused about which topic to pursue. I then decided to write about confusion and fusion (unpublished paper). This illustration is taken from the 'clinical' paper which straddled group analysis and art therapy in respect to confusion and fusion. The location was in the therapeutic community: confusion here was fronted by one member being the focal point with the others doing much work to get the person sorted out, which at times became obsessional. It is worth noting that the struggles in this session ensured that the group was unable to move beyond the absorption with one individual's concrete imagery at the cost of the other paintings/drawings, etc. getting little attention. It is written as a composite in order to protect anonymity.

Two members of this group used this confused method, or technique, constantly. I use the term 'technique' because over a long period, they portrayed on one level a non-understanding and can't (won't) change their position in any meaningful way. On another level what was mobilised was a fused (fixed) stance. The man ('B') was caught up continuously in writing words, constantly giving the impression that he desperately seeks understanding and change through the use of words – the wish for a healthy fusion. On the other hand, words were his captor; confusion serves the purpose of holding the scales in this precarious balance in which there is no solution in a conventional way. Here we see seduction by the confusion and the group members never ceased to fall into the confusion or stasis. Although it came across that he had no control, and in a way he didn't, the whole process was highly controlled. He constantly invited people into his world by leading them down one path and once they were engaged, he would shoot off down another. When he was shown concern he acted surprised at such concern saying he didn't intend to worry people. With this continuous position, there was no apparent answer, only a seduction into blind confusion (acted out by others), with no personal creative confusion, which, if he held onto, may have helped him reach conclusions and solutions.

The second member of this group was a woman ('T') who did similar things to maintain her confusion. Much of 'T's self was fused with external forces outside her therapy. These were different agencies, such as the Department of Health, Social Security and solicitors, whom she saw as making her decisions and last but not least; her religion. She clung to a confusion in which all of these external forces decided her future and she was helpless.

The whole group, even 'B,' struggled with her, but as with 'B' they felt continually frustrated and the confusion persisted. As with 'B' it appeared as if 'T' has no control or power, but it was a pathological fusing, which was indeed highly controlling. Attempts to help her see these agencies as extensions of herself fell upon deaf ears. Seduction was maintained and there was no creative building of healthy fusion structures. Her painting displayed her in a tug of war with the authorities. Unfortunately I cannot show this image but such an image is not hard to imagine.

In Winnicott's book 'The Maturational Process and the Facilitating Environment,' he highlights such obsessional processes, or systems, as I am referring to here:

> In obsessional neurosis we sometimes get a ritual, which is like a caricature of a religion, as if the God of the religion were dead or temporarily unavailable. Obsessive thinking may be a feature whereby every attempt is made to one idea by another, but nothing succeeds. Behind the whole process is a confusion and no amount of tidying that the patient can do alters the confusion because it is contained, it is unconsciously maintained in order to hide something very simple, namely the fact that in some specific setting of which the patient is unaware, hate is more powerful that love.
>
> (Winnicott, 1965, p. 20)

I believe this quotation illustrates very clearly such dynamics in this group with the two members as focal points. Certainly, the whole process was obsessional with the group trying to tidy up but never succeeding, while under this the confusion was visible (breaking through at times) and very certainly hate was the predominant emotion. This whole regurgitated dynamic occurred for over two years. Metaphorically speaking it was like 'worrying the hare' or trying to 'force feed the un-receptive child.' The milk of human kindness soured but persisted. Partial understanding of 'B' and 'T' occurred, but I think this whole process served the group's purpose of using them as a sounding board for their own reflections of not understanding or testing out the acquisitions of new knowledge and feelings. However, this particular struggle did not offset a great deal of positive work over the two years. As long as 'B' and 'T' persisted with this what I suggest is pathological fusion, confusion was kept at bay for them. When it did break through it provided an impact on the fusional states. A certain precarious equilibrium was maintained, with an ideal solution just around the bend but rarely reached. The natural wish here is that all members of the group be cured and everyone should feel good.

New Theoretical Perspectives from 1990

In 1990 I was asked to contribute to 'Group Analysis' the journal of the Group Analytic Society (McNeilly, 1990, pp. 215–224) in which I was pulling together my developments up until that point. In the following I am returning to some key points and how these developed over the next 20 years, along with points raised in further texts and publications. In some ways this 'paper' marked the midpoint of my professional life. Although it was a 'personal perspective,' new points of theory were offered. It was at this point my primary objective was to make a meaningful link with the formal (verbal) international world of group analysis. This would entail my offering ideas, thoughts, illustrations which could be seen on par within the verbally accepted group analytic world. This was not about going 'cap in hand' but an attempt at saying: "consider something new." These developmental points have been elaborated throughout my later publications and at that time were first impressions:

- The creation of a pictorial image to show the content and process of a group session (McNeilly, 1990, p. 219).
- How group analytic art therapy could increase the speed and disclosure in a group.
- The difference between the impact on the conductor is at times intensified during the multiple image creation and the 'processing demands' later in the session via language. Such intensification heralds the importance of immersion:

Often when sitting in an art group, or verbal group, I become immersed in the power of the group. This is similar to creating a painting, composing music or improvising.

(McNeilly, 1990, p. 216)

One difference is that in primarily verbal groups after initial silences, the conductor is relieved from the silence and gains entry to everyone's common language. Whereas in the art group, the conductor has to stay with the groups silence for approximately half of the sessions time while the members create their concrete images.

Although I had been gradually moving away from equations with psychoanalytic terminology I, at that time, was formulating the art making activity on par with Freudian 'free association.' Then, once the concrete images were complete the group moves from this 'concurrent' activity to 'consecutive' dialogue. Beyond the initial group silences, verbal group analysis does not have this format.

The closing part of the 'Group Analysis' paper moved the focus onto an account of the 1989 group analytic congress in Dublin, where there were many hundreds of participants. I had presented a new paper in line with the congress theme on 'Encounter or Alienation,' which I have expanded in this publication. Here I am reflecting upon an experiential art group I conducted with a large group of participants (30–35). This was an opportunity to present my theoretical perspectives, but more importantly to give group analysts from around the world the chance to experience something new.

The congress had been highly intense with verbal dialogue and now the group participants were off the leash and playing with the art materials, someone said: "It's like painting ourselves out of the Congress!", at the end of the week. Freedom was expressed by excited talk, singing, laughing, almost as if permission was given for 'mania.' There was little hesitation with only a few people being timid. Most completed images were abstract or country scenes but one strong painting of an empty chair, not unlike Van Gogh's chair painting, took centre stage once the group convened to speak. This was not so different to a primarily verbal group when one person/topic is the focus of attention at the beginning. This led to dialogue about the empty chair waiting to be filled by a leader. For some time, there were drives to get me to sit in the chair (metaphorically) and this was contrasted with everyone sitting in chairs throughout the week's congress and, in turn, returned to the congress theme of 'Encounter or Alienation.' One can see that by the chair becoming so concretely visible in contrast to an invisible mental image, as would only be available in a verbal group, this facilitated a different set of dynamics to emerge. The chair also became a stable 'port of call' in the chaos of the congress currency of verbal dialogue. In such a congress, mainly structured on verbal dialogue, individual mental imagery can get lost in the melee.

Although many of the group were cognisant of group analytic theory, they were able to have a new visual appreciation, both through their experience and my interventions/interpretations, and were able to translate this into a new concrete form.

Theoretical Expansion

At the time I had been beginning to formulate various ideas which could take a particular Foulkesian theory into the art group arena. I spoke about trying to look at the heart of group analytic art therapy which in a sense was the prototype of 'heartfullness.' Foulkes, probably within this area, was placing concepts of the matrix, communication, resonance, 'group as a whole' concepts but did not relate any of this to the heart. For example, with Foulkes' definition of the group analyst as a conductor in music analogy, I reframed this as a conductor of electricity, which made more sense with the theories on resonance, that is, acting as a conduit, positive and negative charges of energy.

A further addition in respect to the conductor, which I see as a contradiction in Foulkesian terminology, is that a musical conductor usually follows a written score which seems to go against a democratically constituted group analysis, which is free from initial direction (conducting) from the group analyst. Taking it further, as a musical conductor, he/she is in between the composer and the orchestra and is, in essence, leading and controlling the group who has to obediently follow his/her lead. He/she may be seen as the most important figure, along with his sidekick, the first violinist (the most favoured group member), the conductor makes no musical sound on an instrument. The conductor's 'baton' could be ascribed instrumental status, so loud in its powerful quietness. Equally the pauses, silences in the music are not considered in the same way as 'heard' notes, which make up just as important components as the sounds that are heard. In the active life of the group, these elements of verbal noise, silences and pauses are easy to equate with the musical conductor and his/her orchestra.

However, if we conceptualise my re-framing resonance also as an electrical analogy, we can see how the energy is charged and distributed through the conductor and everyone else to equal measure. Sometimes, the power (electrical equivalent) is highly charged, moving between free energy discharge or overload which threatens annihilation and is in need of harnessing. When the medium of art is applied such processes are expressed and worked with on many levels. Concrete images created in such a group gives reign to the freeing charges necessary to create the images; the completed work contains and captures the flow of energy. Such a process is different from primarily verbal group analysis in that group members only have their emotional words and communication skills to let loose and contain things. In this context the conductor has another tool in his box to concretise the group. With this analogy, he or she is a live part of the energy charge as compared to the orchestra conductor, who follows the composer's script and possibly his interpretation of it, with the group following in the same way. This is not to say that he/she is controlling, but there may be a level of unconscious controlling in order for particular groups to follow invisible scripts. In a strange way, in the group analytic art group, the 'making of the concrete images' leads the group, and verbal dialogue follows. It is the completed images that lead from that point, even if one or more pictures are not commented upon. The electrical analogies make some sense today in respect to the heart in which emotions are touched directly and palpably. There may well be 'actual' electrical charges and energy being released.

Further Change and Development

Moving into the end of the 20th century and into the start of the 21st century, there was a great deal of professional change for me, along with my theoretical interests spanning out to diverse and disparate areas. As stated earlier, that by the mid-1990s, my active clinical art therapy was fading, yet still maintaining a strong academic and teaching side. This resulted in a number of papers emerging. Each of these was tackling the ongoing link between group analysis and art groups within the auspices of these subjects:

- Worlds Apart Colliding
- A Smile Makes Six Months Therapy Worthwhile
- Love and Hate in Group Analytic Groups
- Polar Balances
- Failure in Group Analytic Art Therapy (Gilroy & McNeilly, 2000)
- Key Concepts in Cross Fertilisation
- Dualities in Group Analytic Art Therapy

These are some examples that show the way I was developing. Throughout this book, I will have presented parts of these papers accordingly.

Basically, what seemed to run through the range of papers and fuller texts were conceptual spectrums that looked at linear frameworks, such as points of extreme, the coming together or moving apart and what happens in between. If we return to the base position of the patient who first comes to us with their broken worlds yearning to be mended this entails two worlds coming together of the patient and the therapist/group in order to find something new. In my 'Worlds Apart Colliding' paper I said:

Surely one of the most compelling points of collision, is that of falling in love. In such states there is an immediacy that is logically inexplicable, although some biologists may tell us different. When we fall the collision is explosive and consuming. Two separate worlds have collided and forms one new world. If something goes wrong the collision can take another form and the couple moves towards being together but a million miles apart. Physical and emotional tenderness and love can become repulsion/revulsion and silent suffering. On many occasions in groups variations on such scenarios have been shown. The space in the middle when the couple, or indeed close friends and families, can appear so close as to show a solid union. Then when things sour and deteriorate the space between opens up with the release of those darker, destructive, hateful, paranoic dynamics. As stated earlier when I explored extremities and their middle spaces this gradually led me into the concepts of heartfullness and therapeutic love in the ensuing years.

(McNeilly, 2009)

Generally speaking, in a similar way to my earlier comments on differences in conventional group analysis and group analytic art therapy, the pictorial imagery created in groups, on many occasions, had more impact. This appeared more as an extroversion of powerful love elements, whereas the verbalisation of love struggles in the conventional verbal group held on to more of an introverted position. Words, although exposing, did not release the fullness of it all in the same way. Think again about the first contacts between patients and therapists worlds coming together I said:

> Possibly, some of us will establish an alliance/connection in which the patient 'tells all' and we 'tell nothing or very little' of our own lives and personalities. If taken at face value, the patient and the therapist are 'worlds apart', while coming together, and on occasions colliding.
>
> (McNeilly, 2009)

A Smile Makes Six Months Therapy Worthwhile

Just as movements of the heart in therapy created palpable physical resonances of suffering and joy, so a smile can show the movement from misery to joy and hope. This title came to me when one of my patients smiled in a session after six months of highly conflictual, resistant periods. In the world of art therapy, be it individual or group, we initiate and follow the fluctuating nuances created in the development of concrete imagery. Equally art therapists can offer to those therapies built predominantly on verbal dialogue the space to expand their imagination beyond the intellectual and interpretive in concrete imagery and symbolism. Therefore, returning to my patients 'smile breaking through' in those brief seconds and moments, it was a powerful combination of 'so much struggle and battles between us' and 'phew! What a relief, lets continue on.' This meant more to me, possibly us, than many earlier conducive points of intellectual dialogue and interpretations. At this point, we had come together and were joined by the smile which rippled into a joint smile. This, as I was later to formulate in more detail, was a positive spectrum of heartfullness. My long-suffering tolerance of so much negativity had been held in my heart and then rejoiced through the smile, moving into a later positive and fulfilled period of therapy. We had indeed been functioning as worlds apart and at times colliding. The channels of communication were opened up anew. We were able to return to exploring her life struggles – the smile had dislodged this block in therapy. With these areas in mind group analysis, group analytic art therapy, individual therapy, could also be described as a form of psychodrama but not as defined by J.L. Moreno, who was the first to coin the term 'group therapy,' and seen as the father, originator of psychodrama.

When I was writing my 'smile' paper an interesting occurrence happened: I was walking through my local shopping centre. In the crowd I passed a man who immediately made me think: he looks very like someone I know. Then within 20 seconds later the man that I actually knew passed me going in the same direction as the first man. What was communicated to me? Possibly they were twin brothers! Then within another hour I was in a shop and I was quietly looking for a substance called 'blue tack.' As I was standing a little boy said to his mother "mummy, I need some 'blue tack' for going back to school," this was uncanny, especially after the experience of the two male strangers. I said to the little boy: "How did you know I was thinking the same thing as you?" he probably thought: silly old fool. Was this a case of telepathy? In sharing these illustrations I am drawing attention to what initially may seem insignificant communication. As therapeutic practitioners, we pay attention to how communication is manifested, how it may have broken down for the patients in their own lives and how such material is communicated in the therapeutic development. Therefore, if we draw a parallel with the chance encounters I've mentioned earlier, there are notes of interest. For example, our initial contact with the patient can draw parallels to other patients who the therapist encounters. There are times in a therapeutic setting when the patient and therapist are on the same wavelength of 'telepathic like' communication. It is at these times that the therapy is the most poignant, moving, empathic, synchronistic, loving, and as I have said previously, it is a palpable and physical experience at such times. As such the patients smile marked a moving, empathic, loving point of contact between us.

When we experience the sense of being at one with the patient/group as they struggle through their therapy, we will be able to accommodate the physical and palpable aspects within the concepts of therapeutic love and the group's heart. In these respects, we can stretch our imagination to seeing these ventures as forms of drama/dramatic therapy as previously stated. It is interesting that Foulkes was said to have been influenced by Pirandello's dramatic play 'Six Characters in Search of an Author.' So, my suggestion of group analysis being a form of drama is not too far removed. In his beautiful book, 'Wisdom in the Practice of Psychotherapy,' T. Byram Karasu focuses upon 'communicative intimacy' that should develop in psychotherapy

> Despite its temporary status, the bond of psychotherapy contains a special kind of closeness – communicative intimacy – that can go farther than other professional or even personal relationships in its private revelations and breadth of emotions without crossing the boundaries of verbal dialogue. It is also communication through the vehicle of words reaching into the buried recesses of the unconscious.
>
> (Byram-Karasu, 1992, p. 103)

Such a quote echoes the sense of drama within 'communicative intimacy.'

Therapeutic Love at the Time

It was around this time that I began a series of papers, the first being 'Therapeutic Love – Heartsink to Heartbreak.' As the title indicates, the focus had been upon emergent dynamics from clinical settings that were evoked through despair, which could then evolve into one's heart breaking, particularly around the loss of love culminating in states when the heart threatened to break or shatter. By considering this darker end of the spectrum, it moved me to formulate the concept of 'therapeutic love,' which was necessary in moving towards the other end of the spectrum – hope, desire and positive potential. Most of these developments were built upon the primarily verbal therapies I was involved in but could be seen in the group analytic art perspectives. As I said in that paper:

> There was one kernel of new insight that was moving me into something new. Until this point I had been relying heavily upon the concepts of transference and countertransference to account for and conceptualise my work with patients, along with other psychodynamic formulations: one dimension of this was that the concepts of transference/countertransference melted away to be replaced with the sense that I was floating within the therapeutic interface. A marked difference emerged. With transference/countertransference I often felt that this occurred against my will but with this new position my will flowed with it and I no longer minded being drawn in. As a way of concluding this chapter the following group analytic art session will give substance to my earlier commentary.

When I presented the paper 'Therapeutic Love – From Heartbreak to Heartsink'[4] to the Portuguese Society of Art Therapy, I played with a new way of putting across the contents of the presentation. Instead of displaying the finished art work from this group I invited the participants to make their own drawings/paintings as I described each picture. They were free to complete separate images or all on one sheet in order to make it easier to refer to as I narrated the session. For those who did not want to do this, they were free to keep in mind my descriptions as we proceeded. This offer was also a way of helping the congress participants evaluate their abilities in being able to have links between their imaginations and the real thing. It was also of note that this particular group was a long standing primarily verbal group that I converted, temporarily, into an art group for the purposes of writing these papers. This move was unorthodox which, I believe, no one else had done. This group took enthusiastically to the task, like a 'duck to water.' It may also be interesting that a similar exercise could happen with this text. The reader of this book is free to make their own drawings/paintings following my description of each patient's picture.

I will not go into the clinical details of each person in the group, as that would take too long. However, there is a broad spectrum: relationship difficulties; eating disorders; depression and anxiety neurosis. This group met for one session each week for 90 minutes and had been in existence for approximately 14 years, the current members had attended for between one and five years (Figures 5.3–5.7).

Chloe: An abstract image of different coloured lines, squiggles and smudges
Helen: A painting of herself, as a child, and a peer. There is a line between that part of the picture and on the other side her mother and father were watching television.

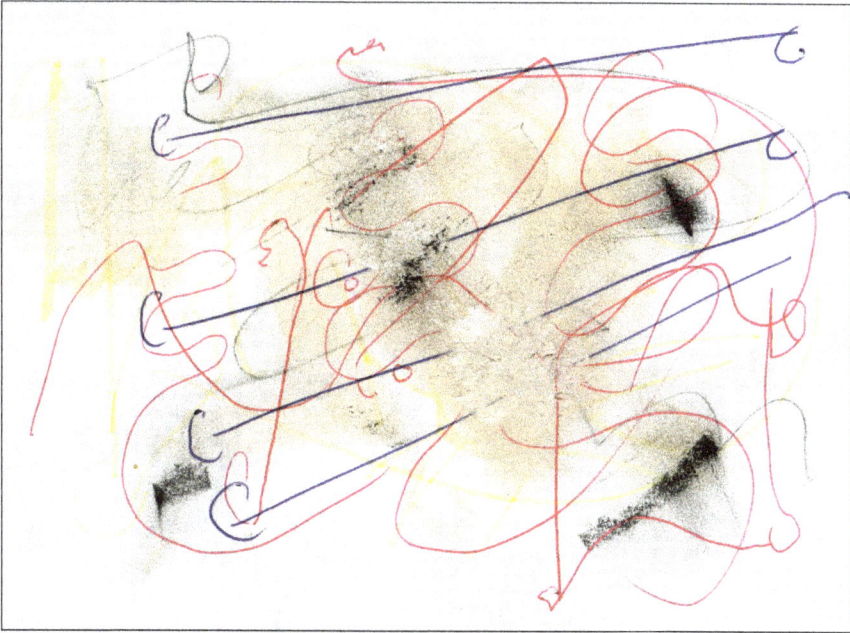

Figure 5.3 Chloe: Abstract image of different coloured interweaving lines, squiggles, black smudges, all within a cloudy pinkish background. It feels like a free flowing dance.

Margot:	A drawing of herself at her desk at work with arrows going from this to a drawing of the other group members. Various arrows are going in between these images.
Alison:	A painting of her psychiatrist on one side of the painting; her general practitioner on the other side; at another part of the painting is her work setting (similar to Margot's picture). In the middle of the painting is a foetus.
Marissa:	A drawing of a film crew shooting a scene where she is interviewing people who have mental health problems.

In accordance with technique/method, each person painted or drew their picture before the verbal section.

Once they had finished their paintings and sat in a circle to begin speaking, there was the usual fleeting 'catch up' talk about the past week. I gave apologies for the absent members. There was a discussion upon last week's session which had been particularly difficult, painful but fulfilling. They had acknowledged feelings last week of loss of support in knowing that the group was coming to an end with my retirement; losing me and one another, although they are contemplating keeping contact. They knew that this will no longer be a therapy group.

Figure 5.4 Helen: Two scenes in one frame. On the left a girl and a boy are argu-
ing. The room has simple furniture and open curtains with the external
view on the right. On the right side of the painting their parents are
sitting watching television. A definite solid vertical line separates both
scenes.

Gradually the focus moved to Helen and her picture. They spent approximately
20 minutes with her as the focal point. The main gist of this was whether she
should tell her parents about a peer having bullied her as a child. She had talked
openly about this at other times in the group. All of them had experienced attack
of one form or another in their lives. There was a very caring gentle and supportive dialogue developing in which they were looking at the plusses and minuses of
disclosure for Helen and what relief or other negative elements would be disclosed.

At times like this, especially if such strong/powerful experiences surface, the
group can only tolerate it for so long and there's obviously other things/paint-
ings, etc. to be spoken about. It would be a mistake to think that when the subject
changes that this is an evasion or flight and sometimes this is so. In this case it was
not. Margot began speaking about her work situation as well as her life changing
for the positive. However, this is on the backdrop of her uncertainty/ambivalence
about leaving the group soon or when the group closes down in six months' time.
There were pressures from her work which added to this as she found it difficult
to get away to be with the group on Monday evenings. She says that her life has
turned around dramatically in the past two years, that is, being no longer suicidal
or obsessional about her weight (this had been extremely low). She is now wearing
more feminine clothing, that is, short dresses instead of jeans and wearing makeup

Figure 5.5 Margot: A drawing of herself typing at her work desk on the left side. In the middle and right, it depicts members of her group enjoying themselves at a bar. There are arrows being sent by her to the others.

Figure 5.6 Alison: It is a drawing in three panels. In the left hand panel, she is sitting between her medical doctor and her psychiatrist. All are looking to the front. The centre panel has a foetus suspended in the air. The right hand panel shows her sitting at her work desk.

Figure 5.7 Marissa: Drawing of a film crew. She is interviewing a woman who has a handbag and a dog. She is the middle figure in the drawing. The cameraman is on her left.

and socialising more as in her picture. They move back and forward in looking at her picture. Probably the most significant change for her has been the final separating/divorce from her husband. This had been an extremely controlling relationship, from his side to her, which had started in her mid-teens. She felt that at last she was growing up. Her ambivalence about staying with the group or not is about 'stopping while she's ahead' even though she knows there are issues that are not fully resolved as well as aspects of trauma from her childhood years still pending. Here she was emphasising how much she had received from the others and myself and also her period of individual psychotherapy with me before coming into the group. Throughout this section the others were gently challenging as well as speaking about things in their own lives, past and present, that is, Helen's speaking about indecision in facing her parents; Marissa was resonating with her own marriage breakdown and independence struggles being successful; Alison, the move from her psychological breakdown and reaching a more solid sense of identity. Therefore, the resonance, associations and communication were in dynamic flux.

In keeping with Foulkesian group analytic theory, the group went further than the personal and familial and took account of societal dynamics, and as such became a 'transpersonal network of communication' (Foulkes, 1990, pp. 154, 229, 253–254, 278). As they were freely speaking, there was a gradual move towards their thoughts/feelings about legal/governmental matters. With regard to the governmental difficulties, this was connected to sickness/invalidity benefits, as Alison, Helen and Marissa were having to attend interviewing boards to see if they warranted the continuance of their financial benefits. There was a collective feeling that such interviews and form filling did not accurately meet their own positions and had little to do with them, but they still had to jump through the hoops. I silently agreed with them. It seemed as if at this point in the session, they were united against the world, but equally it was connected to the points raised at the beginning in their loss of the support of the group against the future demands of the world.

This seemed to give an opening for Alison as there was a clear connection. Having moved positively through a 'psychotic like' experience to her current set of conflicts had been an arduous task. She highlighted in her concrete imagery these matters. She was caught between her psychiatrist who is pressing her to return to work; her general practitioner who is more forgiving than her psychiatrist and is guiding her towards gauging when she feels ready to return; along with the waiting work demands if she does return. She recalled how she'd felt pushed in the past to change things before she was ready. At the centre of all of this is an obsession about an unborn child which symbolises the central driving force of her past breakdown, that is, not being able to have a child. As she became more animated, this sparked the others off, particularly Marissa and Helen who have had very similar struggles with being pressed by such professionals to change before they were able to. As one can imagine the group felt very alive with further references to their concrete images emerging. It was at this point that something was beginning to formulate in my own thinking about assumptions.

The dialogue spontaneously moved to Marissa's picture. She had been asked by the local 'mental health action group' to be their representative, interviewing people with mental health problems, intending to make a film about this. The group enthusiastically supported this, applauding her progress and identifying with the emergent issues. Who better to do this than Marissa.

Thought is formed and changed in the action of speaking. The various elements in the session; the historical factors for individuals in the group as a whole came together in the process of my movement towards interpretation/commentary. I said that I'd felt that there were assumptions in what had been spoken about and in line with their artwork. They implied that they were struggling with mental health perspectives, that is, Marissa's action group involvement but these were variations on 'mental ill health.' They were lobbying against politicians in order not to be stigmatised. I felt that there were variations on a sea of mental health/ill health matters. Such assumptions I felt detracted from the fact that almost everyone at one time or another struggles with mental health matters. This was also relevant to the matter of form filling, that is, did they answer what they thought/felt or was there an assumption that it is not what is being asked for and this will result in being pushed to return to work too soon, whether by doctors or the government. Maybe it would bring relief instead of destruction if they did know. As I finished speaking part of me knew this had been too long, but once my mouth opened it took its own time to complete the process of thought, hence thought being formed through speaking. There was quite a bit of head nodding which led me to assume I had got it right and there were further verbal confirmations that this was the case. The attention moved up and down from the pictures to face to face talking during this part of the session.

As we were coming towards the end of the session, there was a more spontaneous interchange between them with the focus not being held too long from one person to the next. The dialogue returned to the work theme and moved horizontally at a surface level allowing them to see that there was more to work than the Monday to Friday employment, as one point of reference. A lot of work was required in order to move from a confined position known as mental ill health to entering the world in all other ways.

I had not said anything about Chloe who had painted the abstract painting, unlike the others denoting specific parts of their lives. Although such a painting has many possible meanings, it did give some credence to her general uncertainty about being in the group. This was similar to Margot but the difference is that Chloe had not really felt committed to the group and had only been there for about 9/12 months. She had been very erratic in her attendance. However, she was attentive throughout this session and made the odd comment. Possibly the most revealing comment was at the beginning when I said I was able to extend the life of the group by another six weeks before closure and she feigned a humorous, disappointed response: "I thought I was going to get out earlier." Such comments were accepted humorously by the others and at other times she had been challenged more firmly. Although she still struggled to be part of things, the others were very fond of her.

Notes

1 However, there were various separate academic, teaching, experiential courses set up privately or in conjunction with the Art Therapy training colleges.
2 McNeilly, G. (2000). "Failure in Group Analytic Art Therapy", in A. Gilroy & G. McNeilly G. (Eds.), *The Changing Shape of Art Therapy*. London & Philadelphia, PA: Jessica Kingsley Publishers.
3 Which became the book just spoken about.
4 It is of note that many medical General Practitioners have coined the term 'the heartsink patient.' Here the doctors heart sinks in the presence of such people who, in psychotherapeutic terms, more than likely, refers to personality disorders and depressed patients. This paper was second in sequence.

Chapter 6

Individual Psychotherapy

Sally sits, bent over with her hair hanging over her face, slowly tears are dripping down her nose landing on her folded hands. A tear travels down her little finger and disappears onto her dress. Imagine a widening stain. I know she wants to tell me something. This is how she has been in the past while, building up to find the right words. Last week this tension lasted for ten minutes.

I wait!

She shuffles, goes still, gradually the tears stop and she separates her hands, I see the stain I imagined. She parts her hair and looks at me with upturned eyes. A gentle infectious smile emerges through her mascara rivulets:

"I don't know what to say! – I left John!"

Silently I reflect back to last week's session. Has John left her? Has she tried to cut herself? Maybe that's why her sleeves are over her wrists? I want to offer her the box of tissues, but this would interrupt the moment. No! I want to hold her and wipe her eyes. I want her to smile. She feels so near yet so far away, inside of herself. When shall I speak, what will I say? Maybe something will emerge that I can interpret later. Something strange is happening: there is a warm glowing feeling inside me. I feel that there is some movement between us, bringing us together. Only seven minutes have passed. When this started she was so far away, now we feel as one.

This brief snapshot had one of the greatest impacts upon me, giving substance to heartfullness and therapeutic love.

Looking back what comes to mind is my personal assessment by Dr Pat deMare, in 1979, for my application to train at the Institute of Group Analysis in London. He was one of the original 'Founders' of group analysis and a key figure in the newly developed psychotherapy movement in early post-World War II Britain. Although I cannot recall specific details, I remember him as a large, friendly, warm man with pure white hair and beard who smiled a lot. For me, this had felt to have been a loving experience in how he handled the things I told him about my life. Although I did not pursue individual therapy training, I went on to be in group analysis for four years, twice weekly. That experience was no less my own personal therapy than would have occurred in individual therapy. Of course, I cannot be certain

DOI: 10.4324/9781003536857-7

about this. I think that, inadvertently, Pat de Marés style, along with other group analysts who I trained with were fundamental: Meg Sharpe on the introductory course in group analysis; Dr Malcom Pines, my first group analyst; Dr Robin Skynner, who conducted my full period of personal group training; Dr Vivienne Cohen, who was my supervisor and later Dr Liesel Hearst. Each of these people influenced me in a great many ways, but what ran through all of it was their genuine interest in me and others. Although they maintained a professional distance, this was never aloof and in their confronting challenges of me and the group, this was never punishing or malevolent. The sense of their availability, warmth, humour, compassion and empathy, along with their ability to understand and interpret when necessary individuals' and groups' experiences, were key elements. On reflection I, both consciously and unconsciously, modelled myself upon these people, more so in the early years at the Ingrebourne Centre Therapeutic Community, through to my later working in Social Services.

If I was to ask the six people I mentioned earlier would they see my impressions of them amounting to 'therapeutic love' as I define it, I'm sure they would agree. As I developed my own style of initial assessments and way of being in sessions, these five people's influences, along with many others, would emerge from time to time. In various ways I had a love for these people who supported and taught me so much. When I would sit down for the first time with a new patient and ask them: "How can I help you?" these influential figures were behind me. This simple starting move had the intention of depending on them to tell their life stories, as much as they wanted at any given time and this, in turn, enabled them to depend on me. Of the many patients I saw there was, in most cases, expressions of 'therapeutic love' in its many forms. It is only in retrospect that I have reformulated my experiences as 'therapeutic love,' whereas in the more distant past, such descriptions would be formed in 'given' psychotherapeutic parlance.

Meanderings

I reviewed hundreds of sessions over a 40-year period and drew out points of focus which elaborate therapeutic love. I shall not be expanding on each individual's diagnosis or symptomatology in this chapter, unless it is necessary. I will be extracting from different sessions in different years, meandering, in line with the book subtitle. To begin with I would like to present some brief vignettes.

- In a session, the focus was on a new heating appliance that had been installed in the patients' kitchen. Much of the dialogue was related to growing warmth in her personal relations outside and with me. The heating appliance was symbolic of this and I suggested this was the warm heart of the kitchen which she agreed to. At the end of the session, I said that maybe it was her heart that was getting warmer, and she responded with a large smile. In a later session, she spoke of a growing dependency on me, which she initially saw as a weakness, but I reframed this as being positive, a way of acknowledging mine and others importance to her. She, with a degree of seriousness, wanted to meet with me every day. I was tempted to interpret this within the dynamics of interdependency, but it was more loving to just accept her wish but not comply with it.

- Another patient was dealing with her mother's terminal illness and death. When she told me about her mother's illness and funeral service and the amount of involvement in her mother's final days, I felt in awe of her strength as it was a truly horrific period. From a very distant/cold relationship, they had not recognised the love that they both had been denying for so long. She asked me about my spiritual beliefs in these matters and I said that although a part of me would like to say, I did not feel this to be appropriate as I would be guiding her, which goes against my role as her therapist. I should have told her. As the therapy progressed she moved out of feeling that she was living in a bubble and most aspects of her life had improved. As grieving intensified, I equated it to being in two places at the same time which she couldn't understand. (1) Acknowledging the physical loss of her mother and (2) an emotional presence of mother that she need not to let go.

Reflecting on some of these points, which in reality were over a few months of therapy, the therapeutic love elements became clearer. I saw this lady on four occasions of therapy over an eight- to ten-year period. Although at times I was formulating my work with transference and countertransference in mind, this became less and less important and was replaced with simple dialogue on thoughts and feelings. It seems that in my not being over concerned with such former psychotherapy parlance, the ingredients for therapeutic love – holding, empathy, respect, gentle guidance, support and responding to emergencies – were more important and relevant and may have been counterproductive if the classical methodology had been used. Understanding such an intensive therapy was not devoid of classical transference and counter transference issues.

Sometimes, when psychotherapists interpret problems as psychological symptoms of illness, the patient then question, 'Are you saying I'm imagining it?' At such times, the words of the therapist can either be seen as embracing and comforting, or like a surgeon's scalpel but without anaesthesia. With therapeutic love, we aim to the former

- Moving our focus briefly to groups, while considering the individual, Barbara, with a mischievous laugh, said: "men go bald in front through thinking about it" (obviously sexual activity). I jokingly said, "So that's what causes baldness!" (I was going bald at the time). There was a lot of laughing which increased when I asked, "How does it show in women?" No answer. Generally speaking my groups would often interact with me through play and jokes – also in a large percentage of my work with individual patients. One patient said; "you say weird and wonderful things, but we have to put up with you." Psychoanalytically this could have been interpreted as a power struggle with me. I saw, and still see, their way of using me in this way as a form of affection. Looking as far back as early 1980s, I recorded that I was proud of the way patients interacted in a more relaxed, humorous way with me in individual therapy and with 'one another' in groups. In contrast to this, there have been times when I would defensively search for too much meaning in the patients/groups humorous attacks/challenges of me, instead of these being acceptable, affectionate gestures. Therefore, I missed making better use of more conscious life affirming attributes which tasked people with not having to push themselves unnecessarily. Of course, there were times when such processes had to be dealt with otherwise.

Reflecting on these meanderings overall, I now see the early seeds of therapeutic love in contrast to the conventional psychotherapeutic armamentarium. With therapeutic love the following points are of note:

- The therapist's response to patient's challenges, accepts these as legitimate aims at bonding or rejecting and a re-establishing the therapist kinship with the patient.
- Simple non-intellectual interpretations and interventions helps to promote change as compared with my earlier over-elaborate interpretations, which I have illustrated throughout the book.
- The extremely important factor of establishing a meaningful contact with patients on first contract.

Dr Vivienne Cohen, once said: "Gerry, you don't have to keep trying to prove you're smart, you are." This was connected to my inferiority at the time. Out of 11 group analytic peers, I was the only one who had a basic education, without any academic achievement from my early school years. As such, I had a tendency to over compensate for what I thought were weaknesses and failings in my academic ordinariness. I often felt ordinary in comparison to my colleagues but maybe this was a blessing in disguise.

This was in contrast to a beautiful quote I came across and intended to use in full. Unfortunately, I over looked recording the details which I was unable to find, even with extensive searching. However, I recall two sentences (not verbatim):

"To be ordinary does not seem attractive" and "To deal with the extraordinary stories of our patients, there is a need to be ordinary."[1]

Both of these sentences, within the context of the quote, are addressing the many ambitious strivings in trainee and trained therapists wishes to be recognised. Hopefully, if the author of these sentences comes across them, they will forgive my borrowing their nuggets of gold.

How our patients see us is a central question. Psychoanalytic language has many daunting descriptions, that is, we are an object to be related to. Such a depersonalised description! Although on many occasions I have been seen as the distant analyst, with my growing years, this was minimal. Many times, I was seen as the wise man where patients waited for pearls of wisdom to drop endearingly; at other times the invisible man; the person getting in the way (primarily in group) and sometimes a serious wish to expel me; the honorary woman in female groups; the one responsible for symbolically impregnating female group members and individuals patients. During one year eight women got pregnant, three in one trainee group.

Hearing such personal views that patients and students had of me corresponds with the following quote in that their views has taught me greatly. George Groddeck in 'The meaning of illness' tells us:

> The patient helps the doctor make his unconscious conscious. This is why I believe that the doctor should be grateful to the patient. The patient is the doctor's teacher. Only from the patient will the doctor be able to learn psychotherapy.
>
> (Groddeck, 1977/1988, p. 221)

This is in keeping with Pontalis' earlier quote, and:

> The doctor does not need a knowledge of people, but a knowledge of the human heart.
>
> (Groddeck, 1977/1988, p. 231)

The following illustration is taken from the closing weeks of an individual's therapy. By this point Mary is adventurous and relaxed in how she speaks with me, that is, "hello Rudolf" (I have a red sunburnt nose) when I came into the consulting room. She goes on: "it feels like you have a wall around you." This was how she herself felt at the beginning of therapy. She says: "It's like we've swapped roles," "I would like to be tucked up in bed" and "does anyone ever go to sleep on you?" At the time I felt she was trying to de-role me and over the closing weeks wanted to know more about me and my friends by the close of therapy. She feels I know more about her than anyone and she knows so little about me. She feels she doesn't need me anymore. She says: "I've hurt your feelings, like I'm dismissing you! Do you care about the things in the world that I care for?" We looked at our time together and when we needed to uphold conventional boundaries, this developed into seeing how we could have a more friendly relationship if we met outside and how I was not afraid to be close to her. In fact, we were close.

As seen at the beginning of this illustration, Mary was playing with me. Another patient says to me; "it is like playing a game of ball with you, the ball is going back and forth in the things we speak about." This was almost the same sentence verbatim from Robin Skynner's Foulkes' annual lecture some years ago in which he described learning from Foulkes was like a ball game. This process had mobilised her to play more with her children which had been a major issue for her in the past.

Looking at a final session with another patient, I had a warm feeling of fondness for her which I voiced. I said that I found it as difficult as she did to say goodbye. Both of us were sharing our sadness. She couldn't put her finger on why it was difficult to say goodbye. Our relationship had been more important than with her closest friends. A central focus/symptom over the years had been her somatization, with feelings being transformed to physical symptoms roaming around her body. Now she was more able to hold emotions without somatization and this was at play in holding onto her loss and sadness here and now. The life of the therapy was inside her. She began crying silently and we were still for some minutes.

She said, "I don't know what to say, but thank you."

Me: "That's enough, we have been through a lot together! I'll miss you too and I enjoyed working with you."

Sometimes language is not enough or elusive when trying to fathom the depths of that which emerges in the session. Although at times particular sessions showed this struggle, and in earlier times I formulated this as a process which allowed space and time being required, waiting and holding until clarity, language and interpretation, could be used. On reflection, it was the process of developing therapeutic love being formed.

The following illustration hopefully shows this: Samantha, at the start of the session gives me a written note. This opens with: "the hearts been taken out of me. I can't find the words" (she feels aimless). It felt like she was handing me responsibility of her note. After reading it, I hand it back, she asks: "any suggestions?" I remain silent. We gradually discuss her difficulties in speaking about the note. She says: "Here (in the room) my voice sounds so loud, it comes back to me." This felt like an echo which resonated to a central feeling of emptiness, which was connected to her anorexia. Words and language are fragmented which is in keeping with feeling that she is in pieces. She felt taken apart by previous intensive therapies: 'The heart had been taken out of her!' All her coping mechanisms had been dismantled. The replacement coping mechanisms they had provided no longer worked. At one point I simply say: "Although they gave you particular coping methods, possibly you were looking for love, caring and understanding. This is similar to being given materially from your parents but no emotional displays of love." This seemed to 'open the flood gates' and she was now speaking freely. This showed me the importance of not giving complex interpretations, as my simply commenting on love and its absence created a strong bond between us. This permitted a space to exist in which elusivity co-existed with the struggle to form communicable language.

Another area of interest is how the therapist understands and takes seriously what the patient feels for them beyond an analytic interpretive perspective. This came home to me when I read my notes of a young woman who, in the early stages of therapy, struggled with staying in or leaving therapy. At one point she began crying and said that she would be letting me down in her wish to move to another part of the country. She felt that I had given her my input and she did not want to stop, but London was calling for practical reasons. She asked if she could continue in London. My response was somewhat trying to be smart and may have appeared flippant. When I read my notes, after 20 years, my heart skipped a beat physically. I was being smart by saying: "It may be possible but not with me." Had I said this in a more thoughtful way, taking account of this young woman's genuine concern for and value of me, then 'therapeutic love' may have developed more than it did. On the whole these vignettes can be seen as heart felt components which can have very tangible results.

As stated earlier, it has not been my intention to focus on hate specifically. One dimension of hate is that of evil. This was of relevance to one patient who carried the strong conviction that she had the devil inside her and that if she had a child, which she desperately wanted, the devil would be born. So, how could love ever get a foothold? This often emerged as the devil telling her that what I told her was wrong and not to listen to me. This brought into relief how, as a child, she had all these dark devil thoughts and could not share them with her parents as she would damage them and be seen as mad. Now she can give me her thoughts but part of her says: "I can do without you; I've had to do things on my own." She had to negotiate a loving relationship with me, and the group which she later joined, in order to exorcise the devil, leaving her womb open to be impregnated. Val's therapy took many years of individual and group therapy. Reviewing her notes showed many technical formulations around transference and other dynamics but the willingness to be with her, 'come hell or high water' (an appropriate metaphor), was a definite illustration of therapeutic love. She did go on to have a child. She is one of the people I hold dearly in my heart. It is possible that she was one of the people who taught me that by acknowledging her feelings of vulnerability it was strong and courageous.

Obviously when people are referred for therapy, this is because of psychological difficulties and possible mental illness. Much of our work then may feel like going against the grain when we attempt to de-pathologise the presenting symptomatology and reframing it as expressions of life experience, human suffering and unhappiness. The following illustration explores this. A woman with alcohol problems had been referred. She asked me if she had an illness which I could define. I said that I thought she was very unhappy but not ill. Immediately she began crying. She had wondered if she was manic – depressive because of her mood changes. I said that I thought the mood swings were more a search for security from insecurity – she agreed. As the assessment proceeded, this de-pathologising created a trusting platform that opened up many areas. In the closing section of the assessment, she spoke about holding her mother's hand (as an adult) and telling her that she loved her. Her mother pulled her hand away telling Simone she was talking through the drink (alcohol). They never regained any closeness. *De-pathologising is a way of promoting therapeutic love.* In de-pathologising for Simone I felt that this freed things in order for her to recall the early battles to be loved and to feel love.

In such circumstances love was always a victim and she was the material evidence. This was evident from many disastrous relationships: giving birth to a child when in her late adolescence; physical violence when she was a child from her father and to a lesser degree her mother. Her confusion arose from this, that is, she said: "why should anyone want to beat you up one minute and have sex the next?" She was greatly surprised when I equated both with intrusion. Sex/intimacy was a form of intercourse; physical violence was a way of forcing in. She was certainly very hungry for me to help her when I offered to take her into therapy and she gasped: "Yes please." As the therapy developed there was a growing sense of hunger and being fed. She had to come to therapy by bus and she often equated this with, as a child, going to her nice aunt's house where she was fed well and could play. Creating a therapeutic love for Simone allowed a movement from de-pathologising to detailed exploration into the distortions of love, sex and violence, and re-experiencing a love between us and later on in the psychotherapy group after a period of individual therapy, with a re-kindling of memories of positive early loving figures, that is, her aunt. There was also a negative side to things. When she later joined the group there were many struggles in regard to her drinking. The group was not a behavioural one like Alcoholic Anonymous and many of her challenges were trying to get us to treat her as an alcoholic only. At the time I was prohibiting her going to Alcoholics Anonymous which had a different philosophy to group analysis and this caused an eventual split. On reflection, I should not have been so rigid. I found that I was being drawn into an authoritarian position, not a loving one.

On the expression of strong feelings to the therapist from the patient, how are these areas developed without recourse to such things as interpreting transference, counter transference, projection, idealisation, to name but a few therapeutic tools. Gabrielle told me she was glad that I wasn't putting limits on her re: drinking.[2] She felt she should set her own goals regarding drink. She'd been angry with me for not being the light to guide her. On the other hand, she spoke of liking owls, that could see in the dark, they were wise, like me. She also equated me to a wooden toy clown that she has: its inanimate stillness provides affection in giving and receiving. I am 'still,' always here. I tell her that she is letting me into her world without a drink. Here therapeutic love is manifested on my permissiveness; her safety in being angry with me while I am both a wise owl and a clown; giving and taking affection.

On my second meeting with a new patient, Sue, she spoke of our first meeting last week having been good. She felt relieved and understood and not under any pressure when she was here and that I did not give her homework to complete. The freedom to speak without restrictions, directives from me had been both invigorating and comfortable. Spontaneously she spoke about her previous counsellor. That had been different as the therapists had led her in particular ways and had not permitted her to speak about what she needed and wanted to. Also in contrast that during the past week she had wanted to contact me as she'd been feeling bad, which she would not have done with the previous therapists. As I said earlier that the foundation for therapeutic love is established from the first assessment and if this happens positively, it is often difficult to move people on to groups or to other therapists. This had been the case for Sue.

Some professionals describe the patient's resistance to take the assessors advice on therapeutic method as a form of manipulation – getting what they want! Well, Why Not! If therapeutic love is developing from the first meeting, why expect this to be given up. By pushing the person away, this can also be an attack on oneself. At times I have been swayed to see such processes as destructive, aggressive, and devious but not now. After all, manipulation is about moving things, making new shapes, taking control and charge. Later Sue in the course of her therapy with me went on to talk about feeling good about what I gave her but was threatened because her sister had been referred to me and she didn't want to share me. I pointed out that a colleague would see her sister. Some sessions could adequately have been described and defined within classical transferential dynamics, that is, dependence. For example, on one occasion after I returned from leave we were speaking about Sue's negative reactions to me. She almost spat back at me her angry feelings coming from a gut level. She then became more relieved and moved onto her fear of losing someone (me) whom she loved. Her struggles with being left were a key point of reference. There were times when she guarded against her loving feelings for me by saying such things as: "you're only doing your job and you do not really care about people." One last point regarding Sue: in one of our closing sessions, it gave credence to how 'therapeutic love' had come to fruition. At the beginning of the session she was tense and silent. She told me she couldn't think of anything to say and this was followed by her hyperventilating and raising her voice, "you're not helping, you're punishing me!" she was seething with fury at me. "You're not leading me to talk about things. You're giving me a hard time." This went on for 20 minutes with my interceding with various responses but to no avail as she threw back the things I said. I was getting increasingly angry to the point of despair but held back. Then at one point, insight came to her, she realised that she was taunting me; trying to get me to reject her; wanting me to show I cared for her. She was testing me to the limits and drew parallels with others outside. She couldn't stop herself. I then shared my own feelings with her. I felt she was barraging me nonstop and at one point I did feel like telling her to 'fuck off' and almost agreed that she should be rejected. Then at the point when she realised what she was doing, I felt close and warm to her and this brought a sense of us being joined together as one. I felt bad in having used the 'F' word but no other word had come to mind and Sue felt ok about this.

Another patient, Veronica, had problems in finding a way of talking to me freely. In one early session she felt there wasn't a common ground between us and she had difficulty in talking about day to day things before opening up more difficult things. More than other patients at the time I felt a strange impulse to take the role of a protective teacher. She moved onto speak of her fear of getting old and getting wrinkles in which she was preoccupied. Then at the end of the session she says; "I've never told you this before but in the morning when I wake up, I get dressed as quickly as possible and I don't want to see my body. I don't like having baths and when I take my clothes off to go to bed I put my pyjamas on quickly." She didn't know why she told me this apart from sharing her anxiety and fear of seeing moles (brown skin spots). I suggested that she may also not want to look at her natural bumps and curves as a woman. I also suggested that if she did look long enough she may see something she liked. Possibly as an aspect of therapeutic love she felt safe and some of her censorship was diminishing. These intimate disclosures emerged in later sessions along with opening up at the end of sessions which became a pattern. Also her dress became brighter and more feminine as we progressed and she began wearing makeup. Increasingly the bond between us became stronger and at times when dealing with painful/sad areas, I was often close to tears with pains on the left side of my chest – heart. This gave substance to one of my central tenets of heartfullness as a physical and tangible experience and one element of therapeutic love. In later sessions she was acknowledging her view that she can go much further in therapy, which was linked to my telling her she was doing well. I had intuitively linked this to my query on whether her father (deceased) gave her praise, which she confirmed that he had. I then said; "so you still miss him!"[3] The floodgates opened. By my saying this simple statement, it was keeping the focus with father, not myself. In so doing, this is a 'therapeutic love' position as compared to transference dynamics. Here my love symbolically enabled me to be silently in the loving presence between a father and a daughter.

Another interesting point of consideration is about having people in therapy who know one another, friends who are either aware of this or not. As Claire was coming into the clinic building, Barbara was leaving after seeing me. Neither knew the other was in therapy with me. Barbara said to her: "at least the two of us are not nuts." This could be seen as them being united in their friendship, it was a depathologising comment. During Claire's session, she spoke about having seen an anorexic patient on a television programme who died, even though she was attending therapy. She described the psychotherapist and me in the same favourable light. She recognised that she is getting better, that is, her fear of cancer has reduced significantly. However, as often happens when acknowledgement of healthy change occurs this can be followed by periods of regression, pessimism and devaluation. This occurred for Claire following this session. This led me to the following comments which at the time I described in counter transference formulation, but in retrospect, I see this now within 'therapeutic love' dimensions. I said: "I feel that I want to protect you from what you're feeling now. I feel good because it shows a bond between us. This is in contrast to how you see your wish to protect people as negative." She agreed with me and felt good about my wanting to protect her. This allowed us to move on more interpretively, looking at projection within her symptomatology, that is, fear of cancer. Another illustration of how she sees me, while speaking to her husband and others about me, she says; "I'm going to see my man", smiling as she says this. She's not sure what to call me. I think 'my man' is a statement of ownership and reflective of therapeutic love. In psychodynamic/analytic terms, this could have been seen as a provocation to her husband, but I didn't follow this line and just laughed with her. There may have been some truth in this as later her husband wanted to come to see me as he was unhappy with Claire's progress. This felt a bit like pistols being drawn at dawn. Unlike her husband, as the external influence, Claire's friend also had to deal with the knowledge of her friend being in therapy with me. As the therapy with me was positive for both of them, this promoted a healthy and fulfilling tripartite arrangement, unlike the pistols drawn between me and Claire's husband.

Contrasting my approach from those early days to now, there are things I would not do/say. Bearing in mind 'therapeutic love' perspectives with Claire and others, in previously trying to elaborate the erotic, as 'that's what a psychotherapist is generally meant to do' (I say this with tongue in cheek) may at times have felt like I was pushing her to do this, although this was only a small part of the procedure. Today I would not make it so dominant and focus more on 'therapeutic love' foundations/frameworks. Possibly the odd psychodynamic comment or interpretation would have sufficed but now I would think more about the phrasing. Claire was able to respond to me at the times when she felt pushed by me, both positively and negatively. Sometimes I unconsciously expressed my connection with her. For example, at one point when she talked about her moles, I was not aware that I was scratching an itchy knuckle on my hand. When I looked I saw that there was a small lump there. In terms of therapeutic love, this could be seen as a sympathetic response. I acknowledged this to her.

Kathy became a very important patient to me and in the early stages helped me to sow the seeds of heartfullness and also someone I carry fondly in my heart. I saw her on an individual and later group basis. There were early signs of the absence of love in all areas of her life: in her strong need to be cuddled by her partner; to be accepted unconditionally; impatient if not immediately gratified. She yearned for a child to bring love to her life. Her persistent disturbing dreams initiated her wish for therapy. These primarily revolved around being attacked in many ways. There were strong waking feelings of emptiness on the other side of powerful feelings of rage and anger. One early sign in her beginning to look for love in or through me was that she stopped her relationship with her new boyfriend. She clearly had high expectations of me: "I'd like you to wave a magic wand!" She spoke of there being many things that she needed to speak to me about. What was also compounded was a prior view of me in her knowing some people, friends, who were in therapy with me. She said she felt good being with me although she had a preconception that I would be difficult. There was also a dynamic that when men jumped quickly into a relationship with her, this to her was love. She had power over them and she was left with her own insecurity when she was alone. There was a parallel with being spoiled in that her elderly grandmother was the most important figure in her life who spoiled her, that is, being spoiled equals being loved. Feelings of jealousy emerged when she saw others being spoiled. Stopping her relationship with her boyfriend seemed to indicate the beginning of her feeling spoiled, loved in this equation, by me through my attention.

The course of her therapy was over a three- to four-year period. I will highlight points which show how the heart ruled between us. I think its success was based on an overall 'therapeutic love' evaluation.

In the early stages she wanted me to sympathise and cuddle her, while push-ing away feelings of wanting to be close to me, especially when I got under her defences. She was uncomfortable when we were silent as that was too intimate which was in opposition to her need to be in control and intensified her concern in not knowing what I was thinking.

One of my approaches was to tell her not to be in a hurry to tell me things, that is, when she said; "there is something I'm guilty about." In laying a therapeutic love foundation this was a way of helping her to hold out on the early wish to jump into our relationship. She found it odd that I should want to hear about her day to day living and not only soul searching matters. In response she said: "there are weeks when I feel I need you, when I'm feeling bad, but other weeks when I don't need to come at all!"

Me: "so you only need/want to come when you're feeling bad?"

It was probably 6–9 months into therapy that her disturbed dreaming stopped. This seemed to go hand in hand with being more relaxed with me and not being so rigid in keeping appointments. Some therapists see missing appointments as a predomi-nantly defensive move. Although this view is valid, absence can also be a positive mark of progress. In one session she said; "I almost didn't come today as I had to put in a 'perm' (hair treatment) at this time in my diary." She's a hairdresser. I laughed at this and said it was the way she said it, very freely. In being able to sit in silence with me she felt was like reading a book with her private thoughts in my presence. Although partially correct I interpreted the aggressive transference elements in such things as: being late; putting in a perm over me; reading a book in my presence as a form of evasion, I think I missed these as being positive expres-sions of therapeutic love. However, she did agree with my interpretation which is broken down as follows:

1 Putting in a perm = "you are accepting my work and you're with me internally at times when I feel I don't need to come."
2 'Sitting in silence' no longer a potential threat but quiet sharing.
3 'Reading a book in my presence' = although evasive of life's challenges it is an intimate silent state of sharing and reverie.

In the early/middle stages of her individual therapy her attendance became erratic which was connected to levels of resistance and ambivalence. The biggest part of this rested upon the central parts of her past experience she struggles to tell me about. I kept restating that I did not want to push her, or she pushing herself to disclosure.

There was an interesting development in that we met by accident one evening after I finished work. This had thrown her into a state of discomfort. One of her friends asked her if I'd said hello, which I had. This was the first time she had seen me in another setting. In a later session, she wanted to know more about what I did outside and I spoke about a trip to London, playing golf and music. She then mused on her thoughts on what I was like socially as when she had seen me outside. This was in contrast to a quiet, gentle figure at home with my books and cats. This seemed to contrast with me as a strong and resistant figure that she wanted to pound with her fists or wanting me to embrace her and make things better. This, in a way, reflected her own strong resistant will which I said was like; "someone with a cut on their hand, looking at it and maintaining that it didn't hurt. In fact the denied pain showed that it did exist."

There was a key session in which she had been telling me about a fight that she and her friend had been involved. This had opened up a lot of her earlier problems with her father, who had deserted the family when she was 11. This allowed her to put into words the deep area of shame that had been touched upon some months back. With her parents' divorce this had left her mother with Kathy in dire straits with nowhere to live, in poverty and hunger. These memories flooded back and she'd not thought about them in years. I said I felt the past and present were united in the room. She was both 11 years of age as well as her current age. Although I made a more detailed interpretation what was more important was focussing both on her rage at her father's desertion as well as her need for him to love her.

In a later session she fantasised what it would be like for her grandmother being here in the room with me and how we'd get on together. This went on to how other family members would behave with me. It was as if she was making me into a family member but also wanting me to sort them out.

As we approached the end of her individual therapy, a lot was beginning to fall into place. She was in a much more stable place with a great deal having been worked through but there were ambivalences about whether she was ready to finish therapy or not. She feared losing her dependence on me. On the flip side of this, she imagined what it would be like to be me, a therapist. Humour begins to become dominant and in one session she is cracking jokes about a woman's appearance. As I was laughing with her she 'told me off' because as a therapist I shouldn't laugh. I pointed out that she made it funny so why shouldn't I laugh with her.

In her penultimate session she was putting into words much more of her feelings on finishing with me. She spoke of wanting to tie someone to a chair in order to listen which she had to do with me symbolically. Also, the fact that her friend was beginning to see me when Kathy finished was an inadvertent way of continuing with me.

In our last session we were speaking about her therapy in a relaxed and mutual way. She spoke of her progression through her childhood and emerging feelings and life events in adulthood. She had gone through extreme emotions of intense sadness and happiness; the permanent knot of tension in her stomach had gone. She was more at peace with herself; liked herself more and was less intolerant with others; her mistrust and suspicion of people was less; her work situation had improved. I smiled as she spoke of work and said that I trained as a hairdresser so could see where she was coming from. When she began to cry I said that "crying was not only intended to express pain or grief but joy and other feelings. I said that her tears may also be a statement of celebration for what she had achieved with me." At the end she expressed a warm thanks to me and 'at last' we hugged, something she wanted at the beginning but it was appropriate now.

Hopefully this limited account of approximately 2+ years of individual therapy shows a love that had been developed between the two of us in its various formations. Kathy carried on in life for a couple of years but then some points of crisis brought her back to me. We both felt that what had been achieved previously did not need to be covered again. To move into a group would allow a new take, looking in more detail at interpersonal issues. She did well in the group.

Shorter Therapy

Heartfullness and therapeutic love does not depend on long intensive psychotherapeutic arrangements. The following illustration looks at a planned period of short therapy. Ingrid was going through a period of crisis while she was on the waiting list for her individual psychotherapy arrangement to begin. One of the initial hurdles was that before I met with her a colleague had undertaken her initial assessment. She had felt that he had not taken her seriously and she was not understood by him. She felt 'palmed off' and was left for too long a period on the waiting list before I saw her. Another reason for my only being able to see her for a three month period was my pending retirement.

Initially with my first impression I was struck by her beauty and softness. There was a tenderness and fragility, which belied her strength. Once I got to know her I saw how strong and resilient she was. In the past her beauty had been taken advantage of. The primary area of this originated from her mother's attack of her. There were also other forms of emotional abuse, isolation, hunger and abandonment. Alongside her questionable 'borderline personality disorder,' there was both severe anorexia and bulimia. It is possible that I was tuning into all of this in my first impressions. Another question arises: *are these first impressions an unconscious activation of 'therapeutic love's' potential?* I felt these impressions so strongly that immediately my heart was touched in those first moments.

From the beginning she was mindful of how she affected me. As part of her overall mental health treatment she was also allocated a psychiatrist. In her psychiatric review with the psychiatrist (I had been present) she told the psychiatrist, that I said the odd line in our sessions. In our following session, she laughed at this as she felt she may have insulted me. Even though we spoke about very difficult and painful events of the past to which she increasingly took risks with me, she would close many of our sessions with a warm and tender smile, clearly appreciative of my input. I was moved and our sessions convinced me more and more on the validity of heartfullness. As time progressed there were positive changes in her eating disorder and she had also stopped self-mutilating. Woven into this was a lifelong concern as to the effect she had on others. This manifested in a pre-occupation/worry about what others thought of her. She felt that throughout her life others spoke to her any way they wanted, which implied others abuse of her to which she felt powerless to change until now. She felt I was different in that I showed her respect. She had a big heart in her care and affection for friends and mankind in general, that is, worrying about others because no one else would worry about them. At one point I said that "there is a difference in one's heart being in the right place as compared to taking your heart out and giving it away." At first she didn't understand me, so I continued, "having one's heart in the right place was based on having good intentions to help others with their burdens but this was different to doing it too much."

In our last sessions together we spoke about her waiting for a new therapist and her fear of regressing. In closing I told her how valuable it had been for me and that she underestimated what she gave me. I, and other therapists, were privileged and honoured in her trusting us with her thoughts and feelings. I said that it was sad that many professionals did not share such perspectives with their patients and were poorer because of it. It was as if her face was a curtain coming down and as she cried said: "No-one (professional) has ever said that to me!"

In a similar situation with Ingrid, Rose illustrates what we as therapists learn from our patients. She had severe anorexia among other things. In one of our sessions, I was elaborating on the dynamics of hunger. Here are some comments from my session notes that illustrate the workings of a session:

Rose was acknowledging her sadness about Corina, her nurse, having moved to another work position and this led onto Rose being able to acknowledge the importance of people to her and the normal process of experiencing sadness. Although I think she was also talking about potential sadness being evoked when I am leaving. We did not really go into this because I felt that this would confuse and interfere with what she was trying to say about Corina. As we moved into the latter part of the session she had been talking about having failed in the 'Eating Disorders Service' where she had previously been treated, in that she was neither a successful anorexic nor had she really changed the position that she was in through the eating disorder approach at the clinic. I queried what were the things she was saying to the consultant psychiatrist and I had wondered if she had asked him why he wanted to know certain things. She said that he wrote these things down in his notes which were then put in her 'file'. This reminded me a bit of her own struggle in the process of taking things in and using them. I questioned what did it mean to have things written down for her and it was as if the file was a big hole that was being filled in, but she really didn't know how it was being used. I'm not sure how we moved towards the aspect of hunger in respect to eating or not eating and I said that if she did eat (she is being pressed by her partner to try new things) then, in a sense, this would be a way of satisfying her hunger, but in doing this she would lose her hunger and it seemed important that she stays hungry while at the same time giving the impression to others that she is not and this is the reason why people are thinking that she is not eating. I suggested that maybe she is very hungry indeed and not only for food but for other things such as affection, care and purpose, and indeed hungry for an arm that has not been slashed, as hers has multiple scars. At this point she was more open with her facial expression and she began crying and said to me: 'how do you know these things?' I wondered what she was meaning. She said that what I said was exactly what she felt. "How did I know this?" I said that I possibly knew these things from having worked with a lot of people over the best part of 30+ years and it was really they who had taught me about these things and not so much about what I know.

I think that for Rose, her question on my knowledge was also a statement of my knowing her inner world. It's not that I entered her world but with each part of the interpretation she gradually, in a matter of minutes, allowed me access, and pulled me in.

With a successful access as this also comes increasing levels of psychic turmoil which has to be processed, a bit like being a victim of one's own success in getting through to the patient. However, I found that I was functioning in a more heartfelt way with Rose. As well as dealing with crisis in her eating disturbances, there were serious suicidal ideology and gestures, along with self-laceration to various parts of her body. Maybe, as her body was the material location for such gestures it may be a connecting point with my own heart and in the process of our work together both of our hearts were communicating. It also seemed highly important for her to shake my hand at the end of each session, possibly a physical way of keeping me with her. Some psychotherapists would run a marathon before shaking a patient's hand. There were times when she showed a beautiful concern for me, that is, one time I had been burgled and had to cancel her session. She was worried in case I had been hurt. I thanked her and re-assured her I was ok. This turned into her fear of feeling bad towards someone (who has hurt her) and as a result something awful will happen because of her thoughts. Here she was worried in case someone has bad feelings for me, she only had good feelings for me. Increasingly in the sessions she was able to begin voicing bad and negative thinking without catastrophes happening, i.e., her hate of herself being translated into repressed feelings for others. I pointed out that, "this self-hate may be more about the absence of love throughout your life from childhood." This allowed her to have a new perspective. There were some quite graphic descriptions of what she was going through and wanting me to rescue her, particularly at times when exploring how she was contributing to and perpetuating her self-hate and the noise in her head. She pleaded with me once; "if a dog's tail is on fire, you'd cut it off to save the dog!" I said, "Maybe so, but the dog didn't set its own tail alight, did it?" thus leaving her to abstract this. Some therapists may have explored the symbolism in her statement.

Deeper Reflections on Individual Psychotherapy

I would like to say that I don't guide them, but in fact that is not true. It is a great mistake for an analyst to imagine that he doesn't. Theoretically you leave patients plenty of space to say whatever they like, but in fact your mere presence distorts the whole picture. They take one look at you and make up their minds either that they are prepared to talk to you, or under no circumstances will they do so. The relationship between the two people is a two-way affair and in so far as one is concerned with demonstrating that relationship it is not a matter of talking about analyst and analysand; it is talking about something between the two of them.

(Bion, 1994, p. 256)

In this quote Bion comes across as more accessible, a down to earth type analyst, than presented in his more austere publications. Although he is speaking about psychoanalysis his words are appropriate to my own way of working. He had been responding to a question in one of his seminars in regard to how he works with patients. The questions about leading, guiding, directing or otherwise are well established concretely in the art therapy world, as elaborated in Chapter 5. Indeed, having initiated dialogue upon directive and non-directive approaches in art therapy (McNeilly, 1983/1984, pp. 211–219) I went on to change my views, suggesting that there was no such thing as non-direction (McNeilly, 1987, pp. 8–11), it was just how we got there and arrived that was important. Finding one's own way was different for everyone.

The following account could equally be described as a 'case study' which in part is true. It is as much a study of 'my case,' hopefully giving an account of a meaningful and authentic therapeutically loving venture. It brings to the fore the more complex elements, looking at various stages in the therapeutic journey. The patient courageously embarked on and embraced her therapy, evolving and emerging like a chrysalis, which had profound effects on her and those around her, not least me. As one will see in the following chapter on groups, equally many individuals stood out as Samantha in this chapter has done. The therapy brought its own particular demands and challenges, both within the sessions and without. There were unexpected challenges and crises; liaisons with other professionals; unexpected meetings outside the sessions. Clinical details will be set beside and compared with the central tenets of 'therapeutic love and heartfullness.'

Samantha

Samantha had been referred by the Consultant Psychiatrist who was part of our Mental Health Team. In the process many overt/covert messages were given within the referral letter and word of mouth. As well as the psychiatrist she already had some contact with the psychiatric crisis team. At a crisis team meeting, which I attended on a regular basis, the psychiatrist asked me if I had met with her yet and I said that I hadn't. I was given the impression, which was conveyed humorously, that she was unpredictable and that I should watch out as she may hit me. When I did see her for the first time I felt comfortable almost immediately. She clarified why others would have given me this negative message as she had confronted the psychiatrist for what she thought was his unprofessional interaction with her. Throughout our time together, of approximately two years individual psychotherapy, I never felt threatened. The opposite was true in that I always felt a close bond with her; the sessions were full of life, trust and pleasure, even when we had to deal with some of the most difficult points of opening up her past trauma. Pleasure does not seem to be the most appropriate word here but more an admiration in her growing ability to be open, is more accurate.

I looked forward to seeing her each week but I also had to develop a tough skin in order to take her teasing; humorous criticisms on my dress sense; when I needed a hair/beard cut, my not being up to the mark as a psychotherapist. My minimal use of analytic jargon, directness and humour assisted the process. As well as her deep seated psychological difficulties there was a range of severe physical health problems.

When we first met, she became open relatively quickly, even though she was speaking about not trusting easily, particularly men. The initial focus was upon her physical health problems and her negative body image due to this. She said: "I don't suffer fools gladly and I hold grudges!" I said: "I better watch my step then!" We both laughed at this. Her relationship with her mother was very negative. There were many separations when she had to be in care due to her mother's repeated overdoses, depression and psychiatric hospitalisation. She said: "my mother never loved me or showed any affection!", in contrast she had a good relationship with her 15 year old daughter. She grew up in extreme poverty in all departments: housing, finance, food.

An extract from one of our first meetings shows how we began our way of interacting. Following the disclosure about her angry/destructive feelings about her mother she asks:

"Why can't I feel empathy for my mother?" (identifying that her mother also has problems.)

Me:	"Empathy is a two-way street and it may be difficult if the other person is blocking you!"
Sam:	"That's true, I'm scared that my daughter is getting the same sort of life with me because of my illness."
Me:	"It sounds like you do love your daughter. You care and do things with her."
Sam:	"Yes!" She agreed.
Me:	"That's the difference then."

Also, during our first meetings she went into the many areas where she had been attacked by others and her life threatening self-destructive acts. At the close of our first session, she felt better and that it hadn't been as difficult as she had expected. In closing she humorously said that she hadn't been carrying knives (connected to the psychiatrists warning comments) and that I may need to search her when she returns. I smiled and we both laughed as she left the room. I think that her use of humour was not defensive (it is often seen this way in some aspects of psychotherapy), but showed a potential bonding between us in which she felt that I would tolerate what she would bring to me. This was in contrast to previous psychiatrists and other mental health professionals. On reflection I saw a similarity with my own childhood school battles with authority and my having been brought up on the margins of poverty, but with more loving. I also tuned into my own annoyance at the consultant psychiatrist/crisis intervention team who pre-empted our meeting with negativity and threat. Why could they not see her feistiness/directness as a positive aspect that had assisted her to deal with, colloquially speaking, the 'shit' that she had to deal with? Using another word here does not do justice. This does not mean that they were always like this as they were a very helpful team.

Hopefully this provides a snapshot of what happens at the start of such therapy. The process involved continual reflection on my own life and how I used this accordingly. Also, from these initial steps into the beginning of psychotherapy weekly sessions, which by and large had varying levels of intensity along with the slow uncovering of past and present life situations, led to varying levels of resolution and change.

In one of our early sessions, she said that happiness was alien to her, apart from feelings for her daughter

Sam said to her daughter: "I love you!"
Daughter: "I know!"
Sam: "How do you know?"
Daughter: "Because I feel it!"

As she was finishing the session, she said to me: "My therapy is the start of feeling valuable, like being loved." During these early sessions her positive feelings for me were maintained. The dialogue moves from exposition of deep feelings and expanding upon the many conflictual events to playful bantering/interactions between us. Equally there were many times when dealing with the painful and unhappy events in her life also brought unhappiness and anger into the session. In respect to myself at a positive point, she says: "You've got the nicest consulting room in the building!" This was true as I had put a lot of work into the room. When I retired I was honoured in that my colleagues named it the 'McNeilly Seminar Room.'

Sam: "You can give me your lamp and painting (a large oil painting) when you retire."

This was a bit like giving with one hand and taking away with another. In this process she conveys a fondness for me in wanting concrete extensions of me when I am gone.

Throughout her therapy there was a great deal to open up and work through. At different times we spoke about resolution. Here the struggle was between undoing and resolution – a bit like the struggle between forgiveness and forgetting. I told her that resolution was a slow and gradual process in which she voiced more and more about past trauma and life events while seeing that there was a lot more good and helpful things in her life; that's reaching a more balanced existence. There were more difficult and critical events in the course of her therapy. During these times I was not always seen in a positive light. In the context of therapeutic love any verbal attacks to me did not detract from our overall involvement. She felt safe enough to confront me if she was unhappy. On one occasion the crisis team were involved again. She had phoned the team at midnight implying intended suicide through drowning and wanted me to be notified, thanking me for my input and it was important to say goodbye to me. The police were informed and she was found on the bank of a river, supposedly intoxicated. The suicidal risk was great but there was something about her need for me to know which implied giving up or losing someone she cared for in some way. She was not in agreement with parts of this account and gave greater elaboration. From this point I increased her weekly sessions and provided out of hours telephone access to me. Some of my colleagues felt that I was being manipulated and that I was overreacting, but Sam felt more secure and I had a greater peace of mind.

Some six/to seven months later, she had reached key developments. In order to reach my consulting room, we had to go along the corridor from the reception area

As we were walking she humorously gave me the 3rd degree.
"You've had a haircut; you need more off!"
As we sit down in the room:
"That's a nice shirt!"
"I like your shoes."
"You should get rid of your beard; I don't like men with beards!"
"You've got new glasses!"

Clearly, she was pleased to see me. During the session, she moved through regrets at not having challenged previous professionals; being more assertive with her partner Bill; thinking about finishing therapy next year and how upset she was about this. I question if she's afraid that she will lose what she has gained, which she acknowledges. She moved on to look at her growing confidence in life and being less impatient and defensive.

In the closing months of our time together I was more able to share parts of my life with her, although the level and timing of my disclosures were carefully thought about and monitored within the therapeutic context, and not sharing for my own therapeutic benefit. Alongside this I was freer with spontaneous thoughts and comments. This increased sharing of the therapist's life experiences in psychotherapy parlance is at times called 'dissolving the transference.' This is a grand term as compared to seeing that we are more on an equal footing now and less concerned about keeping/maintaining a therapeutic distance. During the final six/to nine months of therapy there was rarely a session in which something important emerged which touched both of us deeply. For example, in one session she was in extreme physical pain as well as recovering from a recent family crisis. She had endured the long bus journey to reach me. In my written recording after the session I noted:

> as she talked in a very open and trusting way I had the urge to do more than just listen and talk with her. I wanted to drive her home after the session in order to look after her in a practical way. Eventually, I said to her that I could not do these things but I was here to listen and put into words the things that she struggled with. She said: "that's enough!".

I believe that this illustrates an aspect of therapeutic love which shows the therapist's battle with one's self within the parameters of setting boundaries, while resisting the pressures to move beyond and into offering more to the patient.

In a later session she was quietly looking at me, smiling and I felt uncomfortable. I didn't say anything for a few minutes. Halfway through the session I questioned what she was thinking during this time. She had also been teasing me with some playfully provocative comments, leaving me guessing.

She said: "I enjoy winding you up. You've been asleep since my therapy began!"

Here she indicated that I missed out on something in our time together but she didn't say what.

> I smiled and said: "I'll miss you! I'll miss your being able to feel free and silly with me!"

As the session moved into more delicate areas she began crying while at the same time playfully hitting me with her scarf.

Sam: "It's your fault, you always make me cry!"

I had made some important points/interpretations which were touching her deeply, hence the crying. At the close of the session she apologised for hitting me with her scarf. So! As warned by the psychiatrist, she did hit me, but in fun.

In one of our closing weeks she articulated the meaning of closure for her. I had given her a copy of my last book as a leaving gesture which she had asked me for. The one point that she was drawn to in the book was that I said that 'love and hate were not necessarily opposite.' She felt that the opposite to love was disinterest and indifference. She highlighted that my interest in her had been a loving experience. I wondered what she had felt about reading the book. She liked that I had dedicated it to my mother.

Sam: "One thing that I will think about you in the future is your running around graveyards and chasing girls."

Me: "That bit was censored!"

We laughed at this. I said that the personal comments were aimed at contextualising the theory.

Her closing sessions were interspersed with some unexpected logistic problems which, in fact, meant that our last session did not go according to plan. A number of weeks went by until our actual last session in which we spoke of the critical events that interfered with the closure. However, things ended very positively. Approximately 12/18 months after her therapy closed I met her by chance in a local restaurant/bar. I was just in the process of leaving England to live in Ireland at the time. She was having coffee with her partner. She was still struggling with her physical ailments but the psychological progress she had made was enduring. We were pleased to see one another again and we discussed fairly general changes. In this new accidental meeting I felt the warmth was still there between us. In some ways I was in awe of what she had achieved and also what she had entrusted in me. We embraced and said goodbye.

In closing I trust that this chapter has provided a sweeping account of individual therapy as I have practiced it. Most of this has been built upon short/brief vignettes and illustrations embracing key points of reference which I am confident that many therapists and patients will recognise. There are two dominant factors which has been the foundations built upon: conventional psychodynamic thinking and methodology in parallel, contrasting and at times opposing, 'therapeutic love and heartfullness.'

Notes

1 Possibly attributed to J.B. Pontalis.
2 Clearly I had learned from my experience in having prohibited Simone from attending A.A.
3 Once again the phrase was appropriate.

'Group Analysis – Primarily Verbal'

Chapter 7

Overview

Let me expand on the versatility of group analysis as it has developed across other disciplines and therapeutic applications. I have been out of the professional loop for some ten years since retirement, but I would doubt if S.H. Foulkes' influence is still not prevalent. Group analysis has filtered through to many British National Health Service Hospitals and 'Outpatient' facilities. Although originating within Private Practice and its application to the treatment of Second World War wounded/ shell shocked victims in English military hospitals, it formed one group approach which became a blueprint for the 'therapeutic community' development (Harrison, 2000). As the second half of the 20th century progressed, group analysis was finding its way into mental health hospitals, general psychiatric/psychotherapy services, social services and private practice. Increasingly, it moved into various psychotherapy training institutes and universities. Originally driven by the medical fraternity, it has evolved to welcoming post-graduate professionals such as psychologists, art therapists, psychodramatists, nurses and counsellors. It has emerged from its German/Austrian psychoanalytic heritage through Foulkes, conceived in England, extending to North and South America, European countries, Australia, Slavic and post-Soviet countries. I am not fully cognisant of its development in America or Asian countries.

Looking at my own group analytic development, I have been involved with groups of one sort or another, that is, childhood gangs, clubs and music groups. So, by ending up as a group analyst, does it stretch the imagination too far? In order to reach this point, I first completed my nurse training before embarking on my art psychotherapy training. Within both of these professions, that although these were individually oriented training pursuits, the group factors played an integral part. With the art therapy training, this was set more formally on the group format in all parts of the training. For example, when I was part of a group, it became quite natural to contextualise my experience in concert with other group members. One illustration was my participation in an 'open art group,' which was facilitated by Edward Adamson (a key art therapy pioneer in England) who said very little to anyone as he walked around the room. As I created my paintings I often thought: "What is happening with everyone else and why doesn't Edward bring the group together to speak?" Instead, once the time of the session was finished everyone just

DOI: 10.4324/9781003536857-9

left the room. So much lost! Equally in some other training groups, the leader would promote dialogue between him/her and one student at a time without reference to others in the group. This, at times, felt somewhat voyeuristic and threatening when the focus would come to me. Some groups were led through a 'Basic Assumption' model as originated by W.R. Bion (1961), already spoken about in Chapter 2. Then came group analysis and it was in this setting that every individual counted and the ways of conceptualising groups married each person with the notion that we were all part of a greater whole, while not losing our own uniqueness.

Moving between being a patient in my own group while in group analytic training, and becoming a group analyst, I could see how everyone was involved in the process of healing one another through discovering the many subtle elements which formed the dynamics of group process. Certainly, such developments were 'not a ride in the park' (easy) at times when conflict and confrontation emerged, but the ways of understanding, communicating, working through interpretations by everyone, promoted resolution. This may have occurred either at the end of sessions or over many weeks, months and years.

The remainder of this overview will consider two frameworks:

A The various settings in which I worked.
B Practical, and to a lesser degree, theoretical group developments.

Part A: Settings

There are three periods in my professional development, which correlate with the three settings I worked in. Alongside these settings, there was a wide range of pilot settings, that is, universities, training bodies, international projects and publications.

These are as follows:

1 1976–1985 The Ingrebourne Centre, Therapeutic Community within the British National Health Service: Principal Art Therapist and Trainee Group Analyst
2 1986–1995 Saffron House. A sessional counselling and psychotherapy service within English Social Services: Director/Psychotherapist/Group Analyst
3 1995–2011 The Pines, Warwickshire. Sessional Psychotherapy service within the National Health Service: Principal Adult Psychotherapist (Non-medical Consultant)

Each of these settings had its own distinct and political frameworks that influenced the provision of group analysis and other therapeutic methods. Also, my own personal development played a part with increasing maturity; level of professional achievement; clinical/managerial and political responsibility, all impacted to varying degrees. There was a vast developmental arc in moving from an art therapy role in the therapeutic community, where I played a smaller part within the system, compared with my later role as Director, group analyst with sole responsibility for five/six long-term groups, as well as a large individual case load. Here I had responsibility for one County District in England.

1 Ingrebourne Therapeutic Community in the NHS 1976–1987

Regarding the Ingrebourne Centre I have covered much of this in my previous publications (McNeilly, 1983/1984, pp. 40–48). This was the place where I initiated and developed my group analytic art therapy model. Within this setting, art therapy gained prominence, becoming a tool in understanding and combining individual, small and large (community) group dynamics. My embarking on my group analytic training through these years contributed greatly. It was here that I conducted my 'training group.'[1] This outpatient group met in the Ingrebourne premises, partly removed to a separate 'outpatient' set of rooms, which brought a number of challenges. This, at times, brought into relief my functioning with therapeutic community principles while trying to uphold the basic rudiments necessary as a trainee group analyst. One example was that when particular community events or crises would occur at the same time as I conducted my training group this could be heard as they occurred in adjacent rooms which at times intruded into my training group. Also, there were satellite groups within the therapeutic community that influenced my group analytic approach: large groups, psychodrama; couple's groups, family groups and creative work groups. There was much to contend with in this setting, which I believe enabled me, in later years, to apply these experiences to those groups that met with me once or twice a week as outpatients. One of the elements that ran through the therapeutic community groups was a dichotomy between professionals trained in groups and those with individual training. A recurring conflict centred upon individual interventions/interpretations and those of us trying to convey the group modality. Sometimes, this felt like a diatribe that had to be sorted out in staff group discussions.

2 Social Services 1986–1995

At the time, in British health care delivery, there was a formal split between the National Health Service and Social Services. Therefore, when I was appointed to create a new 'Service' which combined both agencies, politically and financially, this was a radical and courageous gesture. It was a blank sheet with exciting prospects. Not only was I charged with creating a new service but also employing a staff team. In a similar way to Foulkes' original Northfield Military Hospital, which brought together the different parts of the system and looking at this as a whole, I knew that much rested upon looking at the whole geographical community needs. This entailed networking with other services such as medical General Practitioners, Social Workers and Psychiatrists. Equally, all of these professionals/agencies played an active part/role in the new services development. A guiding principle was that this new service belonged to the town, county and the community, it was not my sole property. Group analytic thinking and action ran through all of the Service, which led to a whole range of individual and group therapies, not only 'group analytic groups.' Unlike the experience of conducting my Group Analytic

Institute training group within the actual concrete building of the Ingrebourne, I now had a brand-new building which had been purposely built for therapy ventures. I was able to create my new groups as a qualified group analyst, having full control of client selection and assessment. This whole experience which I defined earlier as a 'community of therapies,' was instrumental in the next landmark in which I was returning to, the National Health Service. Having completed the creation of a highly successful 'community of therapies,' this enabled me to embrace the next stage of development.

3   Psychotherapy Service in Adult Mental Health 1995–2011

With this new setting, I was entering a well-established department with a larger team of qualified therapists and group analysts, which was also a teaching service for a number of psychiatric and psychotherapy institutes nationally and internationally. In a similar way to my last 'community of therapies,' I was charged with expanding this service to a much broader County geography. So, in a way, it was a new service.

This was based on two elements:

1   To establish a thriving psychotherapy practice for a larger populace in the Stratford on Avon District.
2   To create a professional network of general medical practitioners; mental health professionals; children and family services; social services and psychologists.

It was important to see that the success of such a venture would not have occurred if these external agencies had not been closely involved. Foulkes' view of group analysis being a 'Network of Communication' (Foulkes, 1964) has a greater chance of success if the external networks are working in harmony.

Probably that for the last ten years before I retired the psychotherapy service was continuously under threat of staff reduction and closure, even though it was one of the most successful departments treating large numbers. Many of these people could not be treated by other services due to their complexity. Hence, it was a political struggle revolving around finance and psychodynamic psychotherapy became an easy target: the 'poor relation.' These struggles were similar to what many psychotherapy services were facing throughout Britain at the time. One way that the threat of closure played a part was that it fed into a great deal of uncertainty about the continuance of patient's therapy, raising levels of anxiety, despair and hopelessness. Indeed, both my patients and I resonated with such struggles against the common enemy (bureaucracy) outside. On the plus side, at times it allowed a strengthening impetus to develop against the onslaught, which in turn reverberated with the patients' personal life challenges outside the group.

With the foregoing preamble my intention was to present a brief sketch of the three settings where I had worked. This has been important as it allows us to see that group analysis, like all therapeutic ventures, does not occur in a vacuum. Although the basic principles and rudiments of group analysis are constant in all of these settings, each different environment must be taken into account.

Part B: Developments

How could you spend so many years going into a room with 7 or 8 crazy people and not say anything at the start, waiting in silence? I'd be waiting for all hell to break loose!

The above statement is the type of question that has been put to me on many occasions. Yes! 'So many years,' 'so many groups (as well as all the individual therapies).' 'Crazy? yes! A bit, but healthy and beautiful as well.' 'Waiting in silence!' – eventually it breaks, bringing desire to understand and change, healthy parts to heal the crazy. Yes! 'Hell has broken loose' at times, but mostly Hell's darkness has allowed Heaven to shine through. At other times, we did not emerge, but such life events had to be endured. This, to me, is an example of therapeutic love, giving space for the heart to become dominant.

Bearing these brief flights of fancy, the following accounts are sketches and extracts of primarily verbal group analytic groups spanning over 'so many' groups. During these years, I conducted between three and seven groups on a once/twice weekly basis. Throughout these groups particular patterns, insights, key changes, World events, successes and failures, stages of group and my own development will be considered. A momentous task which can only skim the surface. I cannot stress enough that the quality and value of work colleagues made these services work.

Note

1   The term training group is used to denote the first group analytic group, which is closely supervised by the teaching staff at the Institute of Group Analysis over a course of 4–5 years.

Chapter 8

Early Period

My primary starting point considers those groups which began, 'post' group analytic qualification, at Saffron House, Social Services. Hopefully, as we progress, the early references to love as a therapeutic factor will emerge with some clarity, and how it became a dominant focus in later years.

Some of the areas which I intend to address are as follows: setting up new groups; new members joining existing 'slow open groups' (a term to define those groups which meet for many years. The therapeutic process is slow = 1–5 years, members start and finish at different times); dealing with major individual and group developments; working with crises. These brief headings encompass and incorporate areas that have a great deal of complexity. However, sometimes the simplest things can evoke a lot and with so much meaning.

For example with respect to simple processes in one session Mary says

> When I was in the supermarket and my teenage son was with me, he was speaking to his girlfriend on his mobile phone. He said "I love you." It surprised me that he was so open. I was pleased that he was happy and I felt contented!

Me: "Is your contentment also connected to your own loving feelings for John (your partner)?"

Mary: "Yes! but I didn't connect such feelings before."

The group then runs with a range of things connected to love and contentment.
On another occasion when love is a subject of attention I ask:

> Is it better to find love after looking for it so long, only to lose it?

Janet: "You've hit the nail on the head. My father only told me he loved me a few days before he died."

With the start of newly formed groups, for some people there will be hesitation, anxiety and trepidation. If this is not dealt with through alleviating such thoughts and feelings (mainly through the group analyst and more stable members), the group can

DOI: 10.4324/9781003536857-10

become highly charged and can take off, like a dog being let off the leash. This may be manifested verbally through such things as pre-mature disclosure, silence or a whole range of physically agitated or withdrawn postures. At its worst people leaving the room in agitation. However, many new groups will comprise of members who quickly create an atmosphere conducive to the development of group analysis, which does not call so much on the group analyst to be the negotiator, helping to develop a maturing foundation.

In the case of new members entering established groups, there can be recurrences of such dynamics. During these times, it was important that I handled and contained these elements by being more active. A new group is not a group from a group analytic perspective, it needs time to develop. At these times I needed to be more individually orientated which, gradually over the starting sessions, the group would settle and I could fade into the background. Sometimes there can be a search for intimacy too soon, or a wish to ventilate a life of sorrow and anger. I may intervene by saying something like

what's the rush, we've got at least another year or two!

One of the difficult times in these early anxieties is people's difficulties in listening to one another on top of their own internal script, but usually within 6–12 weeks this settles. As things progress in the early stages, when the groups become more trusting and risking, it is not uncommon for one or more to bring in new experiences that emerge in between sessions, many of which will have been triggered in the previous sessions, that is,

Vicky: "When I was in the waiting room earlier, I remembered when I was six and was playing happily with the teacher. Where has my happiness gone?"

Such strong recollections as this can have such an impact, as it did. Nearly everyone responded with their own happy memories and their loss. As their lives had developed conflicts emerged, particularly Society pressures, being born into less or more favourable environs.

At times groups often move towards particular political and societal events of the day, that is, a rise in crime, health service cuts, election of a new government. Previously, I spoke about the psychotherapy services occurring within a wider community network. Therefore, in selection and formation of groups, new and existing members may know one another outside and this has to be carefully manoeuvred. In small communities, there can be greater connections between people and potential threats to privacy and confidentiality. This, in turn, highlights the need to have personal space to grow both within and without the groups, to be close to one another, but not too close. In these early stages of the group's development the working around and transition through: negotiating space, personal boundaries, stepping into one another's space through such things as empathy and challenge, reassurance and gratitude, may be dominant in the group. This is mirrored in how each member's interpersonal activities outside the group are understood and developed. Sometimes, especially if transactions in the group are too complex to be processed the group can erupt into some form of action, that is, shouting, threatening, insulting and exiting the room. It is as if the specific matter has been unprocessed and deposited in one or more individuals and ejected. This has occurred in many group sessions over all of my years. Then, when the group reconvenes, there will be the need to explore what this has all meant. Hopefully the 'escapees' have returned. However, to kiss and make up is not necessarily resolution, although a key starting gesture and, dare I say, an aspect of therapeutic love through people's willingness to be together and care for one another.

Throughout the years my groups have been comprised of people from many walks of life and different social cultures. They come with a range of clinical formulations/diagnosis and age groups. However, this does not include those people suffering from psychosis, although some have had 'dissociative disorders'. It has been: 'that which brings us together as sets us apart.'

Sometimes in the process of exploration groups may turn to the use, overuse of sayings and clichés: 'don't reach for the sky,' 'more than one pebble on the beach' and 'grass is greener on the other side.' In the early group years, this was dominant or I noticed it more now. I suppose that one purpose of such statements is to bring a succinct encapsulation of common, complex matters. There is a vast world of complex meaning which is reduced to a few words. Conversely, I found that in these early groups I would try to conceptualise multiple statements and return them to the group through some intervention or interpretations. I felt that I had to draw the individual strands together, hopefully not missing anyone. This was also in contrast to the times when I said little or nothing so as not to get in the way, or my tendency to waffle and over complicate things. Thankfully I was not afraid to say: "I haven't a clue about what's happening here!" For some this was endearing and they responded with warm laughter, for others they were annoyed that I was not doing my job. Within these processes, there is the contrast in my showing/proving that I was an efficient group analyst (in fact I was newly qualified) and the developing view that I didn't always have to understand things without too much anxiety. Maybe some meaning would emerge. It was not the end of the world to not know.

There were times when a particular struggle between one individual and the rest of the group taxed the group's reserves. Here the battle was about resolving the antagonism of one individual with the others reactions in order to reach level ground/parity. Here I could not just sit back and say I didn't know what was happening. I had to grasp the many strands of each personal resonances and reactions against the one antagonistic individual in order to understand the 'group as a whole.' Undoubtedly it was possible to conceptualise the projected struggles of the whole group along scapegoat concepts as one dynamic, but it was often more difficult to defuse such sparks of antagonism in order to reach a collective sense of despair and desperation. It is at these times, there was merit in taking the complexity of things apart (each individuals personal associations being reframed in common sense dialogue) in order to reach a simple feeling of ease, calmness and understanding. When such group sessions occur, they may not be resolved for varying lengths of time, but if understanding and resolution occurs this will, on the whole, strengthen the group functioning and may contribute favourably to life outside. Unfortunately, if the antagonistic individual has problems in processing what is happening, this may have negative reverberations outside. If an individual was expressing antagonism and fighting with everyone this was some form of engagement. I recall a woman who, for a two-year period attacked and rejected everything on offer. She saw it as unhelpful, useless; it did not work. 'I was shit at my job,' no one was listening to her. Eventually I told her that she was right, 'We' were not listening to her and I was 'shit' in her eyes, even though I didn't agree with her. Everyone in the group had good intentions in trying to help her but this was 'falling on stony ground' (group seeds could not germinate)

Me: "when would you like to leave"

Mary: "you're trying to get rid of me" (I'm sure many therapists will share this dilemma with a gasp of breath.)

Me: "you've been telling us all this time that it isn't working and now you're upset in my agreeing with you!"

Returning to these earlier years, there was the push/emphasis to help people stay in therapy, sometimes against great odds and a sense of failure if we could not succeed in holding people. One ultimate fear was that such individuals would deteriorate or even end their life. With growing experience, we learn to accept that therapy groups, in this instance, do not work for everyone. In those early groups/days I took it as an affront, a personal failing, in either having gone wrong at the assessment stage or contributed to their not improving with the group. During another session there was a case in point in which it was Harry's last session. He had been in the group for about 15 months and had spent most of his time with his 'cards kept closely to his chest' (withholding and suspicious), while he provoked and seduced people to get heated reactions, thus everyone else 'danced to his tune' and kept everyone at a distance. His excessive use of expletives added colour to this position. In his last session, he sat back while others tried to create some dialogue about his leaving. This eventually moved away from him into a wider dialogue upon suicide. It was as if his leaving was seen as his symbolic suicidal intent and they could do nothing about it. As I said previously that in the earlier years, I felt a need to be more active in bringing things together. With greater understanding and experience I was able to focus my interactions with more precision and simplicity. For example, if this session was happening many years later, I may have said:

Harry is leaving, knowing he's used the group up to a point. He's not committing suicide. However, for the rest of you, you have your own feelings and experiences with suicidal attempts that needs you to stay to keep talking.

Themes and Group Interpretations

Historically, both group analysis and art therapy have been built upon themes and interpretations as they emerge spontaneously or via conscious direction.

As I had written about the place of themes in one of my earliest papers on 'Directivity' (McNeilly, 1983/1984, pp. 211–219), my thoughts turn to connections between themes and group interpretation. Some other forms of group therapy build their practice on either setting a theme at the beginning or arriving at the 'theme at the session's end. It is not uncommon to hear group therapists/analysts state that the theme of the group today was 'failure.' Therefore, how does this equate or differ from a group analytic interpretation. In formulating group interpretations, this is intended to help the group find common ground on apparently singular individual commentary, create new levels of understanding, stimulate deeper exploration, keep the peace and contain varying levels of emotion. However, could this also be ascribed with it being reductionist. We think we are 'adding to,' as compared to leaving the group with the 'balls up in the air' or 'the plates spinning.' In these early years, I felt I had to stamp my authority through my interpretations. When I would leave the room having said very little, or gave no closing commentary I felt that, as did group members, I was 'short changing' the group. With developing years I progressed towards uncomplicated group interpretations; the lessening of a sense of obligation to say things or the bearer of closure commentary; my verbal contributions were less forced. In many ways, the progress, in simple terms, was from an early self-conscious pre-occupation to 'Be The' group analyst to a more natural, spontaneous free flowing group analyst. Although matters of love came through in those early years, it was not until these later personal changes in my practice that ideas and concepts of 'heartfullness' and 'therapeutic love' got room to breathe.

Silence and Individual Attention

In my earlier years, and indeed throughout my career, I would have had a range of thoughts and feelings before entering a group or individual session. These may be:

> I hope there won't be too much silence; I'm looking forward to or dreading it; I hope Sean comes, I hope it's not a replay from last week. I'm not feeling up to it.

At the start of the session, there may be a silent uncertainty as to who will break the silence, how long will it last. There's so much to speak about, it's hard to start. One or more members are so repressed it will make the whole group silent. More positively: people are more relaxed and silently mulling things over, gently approaching verbalisation.

There are many accounts, stories and vignettes about silence which have been developed in the literature. As I gained more knowledge my confidence in working with silence improved. However, I on most occasions, felt better once the group, or individual patient began speaking. Where it became more demanding was when

I entered the room and clearly, one or more people were obviously upset about something. Their heads were bowed, they were rigid, possibly crying. The others were uncomfortable but the silence continued. I may need to intercede at some point after 5–30 minutes, if no one else takes the reins. In a strange way, the silent/depressed person at this point is the group leader. In those early years, on reflection, I permitted longer silences than were necessary. This may have been experienced as a sadomasochistic enactment. In discussion with other therapists regarding whole sessions that were conducted without verbal dialogue we believed that this was permitting the patient/group to tolerate frustration and psychic strengthening. On reflection I regret having taken what I now see as an idealistic position. There was some value in short amounts of silence, but it was also a maintenance of struggle and pain. The intellect was engaged but it was stopping the heart from emerging to reach an empathetic realisation. At such times therapist and patient are in close proximity, but they are also far apart emotionally. However, sometimes if the silence is not charged with conflicting emotions, longer periods of silence may be comfortable and generally verbalisation emerges more easily. In the working through of those difficult silences, where there is a type of invisible wall around the focal person, there can be an avoidant reaction to him/her in which the others start speaking about other matters. This is a double position, that is,

> We're talking because we want to give you silent one's private space so as you do not feel you have to speak, as well, we don't want to intrude.

Then when bridges, links across the silent group chasm emerge, a great deal can be achieved. In those early groups I was conceptualising these developments as points of communication being stimulated either through resonance upon the silent vibrations or moving towards verbal communication. In retrospect I now see periods of silence as people's hearts being touched, thus feeling acutely, empathically and physically, which allowed everyone to progress through such difficult experiences. This, I postulate, as being an enactment of therapeutic love. Also, in the early years that when such events occurred this brought into relief the debate which revolved around whether the group analyst holds back more or feels they can 'treat' the sad/depressed, silent person as if they were in individual therapy in the presence of others. A group analytic directive states that one should trust the group to deal with it. This stance, in a way, goes against such a directive, overlooking that the group analyst 'is' a part of the group and is free to speak when the spirit moves them. As time has passed, I was rarely concerned that I was amiss when I spoke directly with the individual. By giving my verbal input I allowed my heart the space to be.

Practical Considerations

S.H. Foulkes has suggested that the optimal group membership is seven to eight for once/twice-weekly sessions of 90 minutes. Regarding attendance, although of high importance, will at times be difficult for a whole range of reasons. Therefore, over the years I had to adapt when group numbers dropped. Regular attendance is necessary as a mark of commitment and it is the individual's responsibility to organise this, that is, work schedules; taking vacations at set group breaks (summer/winter vacation). In those early years I erred on the side of enforcing the 'guidelines' as if they were rules with consequences if broken. The principle of reducing and stopping anti-depressant/anxiolytic medication was another guideline (in careful planning with the individual's general practitioner) which was hard to uphold. Over the years I became more flexible, not necessarily seeing medication as an obstacle to therapeutic involvement and change. Many people reduced such medications and stopped in their own time without pressure from me.

One of the functional aspects in respect to group numbers was when the attendance dropped below four in a session. In the early years I would stick rigidly to keeping the group 90 minutes, even if it was only one person. I recall my own group analyst, Robin Skynner, saying to me "this is your worst nightmare" when it was only him and me in the room. I know that he was right, but I can't recall if we stayed for 90 minutes or anything about the session. When three members are present, this is not so difficult and the dynamics may be like a smaller version of the larger attendance. However, at times the session moves into a sequence of pairing, with two separate onlookers. The single patient left out cannot set up a dialogue with me as if I was another patient. When there are two patients the 'die' is cast into a dual interchange. All is well if these two get along, but if they don't then the session may be extremely difficult. They may then feel the experience to be punitive or persecutory. Then the ultimate scenario of when only one person arrived and the group was potentially replaced with it being turned into an individual therapeutic session. It would not be uncommon for the patient to ventilate his/her difficulties about the absentees or indeed share something they couldn't with the others with me. Part of the task for me would be to encourage him/her to bring back to the group what we had discussed. Often this did not materialise. Then there were those individuals, who did not want to be alone in a room with me. There were also those extra-ordinary events when no-one would turn up. I cannot fully recall which group analytic supervisor/teacher who suggested that at such times one should sit on one's own for the 90 minutes in order to: 'keep the group in mind.' I dutifully obeyed but eventually thought this was rather silly and pointless. I also recall trying this when my individual patients did not arrive. I stopped this as there were plenty of other things to do with my time. What was the solution?

Generally speaking, smaller numbers bring greater stress and pressure to feel free to speak or not, even though with groups that are 'meaningfully' engaged, this can increase levels of intimacy. Thinking about such groups with my newer theoretical developments, groups that have reached this level of functioning are driven by the 'heart bond' and have become a therapeutically loving group and were able to deal creatively with lower attendances. Eventually I reached a decision in which some of my colleagues thought that I was breaking group analytic rules. For the sessions in which one or two patients arrives, without notice from the others about coming late, there was a choice to be made after 15–20 minutes of stopping or continuing for an hour if the absentees did not arrive. If these two people did not want to continue, we'd stop. This removed the pressure of 'having' to talk. This pressure would not normally be there when everyone is present. On a negative potentiality if it is two people who struggle with the others, then by stopping, or having limited time, it safeguards against a collusive pairing using the session to join forces against the others in following sessions. When only one person arrived I offered a period of 20–30 minutes and I purposely guided the dialogue towards a more general 'catch up' on the patient's week. For some this is all that was required. To not have any time would be punitive as they were the only one who turned up. Some people welcomed this as an opportunity to get closer to me; ventilate that which is difficult in the presence of others. By reducing the time in each scenario this also gives me the space to be different. By and large, these changes kept the desire for individual therapy at bay and enforced the dominance of the 'group' ethos. In each of these I took a more active part, allowing for more spontaneity.

Some Notes on Closure of Groups

In the closing months of my period with the Social Services, approximately 1995, I had to close down five long-term groups. Each group brought their own specific and special dimensions. In the literature I have found that some writers maintain the use of the word 'termination.' For me I find the word insulting and cold. It is a word that is so closely linked with death or the act of ending a pregnancy. Some group analysts and individual therapists explore closure of therapies by drawing on extreme loss and death comparisons as compared to dealing with the immediacy and impact of what is currently lost. This comparison does not fully grasp that this closure is a stage of development in which members move on, hopefully, to better stages in their lives.

Backtracking a little I recall my last group experience at the Ingrebourne Centre. This was a large community group comprising patients, staff and a television crew. The television crew was preparing a documentary in the coming weeks after I had left (Morrison, 1986). The main purpose of this session was to say farewell after a ten-year period. This was a forum for a more personal exchange of what people thought of me and space for me to say goodbye. As with previous groups when staff members were leaving there seemed to be an unwritten rule that the leaver has a 'back seat' with their colleagues being more verbally active. In the past I would often have taken the lead. In this, my last session, it still felt as if the community wanted me to continue as before. There was about a 20-minute silence which I hoped that someone else would break. For a group of 40+ this seemed longer in time. I eventually broke the silence, if only to ease my tension, although I can't recall what I said. From here, most people contributed in sharing their feelings of loss; my importance to the community; those remaining feelings of annoyance and anger at my leaving; closing accounts of happy and humorous past events, of which there were many. On reflection my heart was breaking as I went through this session in closing up ten years of my therapeutic life. It also felt as if the staff team was split between those who valued me and those who thought I was a loose cannon and were glad to see me go, and those whom I shared a heartfelt warmth, as we were often on the same wavelength.

Hopefully this illustrates how a closing group session can contain so much that needs attention, both on an emotional and cognitive level. This last group session is embedded in my psyche and has been a template for many closing group sessions since. The following illustration is taken from when I was leaving one of my other work settings and the group was in the process of closure.

Nigel to me:	"You've made my decision easier to leave now that you're leaving. Can we grill you before you leave?"
	Group laughter
	Annette is silently tearful to begin and later she tunes into Clare and Kim's views.
Kim:	she is shocked and upset that the group was finishing
	"I've only just started in the group and feel like closing things up!" (She had only been in the group for six months). "I've spent 10–20 years getting to this point only to have it taken away"
Kim to me:	"I know you're moving to another job, it's not your fault."
Me:	"it is my fault, I decided to leave."
Rosalyn:	"I feel the same as Kim"
Graham:	"I've gotten so much from the group; I feel I still have a long way to go" (attending for 3 years). "it's like being made redundant."
Craig:	"I'd sooner lose my job than the group"
Alison:	"I'm not sure what I feel. I'm like a square peg in a round hole!"
Jacky:	"I'm sorry for the rest of you because you've not had the amount of time I've had and almost at the end of therapy and I have resolved so much." (5 years)
Claire:	She was very upset and attentive but couldn't put things into words, eventually she says: "When I heard last week about the group closing, I felt awful. It was the same some years ago when I was rejected by a friend and I did not eat. I wanted sleep and oblivion. I was afraid of slipping back to that but I didn't. During this past week I realised how much better I am. I'm going to get over this (I think)!"

I did not say anything at this point but I felt like crying, being both happy and sad as I listened to Claire. Both Kim and Annette echoed Claire's fears of regressing back as well as determination to progress. Eventually the group moved on to want to know about my new job and how I felt about finishing but not as Kevin wanted: 'a grilling.' I felt free to respond directly to this and also about my loss of them. I was more open in sharing what I was going through. This was heart-warming and another expression of therapeutic love.

Confrontation

In general terms, there have been various points of emphasis on 'challenging' in the different settings where I worked. Confrontation was a key component in my therapeutic community period. To a lesser degree, it emerged in my outpatient work in Social Services and the National Health Service Psychotherapy Department years. With the previous comments on silence of the individual/group, this is also a form of confrontation: the silent individual confronts their internal self and the group has to confront a silent obstacle. Many therapists/analysts will be familiar with phrases which are used in the profession: face your fears, you're avoiding the issues, the group is not dealing with this and you have to face your demons. Even some interpretations are confrontations or the way they are conveyed can be confrontative. Over the years I moved away from using confrontation principles or measures. Having reached formulations on therapeutic love this has made me see that such confrontative interactions could be damaging to establishing therapeutic love. Such confrontative gestures would hit the heart first before being transferred to the brain. Some secrets may need to be safely held and not confronted. The following is an example of my earlier, crude use of confrontation.

Timothy has a long history of avoiding things in his life outside which come into force in the group. By this stage, 12–15 months of his membership, we had all reached an impasse or crescendo. For some months he had maintained a sullen, withdrawn position, throwing provocative comments in from time to time. Others were withdrawing from him and likewise avoiding the problem. In this session, there had been dialogue around aspects of distancing. I turned to Timothy and asked:

Are you going to sit another session out?

He did not respond and the others carried on talking. After a few minutes I came back addressing the group: "Every time I or others comment on Tim's position it goes nowhere. Either he stays silent or gives a brief response."

Tim: "I don't have any feelings and can't contribute!"

My feelings reached a crescendo and I said:

Don't talk crap. You're an angry man. You're denying your feelings. Others in the group are feeling the intensity of your avoided feelings. You're turning the group into a mirror image of your family at home. You know very well that you should do things at home, just as here in the group. Either you start using the group or you go elsewhere.

I shocked myself here. There was a stunned silence, which lasted for about five minutes.

Mary: "Gerry you're angry, I've never seen you this way!"
Me: "Yes! I am but the biggest part is my reactions to Tim's projections but I will also have to think about what is my personal position."

Tim did respond and spoke in some detail about his life; the times when he feels/felt worthless, lonely, isolated; probably for the first time. The others were very moved and pitched in their own associations. There was also relief that I had challenged Tim.

Cynthia: "Tim, you need to come back and keep speaking about these things."

On reflection there were things going on for me outside the group which made me speak as I did. There were a number of demands being put upon me which echoed Tim's dilemmas. Were my actions abusive or carried any semblance of therapeutic love? I don't believe this was abusive but I was telling Tim that I'd had enough and there was caring in my frustrated anger, which helped us to move onto a valuable sharing of Tim's deeper feelings and allowing the group to see my human side. The following week I apologised to Tim, and acknowledged what it was in my working life outside of this group that made me speak to him as I did. Tim took the lead in the session, and although he said he felt angry with me, he was also appreciative that I took him out of (his) 'my self-exile.' He was doing more at home and saw how this was affecting his family. The others felt glad that I'd acted as I had but a little envious that none of them had broken the impasse.

Me: "Well you've all tried at one time or another in the past."

From here the group moved very freely from one to the other in which much was sparked off about their past and present life situations. Subsequently I was able to sit back more, which allowed me to have a broader view of the group. It was as if the group had been somewhat constipated until my intervention the previous week. I told them that last week when I had used the word 'crap' in respect to Tim I was daring to question his constipation of emotional trapped energy. This then progressed to all of them offering up similar situations which they were dealing with. What started as Tim's silence, and, following this, the whole group's silent obstacle, was conceived as Tim's withholding presence. Here there is a paradox of consuming fear is consuming power, that is, the initial silence powerfully induces fear with the group being consumed, developing into a powerful strangulatory stronghold.

In earlier years, I was too ready to deem it appropriate that I had the right/responsibility to engage in confrontation with patients, under the banner of translating this as the patient's neurotic symptoms or other pathological states need to be challenged. In a group I, at times, would see this as my enacting something that the others were reluctant/loathe to do as a form of modelling. An intent in this was that hopefully group members would have felt freer to come forward in challenging ways. On reflection I now see that I may not have been as open to the impact this had on other group members, even though there would be some wider acknowledgements and benefits. Such events were not so dissimilar to myself and the given patient being like parents, couples, having a row and not seeing how it affected the children (group members). I recall one group session in which I had an openly angry dispute with Kevin, who was in his first weeks of joining the group, and he displayed an extreme hostility to the group which I felt that I had to take on as there were good reasons why the others were struggling with tolerating his attacks. Following this session, he contacted me to say he would not return, giving practical reasons for withdrawal. When I told the group about Kevin's decision to leave they said that they weren't surprised as they thought he had joined under duress from other professionals, that is, psychiatrists. In fact I had been pressed by my colleague to take him into the group. The one thing that had shaken and frightened them was my behaviour, as they had not seen me being so openly angry before. Marie, who had missed last week's session:

I wouldn't like to see you angry Gerry!

They felt that Kevin could not accept what I was offering him. I had pointed out that Kevin was safeguarding himself with little understanding of his intense anger. On reflection I see that I did not own my own anger and resorted to an intellectual description of narcissism in the colloquial phrase: 'what's yours is mine and what's mine is my own,' which I had said to Kevin, that is, the world revolves around him. I told them that Kevin had asked me, as we were leaving the room last week, 'was I angry with him?' and my response: 'we can take it up next week.' This may have been like rubbing salt on the narcissistic wound and he felt that he could not return. Thankfully, the group was able to acknowledge the depth of their fear of my losing control and potentially attacking others even though, up until now, I had been seen as warm and caring. Although I had been able in other groups/sessions to be more balanced at such times, why could I not have said to the group something like:

This must be hard for you (the group members) to say how Kevin and I are affecting you!

I wasn't able to do it on this occasion.[1] As therapists I think there is, at times, an under estimation of the impact of our words and personality on our patients. What may at times feel like an accurate, helpful comment or interpretation can cut like a knife on the negative side, or lead the patient into the view that these are pearls of wisdom. However, maybe wisdom is something which the wise rarely feels belongs to them. Maybe it emerges at those times when I feel direct channels opening up between me and others and at times when it is expressed in its simplicity. Therefore, wisdom as described in this manner has its own voice. It is a central element of therapeutic love, emanating from the heart as compared with the hardness of intellectualisation, which can go dramatically wrong, as occurred with Kevin, myself and the group. A closing point of note was that when I recorded the session of dispute with Kevin, I accidentally had pressed the wrong dictaphone button which wiped everything from the recording. Originally, I described this as my unconscious counter transference acting out but to do so puts the emphasis on Kevin projecting rather than my own unconscious. This has been one of the factors central to my development of the concept of 'transference constellations,' in which it became a circular process in which one minute the patient's material is the driving force; the next it is the therapist's. There are also times when it is simultaneous, that is, when the patient and the therapist mirror one another at the same time synchronistically. Therefore, if we can formulate and define transference/counter transference, as has occurred in much of the literature to date, with the patient as the initial focus, then why not the therapists? On reflection a new thought emerged which I tentatively suggest = transference is one of psychotherapies greatest errors in that it has been given 'crown like' status, thus blinkering us to so much more.

In with the New – Out with the Old

There are many elements to be considered in 'slow open groups' life span, when accommodating patients starting and finishing at different times. Groups that are less than a year old tend to be seen as pre-mature and those well-established, in excess of 2–3 years, are deemed to be mature. However, to reach these developmental stages entails many factors. Much thought goes into when it is suitable for people to join an existing group as well as the planning required for peoples exit. Sometimes unexpected things can arise, that is, a plan is made for someone to start and with little notice an existing member decides to leave at the same time, possibly not in keeping with the original exit plan. An example of this occurred in one session when Colleen came to her first session. It was Hilary's last session. Interestingly the opening dialogue revolved around dramas and plays they had been to at the theatre. This reflected the 'opening curtain' for Colleen and the 'closing curtain' for Hilary. At one point Colleen is quietly tearful and rises, going to stand silently by the window. The group has now become an action drama. I gently persuade her to return to her seat, helping her to not feel she has to get everything out. It was then, as if the old and the new came together, with Colleen and Hilary appearing to get close with so much in common, with the others becoming the audience. There was pleasure that Hilary and Colleen had met but disappointment that it would be their first and last time. There was further dialogue about some of the members who had left the group previously and how they were doing. I had drawn the parallel between the group and the dramatic play which had a script, the group did not. Colleen and Hilary were the curtain raising and falling. At the end of the session Hilary contemplated staying longer for Colleen's sake. I said:

So, you want to do an encore!

This brought laughter and a sense of closure.

Open and Hidden Messages from the Conductor

According to group analytic principles, the group analyst does not initiate the lead or direction for the group. This carries an overt message, primarily established through his/her entry to the room, saying nothing and waits. This implies:

It's up to you.

However, there is a covert expectation that the group should eventually begin speaking and sharing with one another, which is a covert silent directive. No group analyst wants to bring a group together to stay silent for a whole session or many weeks/months. For example: Diane joined the group recently and last week disclosed that she had recently overdosed. This week she'd found it strange that the others had not asked her more about this, when she had told us. The others explained the protocol of leaving new people alone so as not to pressurise them into saying too much. This may have been odd to her at the silent start of last week's session.

Ruth: "That's the hidden message we get from Gerry!"
Dianne: "So, he's (Gerry) to blame!"

As stated earlier that from the initial stages of assessment leading to a group entry, and throughout therapy, the group analyst conveys open expectations, that is, group guidelines; the expectations that what is said in the group is confidentially held by everyone; that members should do all they can in using the group to change their lives outside. The group will pick up on much that the group analyst does not openly admit to expecting, that is, through facial/bodily mannerisms; his patterns of response; his attentiveness or not; his use/overuse of his personal reactions to events; his/her aloofness, coldness, warmth, tolerance. His use or overuse of theoretical jargon or his common sense language.

Affective Change

In a similar way to the overt and covert expectations, there is also an overt desire that through group dialogue things will be uncovered/discovered and hopefully more substantial or positive concrete change in symptomatology. This can also be assisted if external areas in peoples' lives will work in harmony and is supportive of the patient's therapeutic journey. For example, when one group was discussing 'actual' changes in their physical health they were seeing this as direct responses within the group's progress. Annette's 'thrush' had improved to the point that her gynaecologist felt the change was due to the group's intervention. In the same session Alex, Jackie and Bruce highlighted how all of their anxiety symptoms had rescinded markedly. They could not fully understand why this had happened. Sonia had become pregnant and gave birth during her time in the group. A central fear/anxiety before entering the group was that she was possessed by something evil which had stopped her giving birth in the past. Of course, there was much more to it that had been explored. On a number of other occasions with other patients who had problems with conceiving, they did get pregnant during the course of therapy. These major changes did not happen overnight. For most it was after many months and years. As affective change is an intent in longer term group analysis we may also venture that by establishing the group analytic milieu that it is a form of therapeutic love, providing a containing, trusting environment which enables this.

It holds and promotes surface and deeper searching, allowing healing processes to permeate on many individual and collective levels which in turn may lead to 'affective change.' I have covered a whole range of pertinent areas in this chapter, drawing attention to their significance in the 'earlier period.' These are developed in the ensuing chapters.

Note

1 I was able to meet Kevin later to pick up the pieces.

Chapter 9

Middle Stages of Development

What I have written about so far revolved around the first 15 years of my career, moving from The Ingrebourne and into my Social Services Department. By this point, I was becoming more equipped to gauge which clients would benefit from either individual or group therapy, be it analytic or more focused, such as anxiety management, assertiveness or psychodrama. There were times when I was amiss in not seeing that, in my enthusiasm to promote a client to avail themselves of the richness that a group could offer, this possibly missed that the client knew best and would have fared better with individual therapy. What is also of note was that during this period, until my return to the Health Service in 1996, I was using the term 'client' instead of 'patient.' It is difficult to come up with alternative titles best suited to academic dissemination. Although this variance between two title words is hardly worthy of comment, I think it is extremely important. 'Patient' implies a process of 'waiting' to be treated which conveys a passive dynamic. Although it is similar, 'client' alters the arrangement to some level of mutuality, that is, the 'purchaser' (client) and 'provider' (therapist). Although passivity cannot be ruled out, action/activity becomes more dominant. Increasingly, there were both existing and new theoretical and practical developments as follows.

The Group/Individual Dichotomy

Broadly speaking we are attentive to the individuals overall need in the pursuance of group membership. There are times when we have to pay more attention to one or more individuals during a session, or for example, at times of concern or crisis. Also, there may be times in the course of a session an individual may leave the room upset and the group analyst, or another member, follows to attempt a return. On the positive side, there are particular individuals who, because of their unique personality can bring something to the group which adds greatly to the whole group's potential development. These are: those who take great risks with disclosure, empathy, humour, insight and motivation to help others. In line with my newer 'therapeutic love' hypotheses, they ooze love and hope, showing that it is possible to really change as a result of being in the group. If they miss a session,

DOI: 10.4324/9781003536857-11

there is a great hole in the group. It is through these people that I came to see the place and power of the heart as a driving force in therapeutic love.

For example, Samantha joins an existing group and finds her first session too much and runs out of the room in tears. I follow her and convince her to return. Before she had joined the group I had formed a good contact with her through the assessment period which helped her return to the group session. The others were relieved as Samantha was able to open up about what had sparked this off. As the weeks and months developed, she gained in strength and by her willingness to open her heart to people and give others support, she quickly became a leading figure in the group. She, in turn, uncovered in greater detail her past childhood traumas and how she had rectified the parts of her life that had been affected which was an incentive for the others to follow suit. She gradually reduced and stopped her medication and her anorexia was improving. She came to be extremely valued by the others. An added bonus for the group was that it became a caring and trusting group which could also return the love that Samantha evoked to one another.

This brings into relief the times when the dichotomy is of one individual being given an inordinate amount of time in a group session. As with Samantha, the group can be accommodating if there are positive/loving vibes towards the individual. This, in a way, is allowing the others to identify, resonate associate with that which is evoked. One can feel the love in the room. Contrary to this the individual who consumes a lot of time regurgitating negative, pointless, 'heard it a hundred times' dominance, will create hostility and intolerance. This can become an impasse for long periods of time and one of the most difficult dynamics to understand and resolve. It can pull the group apart. Then there are those individuals who are promoted to take centre stage giving a voice for others at times when the whole group is avoidant of a recurring group problem. What group analyst has never said: 'what is Mary saying for the group?' The group analyst has much to do at times like this in bringing parity to the 'Group–Individual' dichotomy.

On reflection when considering dichotomies there is an interesting variant which may exist for many group analysts, that is, giving attention to the individual while conceptualizing the whole group. In my earlier days, these two points were further apart and with later years, as I approached and developed through my middle years, the marriage between the two became less at a variance.

'Being in the Moment' It Gained Greater Importance

This is a term that is relatively common and applied to many settings. Outside the world of therapy, I have to be very much in the moment: that is, the golf course. Golf is a game with such a philosophy and is also built on paradoxes, that is, keep still as you swing the club; don't hit the ball! Response: how can I make the ball move if I don't hit it? Response: It's the golf swing that you make and the ball gets in the way. The ball moves through the swing. If ones focus is on hitting the ball this reduces the swing only to the club face and ball moment of impact, and misses the subtle complex properties of the golf swing. Therefore, such areas as being with the patient; being attentive; group members saying 'I've been where you are'; 'you don't need to justify'; 'It must have been so painful for you'; 'I feel so happy to see how you've changed' describes the need to be in the moment. There are numerous theoretical terms which can be applied: empathy, identification, resonance, compassion, to name a few. For me, the newer concepts of 'therapeutic love' feel more in keeping. For example, Simone opens up for the first time in the group her guilty feelings that she was to blame for her daughter's birth defects. This is very moving and the others gently spoke with her, sharing some of their own guilty feelings. I say that: "It's important for us to just hold onto the strength of these feelings without needing to do anything further." This surprised Simone, that people were accepting and not criticising her. There was more help in this than providing helpful suggestions for action. This way of experiencing such moments goes to and from the individual's and the group's heart. Words and associations are subsequently ways of conveying love. Over the course of time such sessions build up, layer upon layer of progressions, with the group's safety and security established. In turn this will, more than likely, create a permissive environment in which people can be more challenging of one another. Groups which are dominated with the drive to 'sort things out,' a preponderance of 'conflict resolution,' 'breaking down defences,' I feel will be less effective than the loving group. Of course there are times and situations:

When Is Love Not Enough?

There is a song which was written in 1956 which indicated that falling in love would last forever.

No one enters therapy to fall in love and stay forever, as far as I'm aware. However, some periods of group analysis and psychoanalysis can last for a great many years. In my time I have seen some patients intermittently for 9–10 years. Also, some return on a number of occasions after the initial first period of therapy. When patients/ clients have gone through a successful therapy feeling it to have been loving and changing parts of their life, this, in a strange way, will last forever (as long as they live and in the memory after death). There are many patients, probably the majority, who have stayed with me in my thoughts and my heart. Even if the experience has not been satisfactory it can also last the test of time. One day when shopping in my local supermarket a man was looking at me strangely. He stopped me and said: "it's Gerry, isn't it?" At first, I didn't recognise him but then it dawned on me. [I can remember many patients' faces and parts of their lives from the mid-1970s.] I recalled his name and he asked me if I had a minute (that's usually 10–15 minutes). We shook hands and he said, "I was in one of your groups." Me: "How's things?" John: "Good!" You did two of the best things ever. First, you accepted me into the group where others before you had rejected me. Second, you told me to "fuck off" (these expletives were not my words). I would have told him that he was discharged. "That was because I kept bringing beer into the group." We were both laughing at this. On a number of occasions he had been cautioned and, in the end, I had reached my limits after 12 to

18 months. We spoke a little more about his life before we parted. It was interesting that he saw my ejecting him as very helpful as this had spurred him on to take better charge of his life. He also knew at the time he would be accepted back to the group at a later time if we both agreed. Over the years, I have accidentally met ex-patients, sometimes in unexpected places, such as restaurants, pubs and theatres. I recall meeting a mother and daughter who both had been in therapy with me at different times, at a music concert. The fact that they were together indicated a positive change, as there had been marked animosity between them. Also, some patients went on to do professional training in Health Services and it was not uncommon that we often attended meetings as professional colleagues.

In group analytic/psychotherapy language we speak of finishing, as stated earlier, as termination. I am more comfortable with 'It's time to say goodbye!' The 'therapeutic love' in the presence of others is replaced with parting thoughts and feelings and the start of therapeutic memories in the minds of the patient. Certainly, their external world will have been a major factor impacting on the inner world of the group through the course of therapy. Usually, that when the decision to leave emerges there is a lot of thought and management in order to get through this as smoothly as possible. Key to this is to recognise and acknowledge what this has meant for everyone in the group, that is, the leaver's importance to the group and the group's importance to the person leaving. Sometimes people leave abruptly for many reasons, so leaving cannot be processed in the loving arena of farewell. Usually, it is one person leaving at a time, but sometimes more than one, which also raises concerns for the group's continuity. An illustration of this was when three people announced they would leave in six weeks (the pre-agreed time period in leaving the group). This took everyone by surprise. Straightaway Claire sys: "Gerry, this shows how successful you are!" (Group laughter). Jim: "You should be paid more Gerry!" Me: "That's a nice thought, but maybe we shouldn't just see a mass leaving only as success." We then began to explore each of their desires to leave whether it was the correct decision or not. For instance, two of them had been in the group a long time and it seemed appropriate for them to leave. However, Janet, another long-established member had left a few weeks ago and everyone had been fond of her. As I stated earlier about members who are centrally important, Janet was like a linchpin and we were all mourning her loss. Therefore, was this contributing to the mass leaving desire? Janet's love had gone. There was much nodding and agreement here as I shared my thoughts. Although this was shown as a central motive there were other good reasons for those leaving and how this related to those continuing in the group. With this middle stage of development 'well held views' were questioned more and achieved greater sophistication. Hopefully, the following areas illustrate this.

Natural Biological Love

I find it somewhat surprising that many of my group analytic colleagues would freely use terms like 'the new baby' to name a new person coming into the group.

Equally there have been familial equations of mothering, paternal, parenting, siblings, along with conceptualising and explaining psychological desires biologically as in feeding from the breast, as just some references. I recall saying to a patient: "Harry, there are two breasts, you can't get both in your mouth at the same time." He had major problems with ambivalence and decision making, constantly asking for support and answers. At another group session we were going around in circles and the discussion raged pessimistically: "What's the point?" "There's no point in continuing!" "It's pointless, the group," etc. I said: "The point of the breast is the nipple and you can't get the milk unless you suck the nipple." This was connected to how they were fighting against the love and care of the group, while seeing that they also had to give a little (psychological) nourishment to one another in return. Within the psychoanalytic literature, primarily Kleinian, there is a great deal written about the symbolic nature of the breast, but I do not know if the nipple has been specifically written about by others even though I made a substantial literature search.

Considering the impact of pregnancy within groups, this throws up a great deal. Earlier, I spoke about the woman who was afraid of giving birth to a 'Devil' child. When a female group member, or a male member's partner outside the group, gets pregnant, there will be a whole range of responses. One point of interest is that when it emerges it is like having another group member. As the foetus grows there will be a range of positive and negative aspects. It is not necessarily so that the unborn child will bring love into the group, or the group will be a more loving one. The pregnant mother will have their own agenda and equally the group will resonate on many levels according to each group members' associations with child birth and infancy. Also, the pregnant woman may have concerns about continuing with the group in not wanting her child to be affected, whether this is physical or what the foetus absorbs psychologically through her. The prospective mother may also not want the child; it is unexpected, or an outcome of having been raped. On the positive side pregnant women in my groups have found the group a major support. One patient stayed with the group until the week of the birth, returning the week after with the baby for the others to share in her joy. This has happened on a number of occasions with other patients. When this happens I believe that this is a sign of therapeutic love. In the case of pregnant group members this may take up an inordinate amount of time for the nine months gestation and a great deal of investment by all group members. The expectant mother struggles with her own challenges while the others enter the dialogue, or not, driven by birth and infancy matters. This subject could and does demand a great amount of exploration as a separate item, but here I have merely been raising the questions surrounding the points of contact between biological factors touching upon love and therapeutic love. In passing there are other scenarios, equally important and powerful, which could be written about: when the mother miscarries; is ill or dies; if she has an abortion. Other group members may have had similar experiences, all of which have to be addressed and processed in the group. Let me close this section with an illustration which shows when pregnancy announcements are not fully welcomed: Sarah tells the group that she is happy now that she is pregnant after trying for a long time. She felt that she would have to leave the group in seven months to give birth but intended to return within a month after birth. Everyone was pleased for her but the happy announcement did not develop its potency in the session and the group withdrew into an atmosphere of feeling turgid. Sarah was left holding the others unexpressed associations.

The Therapist Changes

One of the purposes of this chapter has been to address the changes in my practice and theory over a prolonged period. However, sometimes I have made changes to myself physically. One point was when I shaved my beard off, after I had it for many years. This had quite an impact on many of my patients and groups. On entering my group room there is an immediate gasping, smiles, eyes widening, a bit of laughter, almost fearful looks with the following comments:

> Where's Gerry?
> You're a brave man Gerry.
> "You look really clean and smart!" (What! I didn't before – my thought)
> No Gerry, grow it back!

Such comments were echoed throughout my other patient/colleagues' responses.

Sophia: "when will you grow it back, as I won't get used to it not being there."

Likewise, Anita felt the same.
  This evoked mixed feelings on whether I should grow it back or not.

Glynis: "You look 10 years younger Gerry!"
Ted: "It must be a woman behind it!" (Trust him to express the erotic)
Me: I told them that I had been curious to see what I would look like without it. "Don't you believe me about being curious about what I would be like without it?"

I had been living with a false belief that my beard was intended to cover a long chin, along with my dislike of shaving. In fact, it was because I didn't have a chin. What this simple change brings into relief is that when we, as therapists, make small or large changes to our body or dress, this will have various repercussions. Consider what happens when the therapist enters the room wearing an engagement/wedding ring for the first time; coming in with new piercings and/or tattoos; when a female therapist enters and their pregnancy shows for the first time? Over the years I have made various changes to myself which sparked a whole range of reactions. Such simple things as dress, gaining weight, losing hair, being tanned after a holiday. In later years I was more able to use these elements within the dialogue, whereas in earlier years I was prone to see the patient's interest in me as an evasion.

Earlier I spoke of my changing from a confrontative approach to being more accommodating and receptive which fostered therapeutic love although at times needing to challenge. During disclosure of critical and painful past trauma the individual is confronting memories in the here and now of the group. There is no need for me or others to confront. As one patient in a session spoke movingly about having been sexually and physically abused, while having some current flashbacks, the group rose to the occasion by providing space for her and gradually bringing in their own abuse histories. Tears flowed freely. As I left the group room at the end of the session the others sat on for a few minutes to collect themselves and as they left the building some had their arms embraced around each other. Such sessions show a non-erotic love which comes into play. In this case it was after the disclosure of erotic abuse from childhood. Therefore, disclosure is a form of confrontation. The following areas entail points of confrontation.

Pregnancy – Trauma – Suicide

In contrast to the predominantly hopeful elements of the impact of pregnancy, as stated earlier, the struggles in disclosure of abuse experiences, the impact of suicidal ideology and actual suicide illuminates hopelessness. My previous illustrations revolved around one particular group and the following commentary is connected to the same group. They were recovering from last week's session where Hannah had spoken about her suicidal attempts and fears of future attempts. She did not attend this week so people were concerned. Sonia wondered if she had been too forceful with Hannah last week. Claire spoke about her husband manipulating her with his suicide threats, so she had been angry with Hannah. Claire felt Hannah didn't want to change, so could not be helped. There was a split between feeling concern for Hannah and anger, also feeling anxious in not knowing the current situation about Hannah's absence. This then progressed into their talking about their relatives and friends who had attempted suicide. There was also concern as to what this was doing to Samantha's unborn child. She was ok with this. There was some gallows humour in the closing minutes.

As the session finished they embraced one another as they were leaving the room. I see this now as a healthy coping mechanism after the direct emotional power of the sessions disclosure. Reflecting back on my comments about the group embracing as they left the building last week (I had by chance looked out of the window as they were leaving the building), I can see this now as caring, loving gestures at the time. In this following session I questioned this as their acting something out that they had not achieved during the session, implying that they were undoing what occurred in the session. Looking at how such a group can, within short periods of time, progress through dialogue on pregnancy, trauma and suicide says a lot for its ability to create a therapeutic loving environment. The heart is being touched first and foremost and not the mental processes which some may feel are governed by the brain and cognitive assimilation.

The Group Takes Care of the Group Analyst

In 1987 my mother died and I had to be away from work. At the time I had a co-therapist for some of my groups which allowed them to continue. Therefore, in my absence this gave space for developing dialogue about how group members felt about me and the grief that I had to endure. Many patients may not consider in any great detail what their therapist/analyst has to endure. This comes into relief if the therapist has to deal with major life issues that the patients come to know about. Some therapists ensure that the patient will know little or nothing of their lives. The more aloof the therapist the less a patient will register that the therapist has their own trials and tribulations, and this disciplined distance is valued and strenuously adhered to. Sometimes a therapist's parent may die on a Thursday and the patient's session is cancelled because of 'unavoidable circumstances.' The therapist buries their mother on the Sunday and returns to work on a Monday, the patient not having a clue that it has happened. Of course this may miss that the patients will, more than likely, pick up in some way that something of import (note) has happened. Returning to familial equations, there is a more healthy position if, during parents own tragedies, that their children can share in these. The children can see that their parents are able to be open about their life and feelings. This is different from parents dumping their load on the children. Likewise, this applies to patient/therapist relations in that the therapist, and in turn the patient, will gain immensely if there is a transparency with the therapist allowing the patient into their lives at such times. I was never afraid to allow the patients to know about major things in my life, like the death of my mother, to be shared if it impacted on my work, or the times when the psychotherapy department was threatened with closure. I shared my fears, anxiety, and anger. I was fighting for them as much as for myself and now it was time for me to focus on myself and my family. They felt sad for me and it was clear that they had missed me. They told me that they were sorry for my loss but were glad that I had returned. I thanked them and although I picked up some annoyed undertones in relation to my absence it was not appropriate to comment on these. I needed to let them care for me. Equally, some life affirming events such as my international teaching which necessitated me to be absent, I would share. This provided truthful reasons for absence. Sometimes it is difficult to allow the patient to care for the therapist if such transactions maintain a strict discipline which is based upon the therapists need for privacy.

Individual Transference in the Group

I am slightly hesitant in describing a client's attraction/pre-occupation with me in the group as transference in the same way as one would within an individual psychotherapy relationship. However, it will suffice for the time being. I recall one woman who became very attached to me over a two- to three-year period moving from individual into group therapy. By and large this turned out to be successful and ended with my moving jobs, while she remained in the group as it was able to continue with another therapist taking over. There seemed to be a central position of her wanting direction and approval from me while also taking a leading role in the group, almost akin to being my co-therapist – even though I had a professional co-therapist at the time. She was both supportive and challenging, defending me at times of misunderstandings by others and attack. She would often translate my 'so-called' analytic language into common sense language which was more palatable. Meandering a little here, I recall language used from my therapeutic community days which was quite scathing to the patients when they tried to help one another. The staff group would often question with a derogatory undertone, that these people, the patients, were 'playing at being the therapist,' almost accusing them of avoiding their own difficulties. It was difficult for these staff members to accept that everyone was a therapist as well as a patient in the pursuance of the therapeutic community ethos.

Returning to my patient, Carmel, there were times that her own individual struggles had to be addressed beyond her individual affinity with me, outside the group room. In one session she spoke of an uncanny, almost supernatural, thought process, that is, she would be thinking about someone and then they'd appear for no apparent reason. She had been thinking about me one day while shopping and then I actually appeared and we said 'hello.' At the time she had desperately wanted to talk with me but felt: "he wouldn't want to meet his problem in his spare time." She had been having a bad week. I previously had a gut feeling that she would request an individual appointment as she couldn't go further in the group session and I was about to go on leave the following week. She phoned me after the group session and I arranged to meet her. The main gist of this meeting was that recently she had become clearer about her feelings/memories about her dead father's anniversary which were coming back and flooding her. She feared losing me and the group. She was able to bring this back to the group. This sequence brought unexpected repercussions in the group. The others had picked up on what had developed between Carmel and me. In the following session Maria was angry that we had met outside of the group even with it being accidently and she felt I had betrayed the group as I had always said that things should be sorted out in the group. She felt jealous as there were times she had wanted to meet with me separately. I reminded her, and the others, of my earlier statements during the assessment stages, that I would meet people outside the group at times of crisis. However, the first thing I always asked when we met was why it was so difficult to speak with the group or could it wait until the next group meeting. Also, they were expected to bring our discussions back to the group. Interestingly, Barry said: "If Gerry sees anyone outside the session it's not individual counselling, it has to be connected to the group."

Rather astute!

Structural Changes

As I look back to my days in the therapeutic community from my 'middle stages' there were many concrete/structural elements which I abandoned and changed over the years. One of the early therapeutic communities called The Henderson was the location where I did my art therapy training placement as a student. At that time, it was residential and its site was an old converted psychiatric asylum. The patients were told that they had to build their own sleeping space in a large empty room (previously a psychiatric ward). This was quite a demanding structural requirement. Lesser structural points were in place in my earlier groups; for example, during sessions people could smoke, eat and drink. They would pass sweets around to be shared. Interestingly it would often be white 'Polo' mints which at one point I interpreted as 'solid milk' and similar to a nipple in appearance, to little response. Another time I recall a student in one of my training groups who brought her supper of fish and chips. In these early days that although a ban was not in place, as later occurred, I tended to apply various interpretations around such things as feeding oneself; the group feeding was not enough; sharing or not; defending against what was an offer beyond actual food/feeding. Eventually over time within groups, and individual therapy, smoking and eating was banned. I reached a point when I would provide water during assessment sessions and permitted patients to drink water during sessions. In the early days this would have been seen as colluding with patients' evasions. In the end, I thought that it was more caring/loving to reduce anxiety and dry mouths. Also, in the early days that if the patient needed to leave the room to go to the toilet it was frowned upon and defined as an 'acting out' behaviour, sometimes it was a physical need irrespective of a full bladder or a reaction to anxiety. At times it 'was' an 'acting out' mechanism. I came to see that such prohibitive guidelines as were originally in place often blocked off further exploration and did little for the overall therapeutic venture.

The Challenge to Authority

As the years developed, I moved through various ideas/views on the significance and importance of the patient/client group being able to challenge me. Whether I was seen by others as the authority, leader, parental figure, or basically someone who was failing to meet expectations. In the early days I think that I placed more importance on patients/groups ability to reach this point with me. In retrospect that although this had varying levels of importance, it may have blinkered me to a whole range of other factors. As I developed I became less pre-occupied with searching for these dimensions. Patients eventually did not seem so concerned with my authoritative position leaving them room to open up. For example, in an early session in one of my groups, which was dealing with the death of one of its members who had died of natural causes, feelings and tempers were high. I was under a great deal of scrutiny. The death had stoked up a loss of belief in the group, that is, people died before they could get better. Claire was particularly angry with me, not holding back in expressing this. At one point she says:

> "I have not fallen in love with Gerry or anything like that." This comment was linked to an intense dependence upon me which was continuously under group discussion.

This was followed by Tim feeling cheated and betrayed and blamed me for not telling him that the group would be like this, otherwise he would not have joined. He then turned his fury on the whole group seeing the others as weak and the group turned into something of a battle ground for the remainder of the session. In some ways this showed an initial struggle with my authority where Claire's dependency was being seen as love and Tim's attack on the group as an extension of his diverted struggles with my authority. With the ensuing years there would be similar group sessions, but gradually a more balanced reaction to group members' deaths, natural or otherwise, developed. Hence grief and mourning could be processed without a similar animosity.

Losing It

There are times, more so in my earlier years where I just 'lost it' – to coin a collo-quial phrase, but this was becoming less of a problem through these middle years. This would be when I would be at a loss as to either understanding something; feeling frustrated with particular people and groups; feeling that what I offered was unhelpful or meaningless; retaliating when I felt under threat or attack. I had to reach a point of seeing that there was some validity in what I offered but was not accepted for various reasons. On the other side of the coin I also had to accept that I was inaccurate or wrong in my own interventions and my groups/patients were quite correct in how they responded to me. For example, in one of my group sessions Mary speaks about identifying with a television programme which was promoting a therapeutic research programme which she felt fitted her problems and she had approached her General Practitioner requesting a referral. There were two newer members in the group and there was an excited dialogue upon the external research group in contrast to the value of *this* group therapy. In contrast to group analysis the research programme was biologically connected to hereditary factors. The momentum in the session gathered force to the 'great hope' beyond. I began to feel despair and spontaneously covered my face with my hands. Eventually, I said: "Mary, this is your therapy!"

She spat back that the person on the television was a specialist who knew what he was talking about. I returned, possibly in my despair: "I am a specialist and this is a specialist therapy."

She was able then to speak more openly about the group not giving her what she needed. In saying I was a specialist I think showed that I'd 'lost it' as I resorted to attacking any positive exploration into the difference between the televised specialism and that of our group. Such processes as this reminds me of a general dilemma of 'having the last word,' which is similar to what I define as the 'and but' syndrome. Mary had her 'words' but I had to have the 'last word.' In this process when an argument/discussion reaches a point of closure, someone says 'and but' – someone has to have the last word, or the dialogue takes a new turn. Possibly, in some cases the therapist may feel that they have the last word when their interpretations are given. 'Losing it' indicates a loss of control and when reached may well be described as a nebulous start of something new without an answer or conclusion.

The Nebulosity of Love

According to the Collins English dictionary nebulous is defined as: 'lacking definite form, shape or content; vague or amorphous' (Collins, Millennium Edition). When feelings of love are directly experienced they are both solid and at the same time nebulous, that is, it's hard to define. One could romantically say there are as many definitions of love as there are stars in the sky. As a central tenet in my thesis is that the heart is the seat/central force of love, the concrete heart is clearly not nebulous.

Egyptian mythology/philosophy tells us that in death the heart is weighed against the feather of truth. If it did not balance the dead could not continue safely. The heart was seen to be the centre of wisdom and the dwelling place of the soul.

Moving back to my own views, nebulous waves of love (or nebulosity) are evoked and freely flows from the inner to the outer world. Some scientists may define this as the emergence/attraction via pheromones. Therefore, in considering 'therapeutic love' within psychotherapy it is a dilemma, that is, when non-erotic loving is felt and expressed in the group. Are these concrete physical/biological experiences for group members through a process of identifying and sharing with one another, or something less concretely sourced, that is, nebulous heart moves? For example, a group was going through a turbulent phase for about six months. Over the past two to three months, they had lost two members who had become too disturbed to continue for intense and complex reasons. The group was now picking up the pieces. There was some relief in that I informed them that I and a colleague were now providing them with individual therapy. There was a general feeling that both patients were too ill or out of reach and although there was relief that they had gone there was guilt and feelings of helplessness. Both patients would run out of the group when they had been questioned or challenged, so could not deal with the groups pressure

Sue says: "I wanted to take Kate (who had left) under my wing!"
Samantha: "After the sessions I would walk down the road with Simone (the other member who left) and I didn't want to let her go."

John: "We didn't try hard enough to keep them!"
Theresa: "I felt a great warmth for Kate but it was impossible to get close!"

One can see that in this scenario the various statements/comments were coming from heartfelt emotions in how they cared for both women and all of the previous attempts were somewhat nebulous. Such a situation is not unlike the 'leftover feelings' of two lovers parting yet still being in love; or the departee feeling no love and the remainder yearning; or remorse as part of the grieving process following death.

Before moving onto my 'Later Stage' of development let me speak briefly about how nebulosity is experienced in:

The First Session

New members entering existing groups is synonymous with the first session in therapy. I recall my first session of entering a new group for my own therapy when I said "What the F..., how can you see each other here?" (The room was dimly lit with side lamps). I feel relatively sure that this was because I was anxious. Although the first session of individual therapy is easier to predict and manage, the group arena is a whole different matter. What holds it together is the transition of my having met and assessed the new person before entry to the group. At that stage I would have conceptualised some understanding of the person and why it would be appropriate for them to join a particular group. Through many years of experience, trial and error, I became more able to avoid errors and mismatching. Nevertheless, in reality first sessions and how people fitted together was always unpredictable. Strange as it may seem the unpredictable carried excitement as well as fear, hope and trepidation. One learns many things from the processes: 'Love at first sight' or 'facing the demons.' In one of my early groups Chris entered for the first time and almost immediately attacked the others saying they were pathetic, *his* were real problems. The others were seen to be moaning and self-indulgent. Understandably the others rose to the bait and mounted a counter attack. Everyone survived this first session and Chris did return. In a later session he acknowledged that he had been defensive and frightened when he first joined. Initially I felt that I had made a mistake in my assessment for him to join the group and intuitively felt that this would end in tragedy. As the group progressed Chris became more reflective and was accepted more, with the group reaching a greater degree of regard and care for one another. Chris' changing position helped create deeper understanding of attack and defence mechanisms. Outside the group Chris had picked rows at work and was sacked. This allowed me to see how my initial counter transference feelings regarding assessment/selection contributed to the urge to sack him from the group. I suggest that right from the beginning we all make 'spur of the moment' views, judgements with first encounters. There is a relatively accepted view that people make up their minds in the first few minutes when viewing a prospective house purchase, based upon feeling. As one may imagine, these early sessions which had been triggered with Chris' entry had a whole range of reactions and repercussions. This is not to say that it was Chris and my potentially faulty selection were to blame.

Tanya also had a similar first session as Chris but her main way of dealing was through heightened speaking, sometimes for 20–30 minutes non-stop. She rarely paused for breath and appeared to hear very little. There was often a hysterical feel in her words and tears, and she had difficulty in tolerating others positions. Once, when Carmen was crying Tanya got up quickly and ran across the room to embrace Carmen. At the time I saw this as Tanya trying to put a plug on Carmen's tears, which Carmen agreed with. At these times I think that there was a caring/loving component in Tanya's action but as the group was going through heated and fluctuating developments, love and the heart were the furthest things from the groups mind. This does not mean that a great deal of positive work was not occurring. At the time I was basing much of my technique and theorising on conventional psychotherapy and group analytic perspectives but views on heartfullness and therapeutic love were bubbling unformed below the surface.

The previous vignettes are more extreme scenarios. In contrast a new person may come into their first group session and maintain a quiet, passive, frightened position. There will be many reasons for this and tends to be less disruptive as the provocative entrant. Much will also depend on the existing membership: how welcoming they are; the current/continuing agenda. This can either help or hinder the new member to begin to take a more active part. First impressions all round will carry their own compositions. With these illustrations that within the various issues being expressed and worked through there will be a prevailing set of nebulous dynamics, rather like the supporting cast, wardrobe and make up, producer and director of a film.

Therapeutic Love Gains a Stronger Foundation

I stated earlier that my thoughts upon 'therapeutic love and heartfullness' were bubbling under the surface. By the time I had moved back to work in the National Health Service I was becoming clearer in my thinking and how this was being used in my work. Probably this was helped through my becoming very fond of one particular group and my liking everyone in it, most of the time. Nevertheless there were some difficult times. What seemed to run through this was that individuals would take great risks of disclosure which then formed an atmosphere of receptiveness and resonance, leading to further disclosure and mutual care and attention. For example, one woman, Lynda, movingly described her traumatic childhood in some detail. I am not at liberty to specify what these details were, however the group was clearly moved, some were crying empathically and supporting Lynda. This led to increasing disclosures from nearly everyone. I initially did not have to say anything. As the starting point of Lynda's disclosure had been initiated through her talking about a current crisis in her family, I focused upon this. I suggested that: 'within the various crises they spoke about they were searching for love but inadvertently the crisis was an enactment which took them away from love.' In a way this had been shown in Lynda's detailed reflections from her childhood and what had been associated to by others. These comments seemed to pull things together and there was a collective feeling of closeness and warmth. Probably, for a group to reach this level of functioning, it has to go through many stages of development.

Increasingly love became a focus in a number of my groups. In one session love was being explored primarily as what one gives and how this is received. John's father had died and during his father's life John had yearned for his father to love and embrace him. Now that father was dead he wished that he could put his arms around his father. Ironically some months later John died and the group then had to deal with not being able to embrace John.

Unilateral Actions (Decisions of the Group Analyst)

There were times when I have had to be more active and direct which may not have been perceived as loving gestures. A number of my group analytic colleagues adhered religiously to the silent position and could spend many sessions saying nothing for extended periods of time, as spoken about earlier. By upholding such a strict position it was almost as if they were leading their groups in line with W. R. Bions distant approach but without the closing interpretations of the 'Basic Assumptions' (McNeilly, 1983/1984, pp. 87–90) of the group developmentally. I also went through this mode of conducting groups, moving on to an increasing freedom in being more spontaneous in my technique. Eventually I knew that I could not develop my thoughts and technique relating to the dominance of the heart and therapeutic love by maintaining such a 'Bionic' stance. In upholding this opaque stance, group analysts, psychotherapists et al gives credence to patients' impressions of them as cold, aloof, uncaring, 'not human' figures.

Prior assessment for group entry is a unilateral action. The process of moving from assessment to joining a group is one of mutuality between the group analyst and the patient. Then the group becomes active in monitoring the duration of therapy and when it is time to finish. This is primarily in respect to the 'slow open' group and differs from groups that have a pre-ordained time limit, that is, 1–2 years. However, there were times when I had to make a unilateral decision of when a patient leaves a group for whatever reason. This has occurred on a small number of occasions. For example, Terry had been in one of my groups for approximately two years and was generally rigid and any potential or psychological mindedness that we saw at the beginning had long since gone. However, the group persevered with him, going to great lengths to help him have some insight and change. In one session, there was a vibrant dialogue around birth, feeding and psychological development. In contrast Terry, as was his norm, disagreed and held firm to the view that this was 'psychobabble.' His lack of emotion and empathy was becoming more obvious and I could see that the group was no longer appropriate. I said: "Terry, maybe you should think about leaving as you are in disagreement that there is a psychological causation." He felt that he had it coming, that I would give him his 'marching orders.' The others were surprised and shocked that I had done this, it was out of keeping with my usual behaviour. Of course, this brought a wider anxiety, that is, would I do this to each of them? I went on to elaborate that if I felt someone had reached as far as they could go then we had to part company. For Terry to continue it would be a way of escaping aspects of his life that needed alternative (physical) intervention or forget about psychological factors. For the rest of the group members it was different as they were benefitting in a whole range of ways.

There are other times when I have stepped outside of the 'wait and see,' 'following the group' approach. For example, there were times when I've had to warn a group member that the threat of physical violence was not acceptable and I became a referee. Other times if someone was having difficulty in over-talking, monopolising, in a state of hysteria, I would say: "stop talking and just listen." "Give your mouth a rest," "just relax." Looking back over my career the early years in the therapeutic community called more upon having to be so active and pro-active. With the middle to later years I had now reached positions where I could hold more firmly to group analytic principles of following the group and did not need to be actively interventionist. Although there were many heated group sessions where emotions crescendoed, no physical violence between people occurred, apart from the odd broken cup, table, glass, door. When such events occurred verbal dialogue was attacked with a shattering of:

Hope and Expectations

It was Bion who suggested that hope should not be fulfilled as it would then kill off hope (Bion, 1961).

> Only by remaining a hope does hope persist.
> In so far as it succeeds, hope is weakened; for obviously nothing is then to hope for, and, since destructiveness, hatred, and despair have in no way been radically influenced their existence again makes itself felt. This in turn accelerates a further weakening of hope.
>
> (Klein, Heimann, & Money-Kyrle, 1955, p. 448)

Another way of defining hope is that it is a 'silent wait' for an outcome which also requires external elements to join forces for the hope to become realised. So, in a way this negates Bion's view that hope should not be achieved. However, possibly it has more to do with not killing off the drive, or the will, in hope. This is central to the process of any therapeutic endeavour. Particular emotional dynamics may well express developments along these lines such as: feeling lonely, alone, or on one's own. In an early period one of my groups was struggling with these disparate states of being which contained struggles of hope and helplessness. Pat was struggling with feeling isolated, alone and lonely. She was envious of Louise who was happy in being on her own and self-contained. However, there were times when Louise felt lonely. Mary felt she carried others' problems and was isolated and on her own with others' problems. I had intervened with a linking interpretation aimed at clarifying the three different states:

> In the struggle to find fulfilment there is the hope that you find another, as in marriage. With this you hope and expect that this will offset a fear of loneliness and isolation. One can feel alone in a crowd and a group. One, at times, can erect an invisible barrier in times of depression, despair and hopelessness: a silent voice not able to cry in the wilderness.

Changing the Subject

In a session in the early 1990s, Annette spoke of a detailed dream involving her father, which was met with silence. This silence was eventually broken by Pat who said that she was changing the subject and proceeded to speak about her ongoing conflicts with her sister. I queried why she thought she was changing the subject as both of them were struggling with conflicts in their primary families. This seemed to highlight a relatively universal dimension in groups in which when one person is disclosing details, the others feel they need to hold back, that is, "This is your time and space!" To either not respond or associate along dissimilar lines feels like taking something away from the first person. Therefore, to bring in what appears to be a completely different subject is seen as taking away as compared to having some tenuous or unconscious connection. In my earlier groups I would be very busy internally trying to detect the linkage between apparently disparate scripts of each person in the group. In this particular session, which was exploring power dimensions and conflicts, it led to a deeper dimension of love. This was shown when they said that in their power struggles with their parents and partners it was hard, almost impossible, to say "I love you" and also to have it said to them by others. The statement was simple yet powerful

Sammy: "How could three words be so difficult?"

But, in fact, it contained thousands of unsaid stories and words. This, in turn, led to a period of silence, almost as if the mention of the phrase robbed the group of its voice. This session allowed me, at a later point, to publish my formulations on 'powerful powerlessness' (McNeilly, 1983/1984, pp. 166–167). This opened up dialogue upon love both in the present and the past. Love lost and found. The sense of togetherness and closeness crystalized in the group with tears, including myself. They spoke about transferring love from dead partners/husbands into their children; being too old to need love and I say that: "love is ageless." They spoke of the fear of 'loving again' in case they lost it. I say, "why should love's importance be questioned, as you would not question the need to breathe or eat. The paradox of love, it is most sought after while it is fought against." So, in the struggles to find love this carries its potential loss.

The Therapist's Loss

For me a constant that was maintained throughout my career has been the dual of sorrow and sadness in letting people/patients go as if a part of me was dying. This was paralleled by feelings of joy, pleasure, pride when people reached a satisfactory conclusion of their therapy. Along with the feeling that a part of me died, there was also a feeling of something gaining life in me with the patient's achievements. Even with those patients who did not do well my feelings of loss were evident but also the lost potential of that which could have been reached 'if only' I, and the patient, had done things differently or had met at a more appropriate time and set of circumstances. During my middle and later years I became more able to deal with these areas. Also, in having many more patients during the middle and later stages raised the bar.

For example, in one session there was an animated discussion about medication for depression and anxiety. Most of them struggled with past and current dependency and how it affected their lives. Claire had resisted using medication throughout her time in therapy even though there had been times when she had been tempted. This was Claire's last session. I said that she had grown a lot in her five years with the group and made great use of it, the others affirmed this. This did not mean that change would stop and would carry on with life processes. I told her that I was sad that we were losing her but glad she had reached this point. The others echoed my sentiments and they spoke fondly about her and their time together. Claire recalled how, like the discussion on 'medication dependency,' she used to depend on others telling her how to lead her life. Nowadays she was surer about her own decisions. I asked her: "In the 5 years did I ever tell you what to do?"

Claire: "No"
Me: "That's good."

The session ended in laughter.

Some Early Therapeutic Love Illustrations

As stated earlier, my formulations on heartfullness and therapeutic love became clearer and confirmed in the final ten years of clinical practice. There were much earlier times when this showed through, although under different conceptual frameworks in line with conventional psychodynamic language as has been highlighted throughout the book.

Regarding permissiveness, one of my earlier groups asked me (through Shirley with a mischievous grin), if they could meet outside for a meal/drink over the Christmas period. I said "No."

John said to me: "You're an immovable object!"

There follows a number of questions to me as to why they can't meet and I reaffirm the need for security of the boundaries as it would move us away from being an analytic group if they went to the pub socially. If these principles were necessary all year round, why change now? I said I felt like I was becoming a Policeman which I didn't like. It seemed that once we got through this stage in the session, this allowed them to begin opening up. Brenda spoke about an interest she had in transactional analysis and produced a letter she had written to her dead child looking at different adult and child parts of herself as well as her deceased child. Eileen had also lost a child and everyone was tearful or on the edge of tears.

John to Brenda: "Does this mean that you can get on with the rest of your life?"
Brenda: "Yes!"

Much of the letter was connected to Christmas and being on her own and alone.

The group opened up emotionally and everyone was tuning in one way or another, in relating to loss, deceased friends/family. Caroline: "why me?" regarding her onset of cancer; some were silently crying for the whole session. Tanya spoke of meeting a man whom she threw out from her relationship once he told her he was falling in love with her. Love became a focus and, unlike previous sessions, the group felt loving through their ability to share deep thoughts, feelings, memories without holding back the tears. I said that

> Christmas played a part in people/families coming together or being apart. It was now understandable that you wanted to meet outside for a drink/meal as you did not want the group to stop. However, there are much deeper things which have emerged now. It feels to me as if there is a lot of love in the room.

Dawn, who had been quiet, then spoke further about her abortion during her teenage years. She had been rejected by her mother at the time and feared rejection now in telling the group. Everyone was very supportive and admired her sharing this as they knew that she had been struggling since joining the group. This led on to Dawn linking her years of self damage in cutting her arms and legs. At one-point Marie gets up and goes to Dawn and hugs her saying that she could see her own daughter in Dawn. In these closing minutes I question that with being more open will this mean that the long Christmas break will be easier or harder?

Unanimous – "it will be easier as it's lifted a weight off our shoulders."

As they leave the room there is a lightness about them as they walk away arm in arm. To have said anything more than I did would not have helped. Neither would it have been helpful to try and interpret or define what happened with conventional psychodynamic language and would miss the point, undermining the group's heartfullness and therapeutic love. I had noted that the simplest way of explaining that particular session was that I felt quietly satisfied that I was with the group. When such a loving experience occurs it is very satisfying, almost as if everything has fallen into place. It is that solid, but at times nebulous, 'arms of emotion' which opens up and spreads around the group in a loving embrace. Thinking about my emphatic 'No' to their request to meet over the Christmas period is a far cry from my meeting with one of my groups some years later for a meal when I retired as I had become much freer in letting the group show their love and affection towards me.

Anorexic Equivalents

Possibly one of the most unloved feeling states/conditions is that of anorexia. On the face of things, it is easy to see those with extreme anorexia. The skeletal presentation will evoke many reactions for the on-looker ranging from shock, disgust, sadness, a wish to feed; fear of damaging if the anorexic was embraced, a wish to save; incredulity that the sufferer could not just pull themselves together and have a real good meal.

It is not my intention to go into the complexities of this condition but I intend to focus upon group equivalents to this individual diagnostic criterion. I have always included those with eating conditions within heterogenous groups so as they are not bound with cognitive/behavioural principles as are commonly used in homogenous groups. It is probably true to say that the majority of therapeutic approaches to eating disorders are based upon cognitive/behavioural methodology, group or otherwise and are homogenously bound. I have primarily considered food symbolically as a 'red herring' in the greatest percentage of cases (a thing that diverts our attention from the underlying causation). Groups as a Whole can exhibit anorexia/bulimic formations and symptomatology, that is, groups declining in number; groups showing a deterioration and failure of emotional affect; a reluctance to engage and anything 'taken in' is 'spat back out.' It is not uncommon that when someone with anorexia enters a group, the other members will, as stated in the earlier potential responses, begin to interact with this person accordingly. Infantalisation of the patient is not uncommon. There may well be similar responses in respect to those with bulimia, that is, focusing on holding the food down, or as with depression trying to help the patient find things to get them out 'of their' depression as compared to tolerating it within the analytic process. It takes time to remove the blinkers to consider other factors. It is sometimes difficult for people to conceptualise the messages from those who cut themselves as a 'psychic itch,' that won't stop itching until blood has been released. For example, in one group session Colleen highlighted how her week had been difficult and the others wondered if this meant a return to starving herself. This had not been the case and it was linked more to pressures at work and with her husband. However, this showed that some members of the group were taking things back to Colleen's physical symptomatology and earlier concrete expressions through actual food misuse. I question this: "I thought that we had moved beyond the physical." Colleen had described herself as a failed anorexic by gaining weight, almost as if she had lost something that had been a mark of success. Further dialogue highlighted how much of this was linked to the group's struggles with security and insecurity. I drew a symbolic parallel, I said:

> that a boat on dry land was of no use. When it was in the water it was useful by being 'secure in its insecurity'. It had to rock on the waves of the water. If it stayed still there was probably a hole in the hull or it had come aground.

So! Anorexia, and the symbolic equivalence with the group, had fixed symptomatic presentations. However, there was a need to find the driving undercurrents. Another group statement was: "anything for a quiet life!" Life's not quiet. The group had now been able to associate upon Colleen's initial contribution to their own presenting symptoms and that which lay behind these.

So concrete food is a currency of limited value.

When the Group's Heart Is Attacked from Outside

More so in these middle and later years a great deal of my work outside the consulting room has entailed time consuming involvement with other professionals and the general public. This has been focused upon creating good working liaisons/relationships with such people as general practitioners, psychiatric and mental health services, that is, psychiatric nurses and crisis intervention services; psychologists, social workers; families, legal services, hospital in-patient and day care services. The opening sections of this chapter presented a wider picture. Over the course of some 30 years this has proven to be a crucial piece of the jigsaw. As well as these services playing a part in the referral process of new and existing patients, a key element was that, generally speaking, these external bodies laid some claim upon the psychotherapy service/department which I directed. Everyone felt, or was, involved in the patient's therapeutic journey. However, there were times when communication broke down or professional differences became negatively/destructively dominant. This is developed further in Chapter 14, Outside the Consulting Room.

There are times when disputes and clinical differences between professional agencies which can lead to more serious and tragic consequences. Pamela, a young woman had joined one of my groups some months previously. Although she had struggled with beginning, she was starting to 'find her feet' and her voice. Up until this point she had strong links with the local psychiatric services and was still an out-patient attending psychiatrists on a sporadic agreement to monitor her general development. Pamela had just reached a stage where she had opened up some of her central problems and it was clear that the group was applauding her for reaching this point. Unanimously the group were fond of Pamela and had a great deal of affection for her. It was probably unfortunate that at this stage either the group was coming to a holiday break, or I was going on leave. When I returned I was informed that Pamela had been admitted to our local psychiatric hospital and had been given 'electro convulsive therapy.' There had been no attempts to contact me or my department and the decision for the electro convulsive therapy had been taken by a junior doctor. At the close of her last group session there was no indication that there had been a negative reaction to her disclosure and I had also made contact with her before going away in order to settle things. She also had telephone numbers of my psychotherapist colleagues if she felt there was worrying reactions during my absence. The psychiatric and crisis services were also aware of our emergency frameworks should there have been problems. It felt as if the psychiatric services moved in with one of their most extreme interventions without any knowledge of what stage Pamela had reached in her psychotherapy group. I was upset and angry when I returned and there seemed little concern from the 'said' psychiatrist that her actions had meaning or relevance to Pamela's group development. I never saw Pamela again. I was then faced with bringing this back to the group who had been unaware of Pamela's hospital admission. One of the other factors was that all of my groups were in the process of closure within a year due to my leaving my Social Services employment and moving into the National Health Service. However, I had managed to organise the facility of other groups and individual therapy being available when I'd left. Therefore, as well as Pamela, everyone was faced with uncertainties regarding their therapy. The group's initial response to my telling them about Pamela was disbelief in that they felt she was doing so well at the last meeting. They were also angry and sad that she had to go to hospital and had electro convulsive therapy. Eventually they moved to other things that were happening, that is, the governing authorities possibly closing the psychotherapy department after I left; Barbara had been burgled; their reactions to having their therapy taken from them was similar to it being stolen. I acknowledged my own anger and sadness in relation to Pamela as if she had been stolen by the psychiatric services and their not consulting with me. I did not say it at the time but the hurt I felt was imagining this beautiful, bright young woman, being snatched from the group and her head being zapped at the time when she was just beginning to open up and make new relationships in the group. Symbolically it felt like a kidnap and torture. It was certainly heart breaking and I often wondered over the years just how she developed. In retrospect there may well have been good reasons for her admission and electrical treatment but there should have been a greater attempt from the psychiatric services to involve me, or my colleagues in my absence, before such major decisions were enacted. Another aspect was that for quite a percentage of the session the dialogue revolved around their depressive histories which seemed to have been triggered off with the imagined impact of electro convulsive therapy on Pamela and the lengths people went to in order to deal with deep depression. We moved onto looking at the value of depression and its purpose which, on one level, made people stop and move into themselves, therefore giving a space for them to pause and reflect on the truer meaning of their depression. This did not negate those depressions which were driven by physiological and biochemical life events. Both of these scenarios show how a group can collectively resonate on the movement of the heart against external forces. It is the group's heart being attacked by others and internally touched through what they share.

Internalisation of the Group

On many occasions I have been asked by people such questions as

"Do you leave it behind when you finish work?" "How do you deal with the intensity of it all?" Earlier I spoke about similar 'questions' so this develops that line of enquiry.

At different times I would respond

No, I don't leave it behind and it bothers me!
At times I manage to set it aside but not forget!
Sometimes I worry a lot, can't sleep or stop worrying!
I feel good about today. Mary made a breakthrough. I worked well today.
In the earlier years I had difficulty in switching off but with experience it does
    not have the same effect.
I share my feelings with friends, but not the actual accounts of the therapy!
I take a lot of my concerns to supervision and my own group analysis.

On reflection the whole of my therapeutic encounters have been internalised in one way or another. It has made me, along with other life factors, the person I am. Ten years since retirement, as is evidenced in my still writing about it; my waking memories; my dreams; recollections of the people who had done well, gives me a warm internal glow; feelings of unhappiness and levels of guilt in recalling failed therapies. These are just some of the remaining residues. Recently I heard about a young woman who was in one of my groups 30 years ago who had died from cancer. She had made great progress through her therapy, which also put her on the road in training as a therapist only to lose her life in her mid-50s. Certainly, I internalised her and was left with sadness at the news of her death. This triggered off another memory of a student therapist in one of my groups who was vibrant, with so much potential, dying shortly after completing her training. As therapists we will have sat through thousands of hours of, at times, intense accounts of peoples' lives which will make deep and lasting impressions in a long career. Although, when asked in my retirement, how I felt after not being so involved, I rather glibly said

40 years of dealing with human misery was more than enough.

On reflection such a response I see as disrespectful because through the suffering accounts there was also a richness and heartfelt accounts of damaged lives blossoming and maturing into stronger/hopeful new life. Even thinking of the many actual newborn children who came into the world during peoples' therapy is a thought worth cherishing. In one of my group sessions the following brief extract shows a point of the group getting under my skin. During this session it was also colliding with struggles I was carrying from my own life outside the group.

Probably the most important feature that is worth commenting on was how I was being in the group. There had been only one point when I spoke when I simply questioned on whether things were really so pessimistic and this was about halfway through the session. I had contemplated saying some things about the dynamics but as the session progressed it was as if I could not find the energy to formulate my thoughts. At the time of recording, I am still not sure why, I was feeling so down that evening. Maybe it was linked to an element of pessimism, a feeling of things not lasting, that was important here. A lot of the focus seemed to revolve around Harriett and her ruminating thoughts which reflected the others feelings of worthlessness/aimlessness. This seemed to be paralleled by her feelings of panic and fears of death. It was as if this was a further progression from her devaluing the group and devaluing others personal changes. To say more this evening I felt would be repetitive but I think I was just tuning into the hopelessness of it. What I perceived as 'it getting under my skin' may well have been my feeling of being caught on the horn of a dilemma: The collective group feelings and my personal life outside were mixed up.

So! At such times when the group analyst is silently engrossed in his own struggles while dealing with the group, the patients may wonder if he's present.

The Group Analysts Presence

Throughout the book so far, my presence in the group has been looked at from a number of perspectives. It is not uncommon for groups, particularly in the early stages of newly formed groups, or new members coming into existing groups, to raise the matter of the group analyst's presence, that is, would the group be better if I left? On one level this may seem quite ridiculous but on another it makes sense. This is often translated to the conflicts arising if the analyst is perceived as an oppressive figure of authority or critical parental figure. The group analyst in turn can respond to this in feeling personally rejected. In one new group this became pertinent. I had set the group up, along with a female colleague, who was studying with me. I was quite surprised about the strength of their serious wish to get rid of us. I refrained from responding until we had discussed in more detail what Val, my co-therapist, and I symbolised. Collectively, they had resonated with parents, teachers and bosses. In the end I said "No! we were not leaving," reminding them that it was a psychotherapy group with a particular purpose and framework, necessitating us to be there. It was different from what was known as a 'self help' group, even though there were similarities to such groups. Interestingly, within group analytic culture/modalities, it is often seen as helpful for groups to meet at times when the group analyst has to be away, such as during holidays, illness, etc. This would occur with long-established groups. In keeping with the general theme of internalisation in this section the push to externalise me/us was a reaction to those critical and negative figures the patient's had internalised to date.

Getting It Wrong

There are times when particular things are overlooked or missed in the assessment procedure, which comes to light when that person enters the group. It is possible that the elements/composition of the group triggers off what was missed in the individual's assessment. Although this may be defined as faulty or resulting from assessment by an inexperienced therapist, it may have needed the group to activate the potentially damaging symptoms. Of course, many positive and healthy elements emerge as part of a group process that may have only been hinted at during initial assessment. In one of my groups this negative strand emerged with some ferocity when a young man, Robin, joined the group. Almost immediately he displayed both a desperate wish for me to cure him through heart breaking, yearning demands that I knew the answers but wouldn't give him. There were many sessions of his telling us about his out of control drinking and drug abuse. He tugged at everyone's heart strings and this raised a great deal for the others and how it related to their lives, particularly substance abuse and jealousy. After many months, with some degree of relief and limited progress, things returned to the impasse. Although further group attempts and later individual therapy were attempted, he dropped out of therapy. The therapeutic love which was on offer from the group was not enough to offset the power of the jealousy. These elements were not detectable during the assessment procedure. Reflecting back on that childlike yearning for me to do something at the beginning I felt, and was, powerless to heal that deep emptiness which wanted filling. Therefore, probably the most pressing symptom of pathological jealousy should possibly be considered as a non-starter to engage in psychotherapy, particularly once weekly groups. Contrary to this I recall some men who had similar symptoms of jealousy, self destructive personality disorders, doing extremely well in my therapeutic community days. There, they had intensive in-patient/ day patient structure and a contained environment, for long periods of time, 2+ years. We may be able to consider pathological jealousy as a 'solid' internalised object, in the conventional psychotherapeutic use of the term, that yearns to be projected onto another, imprisoning and moulding them into the creator's perfect image.

Moving from the internalisation dynamics we can extend our line of enquiry to the internal/external quasi-religious aspects of:

Belief and Faith

It is not uncommon for groups to ventilate/speak about their religious, atheist or agnostic leanings, such as: "If there is a God, whomever that may be, why has he allowed these things to happen to me, to the world?" "Your God is more punishing, permissive than mine!" Religious dialogue can become intense, creating factions and antagonism. Seldom have I experienced a sense of unity on these occasions and attempts at understanding/interpreting such dialogue as a front for other aspects seemed either inappropriate or misguided. However, I have often suggested that faith and belief are not the sole agents of religion and are as of much importance to the group. Entering the group, or psychotherapy generally, requires levels of faith and belief, sometimes blind, that success and change will occur if, like religion, there is an active investment. From the early stages of questions on group functions and wanting answers, to creating layers of group experience where faith in the group bears fruit through insight and actual life changes, will be dynamically challenging. When group boundaries and functioning principles are tested, doubts on its validity, it is as much a battle with faith and belief as it would be in formal religions. Also, the processing of such feelings as guilt, confession, fear of judgement, forgiveness, non-judgemental responses etc. are in effect, similar to religious bodies. I recall one teacher who held a seminar when I was training (I cannot recall his name) speaking of his own interview to be accepted for his training. When he was asked if he had any questions he said: "I only have two questions. The first: this man Foulkes, was he any good?" the interviewer said: "Good, he was the best!" Applicant's response: "Thank you for answering my second question: Do you have a faith?"

Fantasy – Phantasy

As with faith and belief the world of phantasy/fantasy brings into relief frameworks of thought which embraces the fictional and ephemeral. Within the literature there are two spellings of the word and different authors have defined these differently.[1] With regard to phantasy dialogue emerging within therapy groups I also have mixed feelings. A great deal of the psychotherapy literature has portrayed the erotic dimension of phantasy. In my earlier art therapy days within the therapeutic community a great deal of the concrete art images produced revolved around phantasy, erotic or otherwise. In one art group session Mary had let people know about starting a new relationship with a man that had brought back the 'crushes' she'd had at 16. Then she had phantasies about particular pop/film stars. There ensued a discussion about progressing this relationship based on the early past crushes and present realities. Past crushes would invoke the potential for jumping in too quickly and present reality warranted caution.[2]

This in turn moved the group in sharing a whole range of earlier phantasies and crushes. Sonia had a long-term crush on a male stranger in the local town whom she would have married if he had asked. There were playful interactions throughout the session as each new phantasy was disclosed. Harry and the woman next door both had long term sexual desires for one another, which neither acted upon. This highlighted the need to not act as the reality would not match the phantasy. It also brought into relief how others' partners/spouses would be hurt/damaged if phantasies were acted upon. For some there were long time phantasies in which the yearning was not lessened for 20 years and the degree of sadness that this contained. This long-unfulfilled fantasy was the other end of the spectrum, in contrast to the current, fleeting processes of stretching playful imagination through being with the pop or film star, or greater achievements in life, such as financial success, status, owning desert islands or winning the lottery. On another level for a group to be able to share such things is testament to it having reached a great level of trust and security.

In another group session, some years later, this area became more complex. I was unsure as to what stirred me spontaneously to speak about phantasies. Hilary and Clarissa phantasised about slashing their ex-partners car tyres and seats. Hilary fantasised telling her ex-partner's new partner that he had recently made sexual advances to her, Hilary. This had tied in with her own later phantasies about harming herself but it seemed as if this was a rather new awareness. Returning to the more general aspect of this movement towards phantasy I had told them that the area of phantasy was important to allow themselves to be able to be destructive in the phantasy. This shocked them, especially Linda, who said

Where did that come from.

I said: "from my mouth," without thinking.

They were having quite a bit of difficulty grasping this and I said this is not much different to fairy stories which allowed particular things like these to be expressed. Such things as 'eating people up' was there in negative phantasies, as well as in fond affections, such as 'being good enough to eat.'

Clarissa spoke about her phantasy life, that is, stabbing people and throwing them onto a big heap as long as she could bring them back and restore life to them. Another one was pushing people off high bridges to the ground. I said: "not that much different to bungee jumping is it?" What this also seemed to do was to allow an opening for both Kate and Clarissa to share accounts of their aggressive and violent outbursts. Allison had also spoken about smashing objects. Clarissa spoke about the times after she first knew about the affair that her husband had, and how she was like a 'wild woman' and was very unpredictable. She was also able to recognise over time that she had reached her maximum level of pent up feeling of hurt and in many ways her husband was copping it for all the other people who had hurt her and whom she could not get to. Kate also spoke about this in respect of her husband and how she had also flown into blind rages.

In the closing part of the session I was able to highlight how that by allowing themselves to speak more openly about phantasies this had given them an inroad to disclose or open up thoughts upon aggression and violence. They were able to recognise that they had felt better and safer talking about these things now. Added to this, I had stated that unless these external verbal expressions, not the violent aggressive acts towards another, were found, the tendency was often to turn it back on one's self, such as "I am terrible about thinking about someone this way," "I am not a nice person" or "I am being unfair to another person who has hurt me," and, more importantly, self destructive acts and behaviour. Therefore, this process created constructs of oneself which were either inhibiting or freeing. It was also interesting in the closing part of the session that Linda had said that Gerry was able to talk a lot more since Jane had gone and when I thought about this, I said 'well probably you're right' and I had wondered why she thought that this was the case. She responded that today would have been difficult as Jane was: "always wanting you to spout words of wisdom that she would hang on to, but when you complied, she rejected them." Clarissa also spoke about feeling tense about the interchanges which happened between Jane and myself. In this light it seemed as if Jane's presence was an inhibiting factor which had put a lock on such freer flowing dialogue as was now occurring.

Questions

The use of questions in a group can at times be controversial. If too many questions arise between the members this is sometimes thought to be an evasion of personal disclosure, and naturally associating freely, or it can be seen as projection or 'fishing' in order to find commonality, as just some sets of dynamics.

In one session Caroline was recounting her long held anger toward her mother, from childhood, who had taken her 'dummy tit'[3] away and destroyed it. This provoked a high level of questioning by the others about Caroline's infancy. I openly wondered what the questions said about each one's motives.

Mick: "Another one of Gerry's pearls of wisdom."

At first they seemed confused but then there were very animated personal disclosures about each one's earliest years. This ranged from Colins never feeling loved; Michael's father's physical brutality; Sarah feeling safe and loved by her mother; Claire never having a childhood, growing up too quickly; Cynthia's teddy being given to her sister. Within these scenarios the basic/primitive element of the 'dummy tits' importance for Caroline opened the gates through the groups questioning. In such situations this illuminates how questions will have particular meanings in respect to curiosity, concern, projective endeavours etc. there are times when a question can be taken at face value but more often than not, other factors will be driving questions either for the other individuals or the group as a whole.

Thinking back to my earlier years, up until 1995 I discovered that much of my earlier 'note taking' and the points raised in sessions was dominated with an over-concern in locating and interpreting anger. Therefore, if questions became a dominant focus, either to me, or a general state of affairs, anger was never too far from the surface. Many of these questions were getting in the way or avoidant. I think this goes back to my not being long qualified and attempts at maintaining the 'right' therapeutic musings. I could see that this was worded in such ways as to convey the message that I 'was' the group analyst with the purveyance of proper group analysis. As such I could see this in particular interactions with such people as Caroline. I was emphatic in my deliberations with challenging, confrontative and over long interpretations. Contrary to this my notes were well peppered with a great deal of commentary upon love and its vicissitudes. Possibly these were two sides in my evolutionary journey: anger and empathy, among many other valuable dimensions. I also noticed that the patients were equally moving between these two areas and were reaching points where they could see the differences between loving emotions and physical aspects of erotic sex which often manifested in conflict and anger. As well as heated and conflictual dialogue such dialogue could also be *endearing* in its contribution to insight and resolution.

Terms of Endearment

To give a 'term of endearment' is seen to be a conveyance of love and/or affection, esteeming another. It is usually driven by a warm appreciation of a person's presence in the world or a caring/loving gesture to another person. The phrase has been around from the early part of the 20th century (possibly longer) and therefore somewhat old fashioned.

In one of my sessions Caroline was reflecting back on her daughter when she, daughter, was a child. When her daughter was asleep Caroline would poke her for fear that she had stopped breathing. Unbeknown to Caroline a motion picture had been released called 'Terms of Endearment.' The opening scene was of a darkened bedroom, the door opens and Shirley MacLaine, the actress who played the mothers part, enters. Her child is quiet and peacefully asleep. Shirley looks down and pokes the child who starts crying. Shirley says something like: "Good" and exits leaving the child crying in the dark. For both Caroline and Shirley, surely the poking and prodding is hardly an endearing act, but maybe the gesture ensures that the love between mother and child is kept alive, alleviating mother's anxiety that the child would die in its sleep.

Within groups and psychotherapy generally it is a process of prodding one another in the process of endearment, love, affectionate attention, care is an ongoing cycle where challenge goes hand in hand with care and concern for all involved. There was also provocative, negative and destructive prodding. Within this particular session there is another variant which I suggest has similar foundations. Tanya spoke of her impulses to 'grab' stranger's children when shopping in the supermarket and cuddle them affectionately, which is similar to physical prodding, which she sees as linked to her wish to give birth to her own children. This seems to be a term of endearment. Earlier I had spoken about group guidelines and boundaries. When these are undermined or attacked in various ways, this is similar to an enactment not unlike prodding or poking. For example; Harry was having difficulty using the group and on a number of occasions gave religious advice to others as well as sharing religious literature even when people did not want to accept. This was a type of religious prodding. However, this was understandable in the context of this group in that some members had formed an 'after group' coffee meeting in a local café, which was another way of prodding the analytic group. This had been happening for some weeks before it became group knowledge so this was another enactment of group fragmentation resulting from the prodding. With the acquisition of this knowledge we were able to begin to piece together what had been unknown and obstructive and develop new knowledge, thus safe guarding the group.

On Not Knowing

Throughout my career there have been many times when I had feelings of losing my way; wondering if I knew what I was doing; drying up; repeating myself with particular thoughts, formulations, interpretations. At such times I had to tolerate these periods until it would work its way through to some clarification or resolution. Returning to golf analogies that when I would not play well, not knowing what I was doing wrong, the temptation was to try harder, which made it worse. The harder one tries to relax the golf swing, the more the tension may be created. So, it is similar with difficult and confused times in psychotherapy. I recall many group sessions where I had to hold myself back and say little or nothing. It could all be sorted out later through reflection, supervision and my own therapy. It is also interesting that when such processes are developed over one session, days or weeks and once the 'not known' confused fog lifts, new particles and illuminations become evident, almost like sparkling gems being found. This was of note when one of my groups was struggling with finding direction, both within the group and in their lives outside. The notions of loss and despair reigned alongside feelings of trying to set targets with the aim of reaching desired goals. It became more tense and frightening when one member, Patricia, was struggling with suicidal thoughts and plans. She was implying that she would find total peace as a result of suicide when in fact none of us knew what would happen after death, no matter how we believed it would be. But if it was peace that was being sought one had to be alive to have peace because peace was a living conception. Patricia's response was that it was quite logical and made sense to her, almost as if she wanted to argue with this but couldn't. The tension in the group subsided moving into a more productive period.

In contrast there have been times when I have not stayed with a process that needed greater patience and tolerance. At such times I may have intervened too quickly or was in error and at times regretted my actions. In one group session I got caught up in trying to deal with one member, Pauline's, extreme self-destructiveness. I suggested that her wish to be a helper with children now that she was trying to foster children, was another defence/block against other feelings that were there. Here I stated that she was covering up her raging feelings. This was evident in her strong angry feelings for her husband. She responded that possibly the can of worms that had been opened and would have been better left unopened but didn't go any further with this. The 'group as a whole' was lost in the background. On reflection this was far too much at one sitting and even though there was some validity in what I said this did not justify the overall interpretation. The term: 'can of worms' is similar to the 'elephant in the room' in that it is so obvious in its strength of presence, being seen and not wanting to be acknowledged is a form of 'elective blindness.'

The Elephant in the Room

For those not acquainted with this phrase, basically it refers to a very obvious, large object that cannot be avoided as stated above, yet everyone either does not see it, or purposefully avoids speaking about/confronting it. This may either be a particular problem or an event, such as a suicide or natural death. There will be many reasons for this according to the 'elephants' properties and the make-up of the group. In one of my groups Sally was speaking about herself and her female partners wish to have a child. To begin with her partner did not want to. Gradually her partner was beginning to acquiesce. As the session progressed the dialogue revolved around what it would mean to Sally and her partners relationship if they had a child. As this was a lesbian relationship I wondered what was the thinking behind the absence of a biological father. They were not talking about adoption. I simply asked if they, the group, saw the elephant in the room, I said

Where is the father in this, who would provide the sperm?

A silence descended. The elephant had been named but no-one wanted to go down this road. It took some weeks to explore this in more detail.

There was a similar event which was extremely hard not to comment upon. In one of my group rooms there was a period of four to six weeks when I had to have a large number of patient files dotted around my office for administrative reasons. Usually they would have been hidden in other rooms and filing cabinets. When I would meet with patients/groups I would ensure that no identification details were shown, but nevertheless, everyone could see that they were patient files. In some ways I minimized how loaded this was and this possibly contributed to the 'elephant' being avoided. Then one day my group was meeting without me, which seemed to give them permission to speak about it. In that session it had been commented on the fact that for a number of weeks all of the patient notes had been around the room. When they met on their own they were disturbed by this, both in respect to the breaking of confidentiality and the temptation of wanting to look at these notes and see their own notes. When I returned, I didn't get defensive about this, letting them talk about their feelings before I explained the reason why. Practically this was being sorted out that week. I had also raised the point that in respect to the dynamics of boundary and space I had respected and trusted them that they would not break the boundary of the group circle and interfere with other things in the room. They hadn't really considered this from the sound of things.

Another variant of the 'elephant' metaphor is when one person takes a specific stance or expresses something which is unique to themselves to which the others find hard to accommodate. This individual may equally use this position either to impose or maintain their special position. For a time this is held firmly unchanged, whereas if the particular element is worked with it can be of great benefit to all concerned. I have noticed this throughout my career, but for a 2–3-year period (2000–2003), such events were more noticeable; I do not know why it was more evident for these years, or possibly I was becoming more adept at recognising these areas. Some illustrations are as follows:

- Hilary, an Asian woman, joined the group and in her first session she was attacked by Mark for being secretive. Thankfully, I and the others took him to task but not enough to protect Hilary. Mark had a long-protracted group membership and in the last five minutes of his last session, after 4–5 years, he dropped a bombshell by attacking Hilary once again, while disclosing that he had a mixed-race son. This was completely new to everyone – loaded with meaning and five minutes to go, leaving Hilary distraught, with us having to pick up the pieces. Hopefully something of value came from his lengthy group membership. I met with Hilary for individual therapy following this.
- Michael disclosed too much too early and found it hard to ease off the accelerator. This was then followed by a few months of total silence, where he looked and was physically uncomfortable. His internal, psychological disturbance became overt in his facial contortions, looking out the window and avoiding eye contact with the group. Even though other group members identified with some of Michael's difficulties he was unable to let people in and he left after five to six months. Things were uncovered that had not been clear initially that, had I known, I would have considered the validity of psychotherapy.

With each of these individuals, apart from Mark, the outcome was a 'drop out' from therapy of between one to two weeks and a few months. This seemed to show that if a particular element is either too extreme, emotive, concrete, shocking, disturbing, entrenched, pathologic, ossified – one needs to consider if either a group or individual psychotherapy is appropriate. These can have far reaching consequences. I have had to deal with the aftermath of suicide, thankfully on very few occasions. This has brought specific considerations to the fore. One woman in a group had spoken about her depression, describing it as a blackness descending. She was experiencing it as a 'concrete' terror when others were conceiving it as a metaphor image for her depression and suicidal thinking. This does not mean that such extreme and intense scenarios are potentially seismic but it is more to do with each individual case and how this is developed and processed within each separate context. There have been many times in my career when highly meaningful disclosures, which at the time we felt would have serious repercussions, grew healthily into key and important stages in the group's development. Therefore, moving from what feels like potential catastrophic scenarios to healthy change and life's happiness is channelled through love.

Return to Love

I seem to have, on the whole, meandered away from therapeutic love and heartfullness. However, I feel that as with the previous illustrations, therapeutic love and heartfullness has been the foundation for much, if not all of what I am conveying. To have been able to formulate and work with the whole range of extreme topics stated above, are extensions of therapeutic love and heartfullness. Care and empathy are driving ingredients as is shown in the following:

Carmel told the group about a new job interview. Up until this point she had worked in a hotel and had an ongoing difficulty with her boss, Mrs T. For months the group had to go through the many problems and disputes between Carmel and Mrs T. They had been very caring and tolerant of Carmel in trying to help her sort out her interpersonal struggles. With this new interview things were radically different. During the interview Carmel felt the interviewer was bullying her with his questions and Carmel stopped him in his tracks and took charge of the interview. Afterwards she was anxious, thinking she'd 'shot herself in the foot,' but she was successful and got the job. The group cheered and congratulated her. Everyone was so pleased for her and felt that their endless struggles in helping Carmel for many months had paid off and it brought a great sense of hope and achievement. She no longer had to deal with Mrs T. At one point I jokingly said: "Well Mrs T has now left the group!" and everyone laughed at this. Mrs T, had felt like another group member and Carmel's struggles with her had taken up an inordinate amount of time – as if Mrs T was an invisible group member. Hopefully, the warmth is evident in this account and can be described as a 'heartfelt' interaction. The group had lovingly gone along with the many twists and turns between Carmel and Mrs T. Carmel appeared to have eventually exorcised Mrs T through the new job interview.

Mutuality of Verbal and Written Aspects

Earlier I spoke about the aspects of recording and communicating between professionals, that is, general practitioners/psychiatric services and also the mutual sharing of my assessment formulations with the patients. Often such documents are offered as tentative blueprints and the patient may play a part in modifying, adding to or rejecting. At different stages in the patient's group membership I was expected to write reviews/progress accounts. I would then compile my own version and share these with each patient for them to offer their accounts and then this could be developed in the group session. In their contact with other professionals they were rarely given such opportunities as the professionals often kept the notes as confidential reports to be shared with other professionals. Increasingly the British National Health Service was moving towards 'rights of access' for patients to see their notes but in my time it was generally not encouraged. The following 'session' notes relate to a session when most of the group had had their review meeting with me prior to this, not only of them but also myself.

Probably the first quarter to third of the session was taken up with sharing their thoughts about the assessment letters I had completed. On one level these letters had not brought surprises for them but on another they had. I had given Sally, Kate and Marie copies of the letters a few weeks back and they had obviously had time to think about these. There was a general perspective that I had gotten things right and they were surprised that I was able to convey so much about them. However, for Sally the fact that I had stated my prior views that her therapy was not going to be a long and protracted one was obviously wrong. I had an impression that she would pick up on this after I had given her the letter a few weeks back. In a similar way Erin had been talking about my saying that her therapy should be between 18 and 36 months and now she was beginning to feel some pressure in this, feeling that she was coming into the second or third year and she was also feeling at a bit of a loss here. Marie was quite upbeat about her position. There were some things in her report that she had forgotten about and it helped her to think about things anew.

At one point, I had questioned with them the element of the letters that had only been given attention by them i.e., the time factor, and indeed, the other parts of the letters had been about progress and change. Erin had come back and said the thing that she was happy with was my acknowledging certain levels of movement and I returned that this is what we were talking with her the last time we were here (and on previous occasions). Marie also commented that she didn't think she would be here until Christmas but recognised that she needed time to make that final decision and she recognised that she was slow to change. There were clear positive comments in the letter about how she had changed over the years. The focus moved to Carmel, recognising how much stronger and less defended she had become. Carmel had difficulty seeing this. However, there were points when she did acknowledge the changes as she was doing last week and on previous sessions.

With the above this showed a favourable side to the group being given access to what I thought of them. In later years, I was more willing and able to be straightforward and simple in conveying my own thought processes within the clinical notes, in contrast to my earlier defensive and inquisitive reactions to patients wanting to see their notes, such as:

Why do they want to know?
What does their question say about them?
How would you feel if I didn't respond?

When I moved to my new formulations on therapeutic love it was easier to respond directly to questions, requests and how I responded, such as:

> Don't you know that you give me a lot in trusting me!
> I feel honoured and humbled that you told me this!
> As a group I feel especially proud of how far you all have come!

So! why should we not tell the patient that they are lovable when there are no qualms about interpreting defences and neurotic symptoms?

Notes

1 'Phantasy' is an archaic spelling of fantasy.
2 A number of concrete images were created, which were evoked in the following descriptions. I have chosen not to publish these as well as disguising the dialogue for confidential anonymity. They are therefore a simile.
3 Self soother.

Chapter 10

The Closing Years

As I approached my closing years, I felt that I had a large body of work and experience under my belt. I was still conducting between five and seven psychotherapy groups per week, along with two to three student trainee groups, as well as training events in England, Russia and Portugal. Therefore, on one level I felt I had honed my trade considerably, while still making mistakes, but feeling that I was becoming more convinced upon my theories on therapeutic love and heartfullness. As I was winding down towards retirement, I also had to deal with my own decline and loss, while looking toward a brighter personal life in pursuing further writing, golfing and music. It was not an easy transition. A whole range of new perspectives and ways of working began to emerge, as will be seen in the following:

Spontaneity

Increasingly I began to notice that when particular elements and dynamics emerged, there were surprising outcomes. One such element, spontaneity, came more into play although, as stated throughout the book its presence had emerged to greater of lesser degrees previously. In one group session, I had been concerned with Rachael's inability to tune into the other group members emotions and her somewhat rigid/concrete expressions. In the 'group as a whole,' there were a number of spontaneous responses to one another's painful disclosures on child rearing. Suddenly, Jenny began crying loudly, which seemed to spark Rachael on parallel lines which she diverted to me, she said: "something about what you said about allowing ourselves to be spontaneous hit a nerve in me!" I had said: "you can't plan to be spontaneous!" Rachael began to visibly shake and the colour drained from her face, which seemed to reflect her struggle with spontaneous emotions being highlighted. Even by the end of the session, it was not clear why such strong emotions had emerged.

In keeping with the core of my thesis, it is possible that the group analyst, and at times group members, touch the heart without apparent cognitive associations, a currency which bypasses thinking. There are times when, unexpectedly, group members say something which has meaningful impact.

DOI: 10.4324/9781003536857-12

In another group session, sexuality was the focus. At one point I said: "no-one knew how to do something in regards to sexuality until they did it." Jenny said: "no-one says you can have a book in the left hand and a relationship in the right, while you are involved sexually." I also began to notice that some of my groups, particularly those comprising only women, apart from myself, that there was more freedom in sexual dialogue. At one point the dialogue oscillated between bodily functions, physical attributes, erotic sensations, sensuality and responses to physical intercourse. The main gist of this was how sexual urges, passion and romance, were damaged by physical realities, that is, how one is after giving birth; gaining or losing weight; physical illnesses, for example, chlamydia, among a number of other illnesses. I think that at these times, it was a reflection of how mature, established and trusting the group had been. At one point in the last session noted with Jenny, when the attention turned to their male partners outside the group, they fleetingly acknowledged that they had forgotten that I was present. They laughed and jokingly said that I should 'listen and learn' and they carried on unabated. However, I was eventually able to enter the conversation in the closing part of the session when I focused upon the parallels of allowing men to enter them physically and emotionally, while men had to allow a similar emotional entry as the women. What emerged in this session would not have occurred if spontaneity had not been released. It is as if spontaneity is a release from a captive factor.

Early Dropouts and the Relationship to Suicidology

A governing principle in groups and psychotherapy generally is that one has to 'make it work,' as compared with a 'waiting game.' For many reasons, some people will have great difficulty in perseverance in order to feel part of, and gain from the group. For some the task is insurmountable and should not be seen as a failure if unsuccessful. Either the choice of group therapy or individual therapy was inappropriate, or it was not the right time. The patient may have felt that the task was too great and their level of disturbance, fear, guilt, shame was too much to be opened up. Also, the new incoming patient to an existing group may have found the membership unwelcoming; there were things about existing members that the new person railed against; the content of the dialogue in the group sparked off 'too much, too soon' for the new person. A case in point was when Karen joined the group and although she was very guarded in her first months, gradually we thought that she was beginning to settle in. However, this was offset by a pattern of extreme lateness and absence. After some time in one session, when Karen was absent, the others voiced their concerns more clearly. This situation often raises questions such as the validity or appropriateness of speaking about people in their absence. Bearing in mind they had raised some of these concerns when Karen had been present and I said to them that they needed to bring these points back up when Karen returned. The main points that were raised were: Karen's ambivalence in being part of the group; the content of what they spoke about was too explicit and at times frightened her; disclosures on suicide and self harm; the exposure of sexual matters; opening up of depression and sadness. On the brighter side, the camaraderie and humour which they felt was equally challenging and last, but not least, Karen's unhappiness with me regarding my lack of apparent direction. She found the darker humour hard to accept, that is, Sheila not killing herself because she hadn't finished her ironing (of clothes). When Karen returned, the group had tried to raise these matters with her but unfortunately it was to no avail. Sadly, even though Karen returned to the group intermittently she dropped out and did not respond to my invitations to return to the group. The silver lining in the cloud was that I was able to steer her towards another cognitive form of counselling, so all was not lost.

Another aspect in regard to spontaneity was when I attempted to help the group move beyond the surface of presenting symptoms, that is, Claire's obsessional ruminations about breast cancer. I had suggested that beyond this were unresolved feelings about her earlier impregnation and loss of pregnancy, which inadvertently involved thoughts and feelings about her breasts. I did not expect the group response in that all of them broke down crying and shared their own experiences of abortions, still birth, death of older children. This illustrates how some simple, spontaneous comments, can evoke so much. My closing comment following this was:

Sometimes we think that things are deeply buried but are not too far beneath the surface.

It was extremely moving, touching us all. As time progressed with this group Claire moved from her concrete preoccupation with lumps in her breast to a recognition that this was a reflection of her high receptivity to suggestion, that is, many years previously a doctor had instilled a fear in her that she was going to die and this registered and developed like a cancerous growth. She came to be a key group member, as if she was the 'voice of health' as she led the group in exploratory dialogue. She also said that she and her husband were very much in love. Claire is one of many who go through such major developments, which also necessitates a shift from concepts of weakness to those of strength.

Facing the Strength

Increasingly I was moving further from established psychotherapeutic perspectives. For example, challenging defences, as highlighted earlier, which are seen as mechanisms of avoiding unconscious elements. These are often necessary methods of technique within conventional psychotherapy, that is, that patients needed to face their fears and defences. However, the more I thought about it and sat through many sessions, this did not sit well with my change of thinking and practice. I was indebted to Dr Malcolm Pines for his saying: "Inside every sick person there is a healthy part, and in every healthy person there is a sick part" (Morrison, 1986). In these later developmental stages, I was moving to the view of 'face the strength' and 'cherish the defences.' For example, in one session, I was trying to formulate what was happening in dynamic terms. The group had moved to a new building and for the first time I permitted them to bring water into the room as the central heating system promoted dry mouths. Hence, any analytic interpretation on oral symbolism was demolished. Inadvertently I was responding to basic human needs on hydration. Some of my colleagues were aghast at my permissiveness. As the session progressed the focus moved to experiences with animals, particularly cats. I suggested that what seemed to be happening was that they had wanted animals to have human feelings, while they were wanting particular human feelings to be removed from them at times when they didn't feel very human. At first, they didn't get this and, in a way, I wasn't too sure about it myself. However, I said that many of the things that they were talking about was about being human such as dealing with death and illness, and surviving it; feeling depressed and getting through it; seeing that they could change and had greater awareness and insight into their struggles; dealing with illogical fears and coming to clear conclusions were all part of being human and acknowledging their strengths. The more that they experienced this, the richer their humanity would be. However, it was difficult when they felt like shit and just had to get through it, but that was part of it. Tanya: "Gerry, therapists are not allowed to swear."

They spoke about their pets having personalities (why not 'dogonalities' or 'catonalities'). There was a bit of laughter around this and Sheila had come back at me saying it sounded odd, my use of the word shit, as compared to her use of the word pooh. I said: "well maybe this was even more strange as it was me that was saying it." They then shared the humour in this but also recognised that by my using this terminology it made me human. The session ended in a fairly upbeat manner and they seemed quite united. Framing things in this way moves our attention to 'facing the strength' needed for them to get through life. Even if their human projections into animals were a defence, they were emotions being cherished.

In a later session Maria had been extremely upset because her grandmother had died. Before the session started the group had convened in the waiting room and when I entered, they were already comforting Maria and this continued into the session. There was a greater amount of time (about 20–30 minutes) devoted to Maria's situation. It was as if their empathic responses developed into a form of consumption. This brings into relief the dynamics of sessions in which much is channelled through one individual, which I spoke about earlier, when this indicates genuine empathic responses or those times when the individual is used as an empathic channel, spokesperson, for a great deal of material not owned by the whole group. How one deals with such elements is of crucial importance. In my later years, I was more able to go with the dominant individual receiving/group sharing empathic responses, as compared with challenging/confronting this with terms like projecting, avoidance, scapegoating, to name a few.

Another member, Mary, monopolised the group as each session began. The others showed empathic concern for her wellbeing. Quite quickly Mary would start talking and once started it was almost impossible to intervene or stop her.

Sometimes I had to be brutal and say: "that's enough, we aren't doing you any favours in letting you continue." What starts as empathic concern can easily turn to impatience and resentment. In this scenario, the value of empathy is undermined and the human link between the dominant sufferer and the loving care of the others is not fully established. It was at this point that a new thought sequence emerged for me, which I was able to use with other groups and individual patients. I pointed out that empathy was not gaining ground in alleviating Mary's suffering and the desire to help was 'falling on stony ground' and created disappointment. In this process, as compared with insight and change, disappointment was maintained. I had told them about questioning my friends on what they felt if they attempted to sneeze and after a number of failed attempts they could not sneeze. The predominant answer was that they were 'disappointed.' In a similar way, high expectations generally can lead to high levels of disappointment if there is limited, or no, successful outcomes. Therefore, like the sneeze, Mary's position continually set up group attempts at alleviation which ended in disappointment. It also takes varying levels of strength to cope with disappointment which in turn requires levels of flexibility.

The Strength of Flexibility

One wonders if there is an inherent contradiction in the above statement? On closer examination, the word strength can imply solidity, firmness, holding against, resistance, faith, strictness and ambition. The word flexible may be applied to movement, suppleness, permissiveness, acceptance of difference, versatility, to name a few. However, each word depends on components of each other in order to be understood and applied accordingly, that is, strength of a belief is in danger if it becomes rigid and closed off. Permissiveness may be problematic if it becomes too flexible, which may lead to disintegration. The strength of discipline is diminished if it moves into extreme permissiveness, that is, little or no rules or enforced with a heavy hand. Musical improvisation (flexible) without sound basic (strength) rudiments.

With these later points in mind, throughout my career I oscillated between learning and upholding the strength of my theoretical understandings as I had been taught and the need to adapt along with developing the shifts of theory and practice. Within such oscillations the need and ability to be flexible also had to be accommodated. No mean task, as this sometimes incurred taking risks as I have highlighted previously. My adherence to conventional psychotherapeutic theory and discipline in my earlier years was appropriate, but always had to be open to question, adaption and revision. In moving between individual psychotherapy, group analysis, the therapeutic community and art therapy, there had to be greater layers of flexibility, which I believe in the end has led to a greater strength.

There have been many times when I have had to be flexible, many of these events I have already spoken about throughout the book. In another new assessment, the patient wanted to have her dog in the room, which I complied with. The dog was quiet but then began to lick its genitals and proceeded to have a barking conversation with a dog outside the building.[1] Another patient had broken her vertebrae and was confined to her bed in a rigid frame, and I continued her therapy in a modified form, which clearly demanded flexibility of thought, approach and method. In more recent years I accepted a woman into a group who was severely restricted in her sight, so much so that she had the assistance of a white stick and guide dog. I convened her assessment meetings with the dog sitting quietly in the room but there were not the same problems as with the previous (undisciplined) dog. She then entered one of my groups in which everyone had full sight, although some of us wore glasses. Initially the dog came into the first session, which was okay for a while but eventually the dog was settled in an adjoining room, handing over its protective role to the group. I think that if Caroline had been totally blind this may have been more difficult.

With such a scenario this can evoke a great deal. It is interesting that we use the word insight to denote seeing within = In-Sight. Although this is then transposed to emotional and intellectual awareness development, it uses a metaphor to embrace the visual mechanism of seeing. In this respect how does the word 'insight' be conceptualised for those people who are partially sighted/blind. It is all very well my willingness to be flexible in accepting Caroline, but she and the others had to 'adapt.' For Caroline, although she had some sight, she was more restricted than the others in such things as: following verbal interchange with the visual dimension; picking up on the subtle dimensions which brings language in line with sight; non-verbal interactions; 'body language'; seeing how others are being with each other. Potentially feeling left out or threatened when the group enters periods of silence and understanding what evokes such silences. What does a partially blind group member feel in periods of group silence? How does it affect them depending on the length of silence? In respect to the others they had to make space and allowances for Caroline. One other factor to be considered was: how did Caroline deal with her developing relationship with me in comparison to the others? Granted, we seemed to develop a good rapport during the assessment meetings, but translating this into her group membership had its own added dimensions, which the others did not have. Normally, as group members move from their initial views/perspectives of how I am in the group, Caroline had to go through these processes more nebulously. In the normal course of events, members would have to move from my individual attention in the assessment to sharing me, while also seeing how I was functioning with the whole group. Caroline would not have visual clues and at times when I did speak it would be as if my voice, and others, was in a vacuum. This is not so different to withdrawn, schizoid, depressed individuals, although having full sight, being removed from the emotional and intellectual dimensions and is equivalent to 'partial blindness.' One final aspect in regard to Caroline was how she progressed through not having the support of her dog in the room, and of course, how the dog settled in next door. It would be too much of a diversion to speak about 'props' at this point. Her dog and white stick were very necessary and obvious 'props' that Caroline had to relinquish, but group members often go through their experience with some sort of prop. In the end with Caroline's dog it felt as if it became the group's dog, in a similar way as members new born becoming the 'groups baby,' a member present in an adjoining room; or similar dynamics stated earlier for Mrs T. I suppose I was also benefitting from Caroline's presence in that I was becoming more permissive in stepping away from the strict group guidelines, that is, making allowances for her sight restrictions by helping her with physical assistance. This had a knock-on effect for the whole group in my becoming more flexible and relaxed, that is, permitting water consumption, not pressing people to relinquish medication too quickly; if at all; not going over the top with interpretations on five minutes lateness/absence; not being so rigid about other therapeutic ventures working conjointly with the group; not feeling that I was redundant when I had difficulty in understanding and contributing through interpretation. Another facet of flexibility is that of moving away from well held theoretical 'mores' which is built on 'shoulds' and 'should nots,' that is, everyone is equal with no favourites.

The Favourite

There is a view in certain circles that a parent should not have a favourite. This transcends into many other areas, that is, best friends, musical proteges, talented individuals, so it is in the world of psychotherapy and group analysis. I had a liking for the majority of my patients and dislike for a handful within hundreds of patients, trainees, students, whom I was with throughout my career. However, there were certain individuals and particular groups whom I felt particularly fond of. This fondness, I am not afraid to say, was a form of love. One group in particular had a lifespan of 15 years, the current membership ranged between one and five years. In the early years, my fondness was present, but it became clearer and stronger in the final 2–3 years. It was a group meeting once a week. Also, the fact that I was winding down towards my own therapeutic closure intensified my loving feeling, as I knew I would have to lose them. However, with these general points stated, the driving factors in this sense of favouritism was determined by the personalities of the group members, which shone through in their abilities to use the group; to form close relationships with one another; support and empathise with one another; take great risks in sharing and challenging one another; giving powerful support within and without the group at critical times. This group showed a fondness and love for me. Some group members will feel left out or rejected when the group analyst appears to give individual attention, but not this group. Although for many of my groups I felt this fondness and favouritism, but particularly this group, who were dearer to my heart. There is a television competition called: "Strictly Come Dancing." The main host, Bruce Forsythe, who has sadly died, used the catch phrase: "You're my favourite" to each of the dancers and this was sought after by each competitor and when given, the audience cheered. Each time it was said showed how being a favourite resonated with many people. "I want to be a favourite but others will fight me for it."

The following example illustrates these areas.

One individual from another group whom I felt a love for was Cynthia. In thinking about this love, the simplest way of describing this was that of a feeling of warmth and closeness to her, but at a certain distance. She had gone through a very traumatic childhood and emerged with great strength, although she underestimated this, that is, she reached a strong abstinence from alcohol surviving alone from then. There was a sense of beauty when she contributed to her group. She would listen quietly to others and, although she rarely spoke, what she said of others was astute, profoundly understood and welcomed by the others. The sense of togetherness was there at such times which I now see as loving gestures. Sadly, Cynthia undervalued such contributions. There were times when she focused on her own struggles and the group was supportive. One such time was when she reported visiting the hairdresser, a task she always baulked at as she did not like her hair being touched. As she unfolded the hairdresser story she broke down in tears, not knowing why she was crying. I passed her the box of tissues. Others began crying (I think in empathy with her). Cynthia felt she was making everyone cry but the others disavowed her of this. She felt her problem was of little consequence compared to Sarah and Maureen's cancer concerns. The others said that Cynthia's problems were equally important. I did not say a great deal but at one point suggested that for Cynthia and the others this highlighted the conflicts of touching and intimacy. They were also allowing a level of intimacy in the group just now in their sharing and crying. Cynthia said she didn't know why she started crying, and said: "I don't let people know how I feel!"

Me: "Well you're doing it now!"

As the session progressed everyone opened up more on particular parts of their lives when there had been struggles to be intimate. As much of this was sad and painful there was also a feeling of closeness and containment. At times, mainly when Cynthia spoke, I felt the tears welling up in me and it felt good to be in the group. They could also see that I was tearful but they didn't press me to say anything.

Possibly one of the factors that promoted me to experience Cynthia as a favourite was her commitment to the group; rarely missing and always on time; her genuineness in her contributions to others. She, in many ways represented the group analytic ethos. More simply, I just liked her. I found myself smiling when she spoke and almost crying when she was unhappy and distressed. I wanted to protect her and once I had a fantasy that I'd like to adopt her. Her directness and honesty were infective. She had trouble making changes in her life outside, but she kept trying.

The greater dominance of having favourite patients and groups is set above the many other patients and groups I worked with whom, to a lesser degree, provided positive experiences and outcomes. If the sense of favouritism prevails, it is like having something precious that crystalises into a thing of beauty which has to be let go, rescinded, in the closing stages. I do not think it was possible to see these areas so clearly in my earlier years. So, in having to say goodbye to all of these favourites, and other people, when I closed my practice, was both celebratory and a deep loss. All of these people over the years had given me so much and I, like Cynthia, at times wondered how I possibly could have helped. In the closing weeks and months prior to retirement a number of patients and groups humorously voiced a wish to move with me to Portugal, as that's where I had intended to move to. In a strange way they have come with me in my memories, dreams, associations and the current writing of this text.

Note

1 This is expanded in Chapter 15 on humour.

Chapter 11

Convergence

Freud tells us little about love -. Freud's emerging thought: that love pulls us in two different directions. In Aristophanes myth, love is a regressive force by which we yearn to re-establish a previously existing unity. We are, according to this myth, descended from hermaphrodite creatures who were cut in half by Zeus. Love is a pressure within us to restore a lost unity. Aristophanes 'love' impels us to abolish the boundaries between individuals.

(Lear, 1990/1998, p. 148)

I have already alluded to convergence in previous chapters, that is, the various emotional elements which materialise, are driven by the heart and develop into the framework concept of therapeutic love. There are convergences between care and gratitude; compassion and empathy among many emotional duals. Bearing in mind Lear's quote above the variance between Freud's love as 'pulling apart' (possibly due to its confinement to the erotic) and Aristophanes regressive myth to re-establish and restore lost unity, abolishing the boundaries between individuals – the concept of convergence is apt. However, the convergent drive may not always lead to unity, that is, a 'convergence zone': a zone where tectonic plates collide, typified by earthquakes, mountain formation, and volcanic activity (Collins, Millennium Edition). Parallels within psychotherapy are easy to see within this spectrum when destructive forces or the lack of therapeutic love are in play. 'Convergent thinking' according to the dictionary quotation in psychology is analytical, usually deductive, thinking in which ideas are examined for their logical validity or in which a set of rules are followed (Collins, Millennium Edition). This definition, which relies on the factors of deduction and logic would fit with the Freudian perspective on love but not with those purported by Lear and my own meanderings on the heart and therapeutic love.

As I meander through the book convergent processes and points of convergence emerge extensively. For the purpose of this chapter I intend to expand upon two points of reference which were initiated with two separate lectures. The first of these was presented to a Group Analytic Congress audience in Dublin (2008), and the second was the 'Classical Psychoanalytic Congress' in Athens, Greece (2011).

DOI: 10.4324/9781003536857-13

However, both presentations were formulated with the intention of bringing to the fore matters of the heart and therapeutic love to the attention of two polar disciplines of 'group analysis' and 'psychoanalysis.' With the former, group analysis, I focused upon the convergence of the primarily verbal group and, the group analytic art group. With the latter, psychoanalysis, the intention was to move people's attention to non-erotic love and suggested that there was more than two people involved in psychoanalysis, reaching outside, beyond the intra-psychic. Another statement, which unfortunately I cannot recall exactly, or by whom, was that underneath the psychoanalytic couch there were groups.

Desire – Dialogue – Despair

This was the theme and title of the 14th European Symposium in Dublin, Ireland. A basic converging principle here was to provide a theme which would inspire dialogue between the concepts of desire and despair. I found, like other such congresses, there was the tendency to spearhead two apparently opposite/polar perspectives, that is, the forward moving principle of desire incorporating wanting, acquiring, satisfaction, hope, yearning for love if achieved, and despair, incorporating non-achievement, loss, disappointment, unrequited love, depression, regression.

One of my starting points of reference was that a base for desire was a 'sense of wonder.' As stated earlier when I spoke of using music at the start of my presentations I let the audience listen to Van Morrison's song 'Sense of Wonder' (Morrison, 1985), which hopefully touched some hearts as the melody and the lyrics encapsulated desire. I see the sense of wonder which drives desire as an elevated expectancy and infusion. On the other hand, despair is a desolate place where wonder ceases to exist. Desire and despair sit at two ends of a spectrum. Within such a spectrum that when despair is experienced it feels like a depletion of the 'self' when all is closed and desire is the furthest point imaginable. In desire there is a convergent aim, in despair there is a convergence withdrawal. In our work as therapists and analysts we strive to create convergences/transitions from despair to desire, or in other words hopelessness to hope. On a basic level desire, which is predominantly linked to the romantic, erotic frames of reference, comprises of many elements which forms one's yearnings for another, such as love at first sight, physical attributes, intellectual appeal, gentleness, kindness, mutual attraction, sense of humour and sexual arousal. Of course, the recipient of the desirer's attempts at convergence needs to be receptive on some level, or equally desirous for a 'convergent zone.'

My world fell apart when she left me.

This single statement illustrates the power of the move from the convergent 'world' of love to a convergence withdrawal and the world falling apart. If the desirers advances are not reciprocated or rejected; or eroded/destroyed after a lengthy relationship, despair can quickly settle in with potential downward spiralling into regression and depression. The sense of wonder which offered so much at the beginning has been decimated. Of course, the driving constituents, such as yearning, wanting, wishing and hoping, are also present in other forms: ambition, drive, competition, creativity, wish to be liked, homesickness (a desire to return to a loving environment), as some illustrations, not necessarily linked to intimate experiences.

Turning to the matter of dialogue this implies various forms of conversation and communication. In this context, desire and despair are navigated through dialogue, that is, the expression of such positions and the working through to levels of understanding and resolution if conflict exists. In general parlance I would say: I'm going to meet friends for a chat and catching up; meeting for the 'craic' (having a 'good time' is the closest English translation). This last Irish term is more about a total friendship encounter, not just talking. I would not say I'm meeting a friend for dialogue. Therefore, that although dialogue is defined as an expression of conversation, exchange of opinions, discussion on particular subjects, that once such processes are construed, they have a particular or specific purpose which is different from 'just talking' or 'chewing the cud' (the salivation joys of talking without meaning or nonsense).

Returning to the Dublin Congress, as one would expect a great deal of scientific and other theoretical views were shared over a week, with hundreds of delegates, many known and unknown therapists and writers' publications were developed in the congress dialogue. I was no exception in trying to get my points across which was daunting as I was 'preaching to the converted' while trying to show that I was not messing around with group analytic theory as applied to art groups/therapy. With dialogue in mind David Bohm tells us:

> A basic notion for a dialogue would be for people to sit in a circle. Such geometric arrangement doesn't favour anybody; it allows for direct communication. In principle, the dialogue should work without any leader and without any agenda. Of course, we are used to leaders and agendas, so if we were to start a meeting without a leader – start talking and have no agenda, no purpose – I think we would find a great deal of anxiety in not knowing what to do. Thus, one of the things would be to work through that anxiety, to face it. In fact, we know by experience that if people do this for an hour or two, they do get through it and start to talk freely.
>
> (Bohm, 1996, p. 15)

Personally, I think that the word 'dialogue' and its usage has acquired a level of pretentiousness, instilling it with lofty importance as compared with the idea of having a 'chat' with someone. In contrast if we are narrating something it is talking about someone, or something else. Using the term 'narrate' in autobiographical terms gives an impression of being removed from oneself retrospectively, creating a new reflective dialogue in telling the story.

In group analysis there is no fixed agenda as also occurs in Quaker meetings. There is no overt leader, although the group analyst is perceived as one. With

Quaker meetings, possibly God is seen as the invisible leader within the silence and those who do step forward verbally in the 'Meeting.' Sometimes there is nothing said during a 'Meeting.'

As stated earlier that when I speak about conducting groups where no concrete art is produced I have called these: 'primarily verbal groups.' In these settings dialogue is constructed from the spoken word and silence. When conducting art groups the concrete pictorial images/sculptures creates another form of visual dialogue, as well as verbal and silent dialogue. In the primarily verbal group, dialogue depends on consecutive verbal interchanges of preparatory and concurrent processes of silent thinking before and after others contributions. Thus, regarding convergence, we can see the way that dialogue moves forward and backwards through the desire to communicate, work through and aiming at change and resolution. Such processes and developments are equally present in art groups but with the added dimension of concrete imagery, dialogue is formed through each individual act of creation (each individuals inner dialogue with self in the formation of the concrete image) and the overall sharing of the collective imagery when seven or eight pictures (images) converge within the circle of the group when the art work has been completed and brought together and displayed for all to see. However, people are at liberty to not paint, or share a finished piece as one is at liberty to withhold in primarily verbal group analysis. Once the group sits with the completed art work then consecutive verbal dialogue becomes dominant. To be more specific about the intricate machinations of verbal dialogue within a group, before words leave a person's mouth, there are prior seconds and minutes of internal thinking, feeling and weighing things up: thus, an internal silent/self dialogue. We cannot omit the place of spontaneity within this whole process, as spoken about in other parts of the book. However, in its simplest way, within my understanding, it can be seen as another chicken and egg scenario, that is, do things happen in the therapeutic session which leads to and sparks spontaneous reactions or do spontaneous thoughts/gestures lead to further expressions and chains of spontaneous resonances? In a similar way resonance has deeper layers, not only in its particular manifestation/embodiment (McNeilly, 2006b, pp. 37–38/64–65/154–160), so synchronicity will also be multi-layered/faceted. In charged moments such process may be quicker and appear more immediate and spontaneous. On the other hand, heated moments can evoke withdrawal into oneself and potentially a state of paralysis. On a productive spectrum healthy dialogue, creating negotiation and resolution, can occur allowing such individuals to build upon the spontaneous movements from their internal dialogues and therefore creating a vibrant, dynamic, creative composition on the group's canvas. Returning to the initial individuals silent internal dialogue there are parallel processes going on within each member of the group. As one can hopefully see, this is an intricate interplay of all the forces that have to be negotiated (indeed dialogue is seen as integral in the process of all negotiations) through various forms of dialogue and communication.

It is a sense of wondrous desire when it works, but if things falter and fail such endeavours can plunge all parties into states of hopelessness and despair. At the time of writing the original lecture there was a television programme on the secret negotiations leading up to the 'Good Friday Agreement' which led to Irish paramilitary disarmament, 10th April 1998. One of the negotiators (identity not disclosed) said:

It was dialogue and its continuance, which established the agreement, and with each day of dialogue, lives were saved.

Since then, one only has to think of world conflicts – The Balkan Wars; Zimbabwe; Israel and Palestine; mass movements of migration through war zones – in order to see the power of the polarities of desire and despair and the need for dialogue, and more recently, in the Russian invasion of Ukraine (2022).

In the dynamical field of group analysis is it not that despair is part of dialogue as compared to being a 'thing in itself' moving with desire? Picture for a moment a group that is struggling with a range of experiences: the pain and joy of childbirth; loss of children; finding and losing love; emotional and physical trauma; pleasure and success in lifes' ventures, all in a 90 minute session. Throughout the groups life period, despair and desire are evidenced, intertwined and worked through. Such matters require the concept of convergence to illuminate/elaborate the group's to-ing and fro-ing.

I believe that one limits the concept of dialogue if it is only understood and described as verbal discourse. In many non-verbal ways one could describe dialogue as a mechanism of desire, that is, the creation of channels of communication and interaction. Other factors play a part: a smile or a frown; verbal intonation; the presence/absence of emotion; lying and suspicion; humour; seduction, to name a few. Surely the notion that dialogue is only a verbal transaction pales into insignificance.

In September 2019 there was a news item regarding David Cameron (former British Prime Minister) disclosing that he had sought guidance indirectly from Her Majesty, Queen Elizabeth on the Scottish Independence Referendum. The content of such discussions between the Prime Minister and the Sovereign should never be disclosed. Cameron suggested that even her raising an eyebrow in response to his search for guidance would have satisfied him. This shows the power of non-verbal communication as a silent dialogue which in a way is more supreme than language.

This complex interrelationship between the spoken and other communication forms is self-evident in the broad church of psychotherapy. Group analytic art therapy provides physical evidence of non-verbal dialogue in a way that primarily verbal group analysis cannot. The combination of verbal and concrete art expression brings us a three-dimensional perspective to dialogue. Therefore, whenever images are created in concrete form, that is, one or more group members draws/paints unhappy events from their childhood along with desirous wishes to reach happier times, desire is not a mechanism only aimed at some time in the future, but an enactment of the present here and now. The concrete art objects are tangible products whereas primarily verbal group analysis/individual psychotherapy is confined within a linear/consecutive (one person speaks at a time) process. Within the pivotal qualities of dialogue, despair may be seen as a devalued obstacle obstructing hope and desire. In the final analysis should dialogue be seen as a tool/weapon against despair, a resolutory device? Should we not accept that despair is as much a necessary ingredient of the human condition as desire is? Should despair be transformed to desire, or something else, or are these two states equally in need of preservation?

Hopefully, our starting focus on convergence has not been overshadowed. Taking desire and despair as expressions of convergence, I trust that I have clarified some of the complexities of such emotional elements as they touch and separate.

S.H. Foulkes has taught us the value of considering such polarised positions: good/bad; positive/negative; optimism/pessimism, in describing these as two sides of the same coin. In the words of a famous song: not having one without the other. If we are true to Foulkes' teachings, can we not see desire and despair as two sides of the same coin? Like the sound of one hand clapping, there are no single sided coins.

There seems also to be repetition in Foulkes' theories (who doesn't repeat). Many years ago, I visited Elizabeth Foulkes, his ex-wife, in their London home. Michael, as Foulkes came to be known, had died by this time. She told me that she had brought his repetition to his attention by pointing to his books on their shelves, emphasising how similar all the titles were which he was not fully aware of at the time. Possibly, his repetitions had converged into a form of consolidation.

When we begin to explore how convergence is created and developed within therapeutic settings, particular components emerge. In group analysis, there are often times when there is a contrast/conflict between group members asking questions, while on the other hand other members are associating/identifying with one another. In the group analytic art group this is similarly seen in members explaining/interpreting their own concrete imagery and linking with, associating and interpreting one another's productions. However, in many questions there is overt desire (at times rhetorical) and covert (silent) questions in the associations. Psychotherapy, in many ways is years of answered and unanswered (mostly) questions. Within these complex processes care needs to be taken as desire and despair go hand in hand. For example, if we address the matter of psychological defences, they may be as much about guarding against something coming 'out' as compared with a wholesale guard against intrusion by those who are challenging defences. I once had a discussion with a psychiatric colleague about one of her patient's refusal to take off his dark glasses. My colleagues' line of thought was that this was to filter his internal psychotic pictures and voices. I suggested he may have wanted to black out the external world as it contained a past event of accidentally killing his sibling when they were children playing in a field. In our desire to help the despairing elements constituting the defences this may become a destructive desire at breaking down defensive walls. Given time and nurturing, defences can drop like a silent curtain. Defences are not there to be broken and should be respected.

Art Group Illustration

At the time of writing the original Dublin congress paper I did not have an art therapy group in place. Therefore I, for a period of time, converted my primarily verbal groups into art groups. The members were willing, curious, excited and hesitant in changing the format for a short period. Some refused. As far as I'm aware no other group analysts have attempted such a conversion with long established groups, that is, 2–10 years life span. The basic format of the session was that members had free choice in what they painted/drew for the first 30–45 minutes of the session and then began interacting verbally.

Descriptions of each member's drawings/paintings (Figures 11.1–11.4):

Carmel: A figure reaching to the sky with a red pit on the left
Anthea: A woman and a man with a clock/flowers, spiders web.
Catrina: Figure with head exploding, barbed wire in the background
Evelyn: The 3 stages of her life – traveling the world and happy; despair through a painful divorce; emerging smiling and happy.
Zoe: Picture not disclosed

Excerpts of the images are noted in brackets: ( ), in the following accounts of people's paintings in the session.

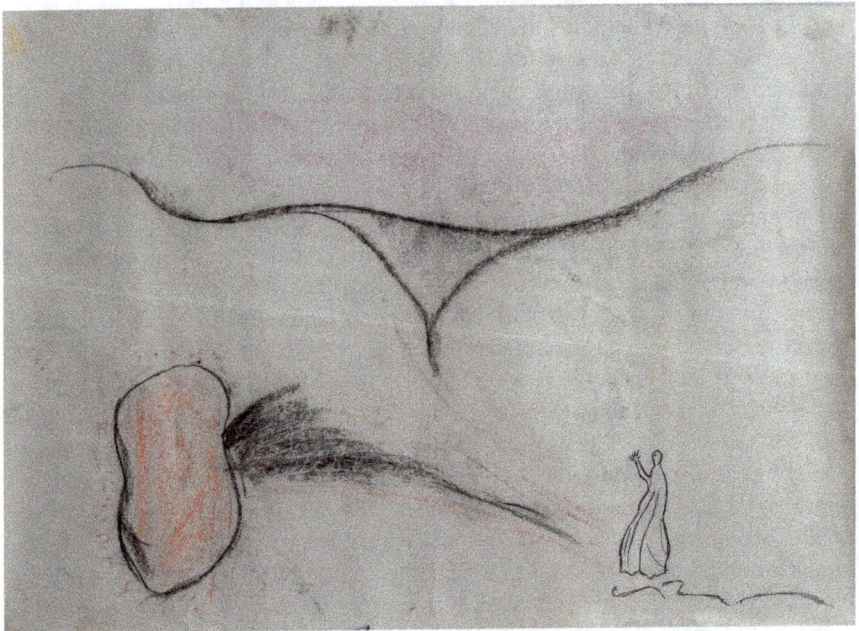

Figure 11.1 Carmel: She is a small black figure deep in a valley reaching upwards to a pink sky. On her left is a red pool of hell that she has come out of.

Figure 11.2 Anthea: A man and a woman in coloured clothes standing side by side by Anthea facing front. Above their heads is a large clock. They are in a domestic kitchen but they are surrounded and encased in a large spiders web.

Carmel, Evelyn and Anthea are longer standing members whereas Zoe and Catrina have only been in the group a few weeks.

The session was predominantly dominated in early part by Carmel speaking about her mother, who had recently died. This revolved around a desire and the yearning for her mother to come back to life and be on earth. This is shown in the picture by her reaching to heaven with the pool of hell or that which is unknown to her on her left. As she was describing being pulled in two different directions she was tearful and angry. In this situation her anger was moving her between desire and despair. Her yearning seemed to be a variant of despair and desire combined.

Anthea went on to speak of her struggle with her husband. Although this was about a row they were having it was the most animated and vibrant that we had seen her. Like Carmel she was also becoming overtly angry. She has rarely shown negative feelings for her husband until today. What her picture was saying and showing was that she felt that she was a prisoner in her own home (indicated by the cobwebs). She rarely left her home without her husband, who helped her manage her symptoms of agoraphobia. She had not worked for many years, but was now

Figure 11.3 Catrina: A green and blue figure standing with their back against a yellow door, legs and arms are akimbo and has a very large explosive head receiving lightning strikes. Two large hands signal NO ENTRY.

Figure 11.4 Evlyn: A downward sweeping curved channel containing arrows in the middle of the channel moving from left to right. The top left of the painting is her travelling the world, happy, showing concrete objects linked to travel. She moves down the channel to a cage, a symbol of being desperate in divorce, then moving upwards to happiness.

showing a desire to begin to think about leaving home on her own to find work. This came across to the others strongly, and it began to generate a sense of hope in the group. Not only were people pleased that Anthea was showing strong emotions, there was a sense of potency in how she was coming across.

Catrina mirrored Anthea's position. Her picture expressed her explosive feelings in regard to a row that she had had with her partner at the weekend. She had felt that her partner was putting excessive demands upon her, and they nearly came to blows (the two hands). In a similar way to Anthea, she was feeling both trapped by her partner, and also had severe agoraphobic symptoms (the barbed wire). This had left her feeling very much in despair, and with this she is spiralling down into depression. However, she went on to speak about a desire to get better by coming to the group. The others were very helpful in exploring the despairing feelings in the relationship, where she feels trapped, helping her to see that the future might bring her more freedom. They moved into a wider group discussion and were able to speak more openly. Within this process it was clear how desire is expressed in different forms, and how easily it could be eroded as despair became dominant.

Although Evelyn had been coming in at different points in the group dialogue, at times very helpfully, it wasn't until this part of the session that she was able to speak more about her own picture and what she had been going through. She related her picture to three stages in her life. The top left-hand part of her picture shows how she used to be very outgoing and happy travelling around the world. She eventually met and married her husband who eventually ripped her off for everything she had, leaving her bankrupt. Therefore, desire for life and happiness had been destroyed, plunging her into despair. She was also associating with Carmel in yearning for her mother, although the actual circumstances were different. She was also tuning in to both Catrina and Anthea's, loss of confidence, which was replaced by agoraphobic symptoms (the central figure in the circular cage). Sidestepping for a moment, it is possible to see that agoraphobia is a way of guarding against frustration and anger, keeping oneself safe against external threats and danger. The third part of her picture relates to how she had turned things around for herself even though she was bringing up two children as a single mother after she divorced her husband. Desire emerged again from the ruins of her despair and depression. The final image of her smiling beside a tree shows this. Apart from Zoe, the others were very involved with Evelyn, even though we all tried to involve Zoe. Evelyn seemed to bring a sense of hope through her experience which united them. This clarified, for me that desire and despair could not be separated.

I was able to bring in an interpretation of the group in which I highlighted the various elements that had come forward. The most obvious part of this interpretation emphasised those points of desire and despair that had been expressed, such as Carmel's struggles in relation to her mother; the various relationship struggles which they spoke of and painted; the imprisoned and agoraphobic struggles. Some points of desire were impossible, such as Carmel's yearning for her deceased mother to return; whereas it was difficult for Zoe to avail herself of the groups hope. Evelyn's contributions showed how desire and despair, within the parameters of convergence, were stages that revolve and evolve throughout life.

Hopefully this group illustration goes some way towards helping to visualise the areas of despair and desire. Granted it was not an actual art therapy session which was set up initially as such in its own right, although it was an existing established verbal group analytic group. However, those who conduct primarily verbal groups may see that within such groups mental pictures/images are continuously created in their own settings. In a similar way, art therapists who work group analytically will hopefully understand that it is through verbal language, silently held while the concrete images (paintings/drawings) are created and eventually co-joined with language, that we begin to make sense of the overall group analytic genre.

Although I have confined my explorations of convergence within the parameters of despair and desire there are many other dimensions which would bring our attention to these dynamic movements, not only in single sessions but in group phases/periods and the overall life of the group. Despair and desire have just been two points of reference.

Psychoanalytic Perspectives

In the opening introduction of her book 'Clinical Values,' Sandra Buechler tells us:

> This vast literature on psychoanalytic treatments informs more than it inspires. It fails to integrate life experience into its body. Too often it is content with explanation rather than wisdom. It cultivates intellect at the expense of feeling and spirit.
>
> (Buechler, 2004, p. 1)

As stated earlier one of the driving factors within the formation of this chapter was the promotion of dialogue with Greek psychoanalysts during their 'Classical Psychoanalysts' Congress in 2013. This was an esteemed audience and one which was difficult to sway from their Freudian world. Generally, they were appreciative of my contribution but as to how much they perceived this as relevant to their own world thinking is impossible to say. As much of the psychoanalysts' congress had sexuality and perversion as its primary theme, love got little attention beyond the erotic. Of course, I may be doing them a disservice as most of the contributions were in Greek, and only one other in English.

Over many years, in my reading of texts and discussions with colleagues at conferences, psychoanalysis has tended to be placed on a rather lofty, secretive pedestal which functioned like an expensive, introverted 'cult of two,' with a dominant master in the psychoanalyst being given access to the analysand's inner world on a regular, consuming and expensive contract of three to five times a week for many years of involvement. We owe a great debt to psychoanalysis, both in its contribution to lives of thousands and their families and friends but to the 'helping professions' as a whole. There is a counter to this in which it has been vilified and condemned as a dangerous practice which leads to destruction. John Kerr brings attention to this in his book: 'A Most Dangerous Method' – The story of Jung, Freud and Sabina Spielrein (Kerr, 1994). It was made in to a major motion picture (2011). Psychotherapists across the board, group analysts, art therapists, psychologists, counsellors, may not have come into being without the birth of psychoanalysis. The move to 'talking therapy'; the creation of therapy which required an opening up of people's inner worlds; the discipline of creating frames to operate within; the recognition of unconscious life; the lack or suspension of judgement; the development of clinical formulations which moved beyond psychiatric diagnosis; the patient/therapist relationship as just a few elements having started in psychoanalysis and have evolved and blossomed extensively. When I lived in England, I recall seeing a notice outside a 'Wetherspoons' pub/restaurant which said:

> "Cheap drinks – born here, raised elsewhere" not unlike psychoanalysis giving birth to the rest of us, but little of it is cheap.

True, they were the first chain of such establishments who radicalised the cost for the consumer. Therefore, instead of continuing to see classical psychoanalysis as an activity functioning royally behind closed doors, what can be offered to psychoanalysts that can be taken back into their consulting rooms. I think that one way is to convey the importance of the heart, in whatever form that may take. Can psychoanalysts find therapeutic love and heartfullness perspectives/ingredients in what Buechler has brought to our attention in her following use of Shaw's views:

Shaw connects the analysts own hopes for the patient with the growth of analytic love.

> We sustain our analytic purpose with even the most difficult of analysands be-cause we hope that they will get better. We hope that what we provide will bear fruit in the analysands life, in the form of his healing and growth. Very often, wit-nessing the fruits of our labour in the form of the analysands new found trust, and hard earned healing and growth evokes and further stimulates our loving feelings.
>
> (Buechler, 2004, p. 43)

At the time of my Greek congress, I was defining therapeutic love as a 'Neces-sary Convergence.' By this I had meant that it was a necessary intent and outcome to discover the heart moves (range of emotions being activated), and how this is experienced by all parties, be it patient, therapist or group; subjective/objective ele-ments; intuition and empathy; merging and synthesis, to name a few.

In previous publications I have described that the love that is created within therapeutic encounters requires a level of immersion, not only by the therapist in the given hour but also from the individual patient or group (McNeilly, 2006b, p. 124). Is this similar to the psychoanalytic concept of 'free floating attention'? Thus, immersion is a form of converging, that is, on the therapist side when they step out of their last patient/group session and into a new one; moving from the 'outside world' while 'drawing it in' at the necessary points when particular ele-ments are touched upon.

I am not a psychoanalyst so I am somewhat naïve as to what actually happens in that setting. I have been struck by some psychoanalysts and psychoanalytically ori-ented therapist's inability, difficulty, resistances in conveying just how they worked or how they arrived at theoretical formulations, whereas I had little difficulty in opening up on such matters. I think that such a reserved, dare I say, withhold-ing position may well strengthen the perception by others of an elitist model that cannot be entered unless the 'Road to Damascus' is travelled through the lengthy period of psychoanalytic training. With that said, I suggest that psychoanalysis is a form of therapeutic love, as stated earlier. For an analyst to agree to accept someone on a regular basis for potentially years of work is a form of love. For this to be successful there has to be a convergent road leading to merging between two people. Unless there is emotional contact, the intellectual pursuit will not be enough alone. The analyst may not overtly convey their emotional reactions to the patient, or make use of his own thoughts and emotions (generally described as countertransference) in the same way as other therapeutic methods but these will be present in a covert way.

Creative and Artistic Convergence

Moving beyond the psychoanalytic/therapeutic frames of reference there are some points of interest in music and general literature which brings further colour as a way of bringing closure to this chapter. There is a song by an Irish singer/songwriter, Declan O'Rourke, called Galileo which draws our attention to the struggles between the heart (love) and the head (science). The following extracts from the song 'Galileo' had a big impact on me, the full song needs to be listened to:

Galileo fell in love, as a Galilean boy, and he wondered,
What in heavens, who invented such a joy?
But the question got the better of his scientific mind,
And to his blind and dying days, he looked up high
And often sighed and sometimes cried...
Who puts the rainbow in the sky?
Who lights the stars at night?
Who dreamt up someone so divine?
Someone like you and made them mine?.
(©Declan O'Rourke, Album: *Since Kyabram*, 2004)

Moving from the world of music to someone with their feet firmly in both fictional literature and philosophy, Iris Murdoch tells us:

Contemporary philosophers frequently connect consciousness with virtue, and although, they constantly talk of freedom they rarely talk of love.
(Murdoch, 1970, p. 2)

This parallels with my earlier comments about the broad church of psychotherapy, when I intimated the paucity of love references against scientific and quasi-scientific psychotherapy perspectives. Extending these views back to psychoanalysis J-B Pontalis, who wrote beautifully about his personal, warm and wise psychoanalytic perspectives:

Eros, that little diabolical god, tricked Narcissus into making him believe that we could love ourselves, when love is what takes us out of ourselves.
(Pontalis, 2003, p. 24)

Commenting on his own standing as a psychoanalyst he says:

When I protect myself like this – all ready to convince myself that the others are the patients addicted to their illness and that I, wedged well in my chair, have stopped being a patient ages ago – I am no longer an analyst. I forget that these men, these women, take care of me in their way. Taking care of me by opening the gaps in my 'normality'. Analysis is, perhaps, along with love, the only experience that takes you 'out of yourself.'

(Pontalis, 2003, p. 83)

I agree whole heartedly with these sentiments, apart from 'Analysis – the only experience.' I see these 'taking care of' perspectives as a form of heartfullness and therapeutic love. From the man who co-wrote the classic dictionary of psychoanalysis (Laplanche & Pontalis, 1983), this small and rich book was certainly not to be expected from such a figure, but it has influenced me greatly in my endeavours in pursuing my views on heartfullness and therapeutic love, hopefully, as a genuine contribution to psychotherapy.

There was a film released in 2017 called 'The Mountain between Us.' It was about a plane crash in the wild snowy mountains in which only two people survived (with a dog) and their weeks of ordeal in getting back to civilisation. The two actors were Idris Elba and Kate Winslet. As they are slowly approaching death through not being rescued they struggle through waist high snow.

Sadly I was unable to get permission to cite the dialogue but there is a conversation which reached a crescendo in the closing part of the film about the matter of survival via the human heart and love from Winslet, in contrast to Elba, the neurosurgeon, who initially views the heart as only a pump.

Convergence and Perversion

Returning to the origins of ideas which were stimulated in my dialogue with psychoanalysts highlighted previously, perversion was central to the congress theme. Considering the place therapeutic love has in relation to perversion it was somewhat difficult to rise above perverted eroticism as understood within classical psychoanalysis. One of my starting hypotheses was that love was removed, diverted and/or perverted in sexual perversion. If we contrast the two words perversion and convergence there are interesting points of note. A dictionary defines perversion as a deviation from particular normal positions. Convergence, on the other hand, is about things meeting or coming together. Of particular interest for me was the definition of 'convergence zone in respect to geology,' which I opened this chapter with and just to highlight again: 'a zone where tectonic plates collide, typified by earthquakes, mountain formation and volcanic activity' (Collins, Millennium Edition). I think that this particular definition is helpful in our work as therapists and analysts. The overall holding embrace of therapeutic love as a necessary convergence and framework allows for internal/external life movement, that is, a mountain can keep moving but stays in the same place. Let us not forget that the planet Earth is in continual moving rotation.

With the psychoanalytic audience in Greece I was certainly not preaching to the converted. To move beyond well held psychoanalytic views of perversion being understood and analysed as deviant pathological expressions with all of psychoanalyses armamentarium, may have been a bridge too far for some. This entailed turning things around to consider such psychopathology as expressions of diverted and lost love? How could psychoanalysts conceive a form of love existing between them and the patient with multiple complex sexual perversions, as Pontalis indicated earlier. In a semi-serious way I attempted a redefinition of the word psychopathology as

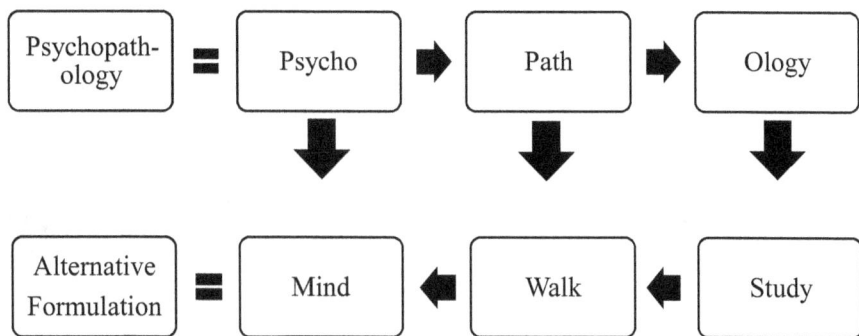

Psychopath-ology	=	Psycho	➡	Path	➡	Ology
		⬇		⬇		⬇
Alternative Formulation	=	Mind	⬅	Walk	⬅	Study

By reading the bottom line from right to left this moves it from a medically severe mental illness as presented in the top line to: the Study (ology) of Severe Pathways (walkways) of the Mind (psych). I do not consider that my concept of therapeutic love detracts or negates psychoanalytic principles, and hopefully begin to see that both can reach some level of CONVERGENCE.

Part 2

The Gap

Intro

The opening photograph is of Mamore Gap, in Ireland. It splits the mountain and could be described paradoxically as an empty gap yet the term 'gap' also denotes the road. I was drawn to the word gap on many occasions, and particularly in my most recent paper: 'Running between Raindrops and Trying to Keep Dry' (McNeilly, 2020). With Part 1 of this book much of what I wrote about focused upon polar points and positions along with what occurred in the empty space.

Figure 12.0 A photograph of a wild Irish mountainous land with a long steep road forming a gap of two miles long. It is intended to spark a reaction to presenting the theme of the gap.

DOI: 10.4324/9781003536857-14

My last book on group analytic art therapy was also constructed on two parts. So it will be with the following chapters, in which I will enter unchartered areas that I think few may have entered. Even though the subject matter of Part 1 has been enjoyable to write (after the blood, sweat and tears), the following has given me more challenges. The focus throughout will be on gaps, not in the same way as Part 1, but more of a movement into extra-curricular areas that are encountered in therapeutic endeavours, that is, The Thoughts I Threw Away, Outside the Consulting Room, The Lighter Side and Humour. Throughout my professional lifetime, these topics have interspersed mine and many of my colleague's work. For example, one simple area, which is also complex, is that of confidentiality, that is, Is confidentiality a firm object or is it a space, a gap between the therapist, patient and the outside world, an invisible dynamic that drives a climate of openness? At times, this leads to confusion between what is confidential and what is private. Within clinical settings once something has been assigned the title: confidential, it carries an almost legal safe set of criteria, and if broken there can be punitive consequences. Whereas, if something is private, it does not carry the same repercussions. Written contracts are more closely associated with the former, that is, confidentiality. This alone could make up a full chapter, but I will meander on.

Chapter 12

Mind the Gap

In 2017 I gave a paper at the 20th Anniversary of the 'Sociedade de Art Terapia' in Lisbon, Portugal, which attempted to question the trend in psychotherapy and art therapy to be scientific. The sub-heading of that paper was 'Caution against a Scientific Approach.' It seems fairly common in psychotherapy trainings to call qualifying theses scientific papers. In my suggesting 'caution,' I was equating these scientific papers to 'gaps' waiting to be filled based on elitist yearnings which objectified the therapeutic contents and processes of various enterprises. The old adage 'publish or be damned' has been replaced with: 'be scientific or sink.' Returning to O'Rourke's song, from Chapter 11, the line: 'But the question got the better of his scientific mind' moves Galileo away from science to the romantic realm of the heart. If the reader listens to the song I think their heart will be touched and moved. It is a love song that touches and reverberates between the head and the heart, which moves between the often undefinable human experience of love. In my last employment, I recall being at odds with my senior colleagues, who insisted on creating research programmes with increasingly elaborate methods of enquiry, in contrast to my drive toward narrative reviews. The corporate idea was that such research would give credence and serious 'clout' in order to validate the Psychotherapy Department. It did not work as the Psychotherapy Service declined to just one therapist being employed. Regarding my holding to the value of the 'narrative' it is a driving force in this book.

Of course, I am not saying that scientific exploration is not of value and has helped in furthering my own and others professions. My emphasis on caution was an attempt to guide us back to matters of the heart which I believe has suffered from inattention in the striving for scientific appraisal and value.

If we look back at our history within the worlds of psychoanalysis, psychiatry, early art therapy formulations, the moves into object relations theories and neuroscience; as some of our forebears have moved, we can see how scientific searches have claimed us. Anthony Storr succinctly illustrates this:

> When Freud first initiated psycho-analytic treatment, he did not anticipate that he would become emotionally important to his patients. He hoped to make psycho-analysis into a 'science of mind' which would ultimately be based upon,

DOI: 10.4324/9781003536857-15

and be as objective as anatomy and physiology. He saw his own role as that of a detached observer, and assumed that his patients would have the same attitude toward him as they would toward a medical specialist in any other field. When he discovered that this was not the case, that his patients began to experience and to express emotions of love and hate toward himself, he did not accept such emotions as genuine expressions of feelings in the here-and-now, but interpreted them as new editions of emotions from the past which had been transferred to the person of the analyst.

(Storr, 1989, pp. 4–5)

So, I have cautioned against a scientific pull in order to fill a gap that demands to be filled in order to give substance, purpose and meaning. 'Mind the Gap' was the first image that came to mind in the congress title.

'Mind the Gap' are words that are written on railway/underground platforms to warn us about getting on and off trains. The gap is dangerous if not minded and especially so for children, the blind and those speaking other languages. It shows us that there is a waiting space between the stillness/permanence of the platform and the stepping onto the movement of the train. We must cross the gap while keeping it in mind. In our work with patients, there are so many gaps. The emphasis on gaps will vary, that is, past-present, emotions-intellect and language-imagery, to name a few. Theoretical terms exist in psychotherapy, such as transitional space, creative space and a place of reverie, to name a few. Particular therapies will either be cautious or careful of entering the gaps that contain threat, fear, despair and hopelessness. Whereas others are more ready to embrace the gaps, even though they may be seen as dangerous and containing creative potential, excitement and a bedrock for psychological growth. To step into the gaps may be full of hope for change and the healthy unexpected.

There is another perspective in which the analogy of the train emerges. Standing on the platform the white letters tell us to be careful. The parallel here is that the patient, metaphorically defined as a passenger, arrives and he has to get off the train or stay on. The journey of his life brings him to the station of therapy. Now the train is still and the patient sees the gap, which is potentially chasmic, if that is a word, in making the decision. The choice is of entering therapy by stepping over the gap or by staying on the train of their life's journey without therapy. If the patient starts the new journey of therapy, there will be many more stops, starts and gaps to be encountered. Possibly one may say that these analogous or metaphoric equations are not scientific. Critics may say "You're not keeping up with the times?" I cannot deny these criticisms if presented. Can art therapy (and other psychotherapies) claim to be scientific just as psychoanalysis has staked its claim? Science requires methodology supported by rigorous research, such as blind testing, placebo usage in medication and evidence-based practice, as some points of reference. What seems to lie at the heart of these directives is the matter of 'proof.' This seems to percolate to a whole range of therapies. What seems to emerge triumphantly are those methods with slick ideas on terminology, that can be practiced and explained through bullet points and homework, with therapies being completed in as short a time as possible, i.e., 6–12 weeks, and are therefore financially driven as the most economic. Such methods are often applied to less complex conditions and may be evaluated through providing proof of their efficacy, such as cognitive therapy, mindfulness and neuroscience, to name a few. Art therapists have also stepped forward pinning their colours to the masts, such as mindfulness art therapy and cognitive art therapy.

I think there is a 'flaw' in attempting to apply science as either a driving directive or being validated through elements that show efficacy. If therapists are trying to show that their method deserves recognition scientifically then there seems to be a 'given' that inherently this requires proven science. What scientific proof is there in the art images encapsulating therapeutic efficacy, if this is the art therapeutic model being followed?

The Core of the Gap

So far, the points that I'm raising draws attention to something that has to be carefully considered: the dangerous potential and risk that the gap poses, something to get over or overcome. However, such perspectives move our focus away from what resides in the gap and in many ways, in therapy and life generally, there is a great value and learning from the gaps we fall into. 'Falling in love' seems to imply that two people or other loving experiences are not fully experienced without falling into something. Possibly one of the most tragic situations in real terms is that of suicide when the person has little concern for the actual writing on the platform as he/she throws themselves in front of a train, and could not be saved or involved in therapy.

Reflecting back on my presentations at congresses since 1997, I now see that much of what I wrote and spoke about, was the importance of gaps and spaces. A portion of these papers raised attention to the pivotal words: *Of – Or – And*. These words filled a gap that either united, as in 'of'; bridged or connected, as in 'and' or pushed apart or set in opposition, as in 'or.' To expand on these historical works would be too much of a diversion, but this has led me to the concept of the 'core' which has many meanings.

Particular Gaps and Cores

With the 'Intro photo' of Mamore Gap, I trust that this gives a clear image. Here are two further gaps:

Figure 12.1 is a fairway on my golf course. Better golf shots have to stay on the fairway – a gap between the rough and longer grass. To reach the green one has to take more shots in order to get the ball into the hole on the green, which could be defined as the 'core' of the green. Hence one needs to keep within the gap of the 'fairway' in order to play good golf which, in turn, leads us to the 'core.'

The second image is of a sculpture called 'The Fid' (Figure 12.2). It is a wooden structure in my home town of Moville, Co. Donegal. A 'fid' is a tool for mending fishing nets. Before I knew this my own immediate imagination saw it as a

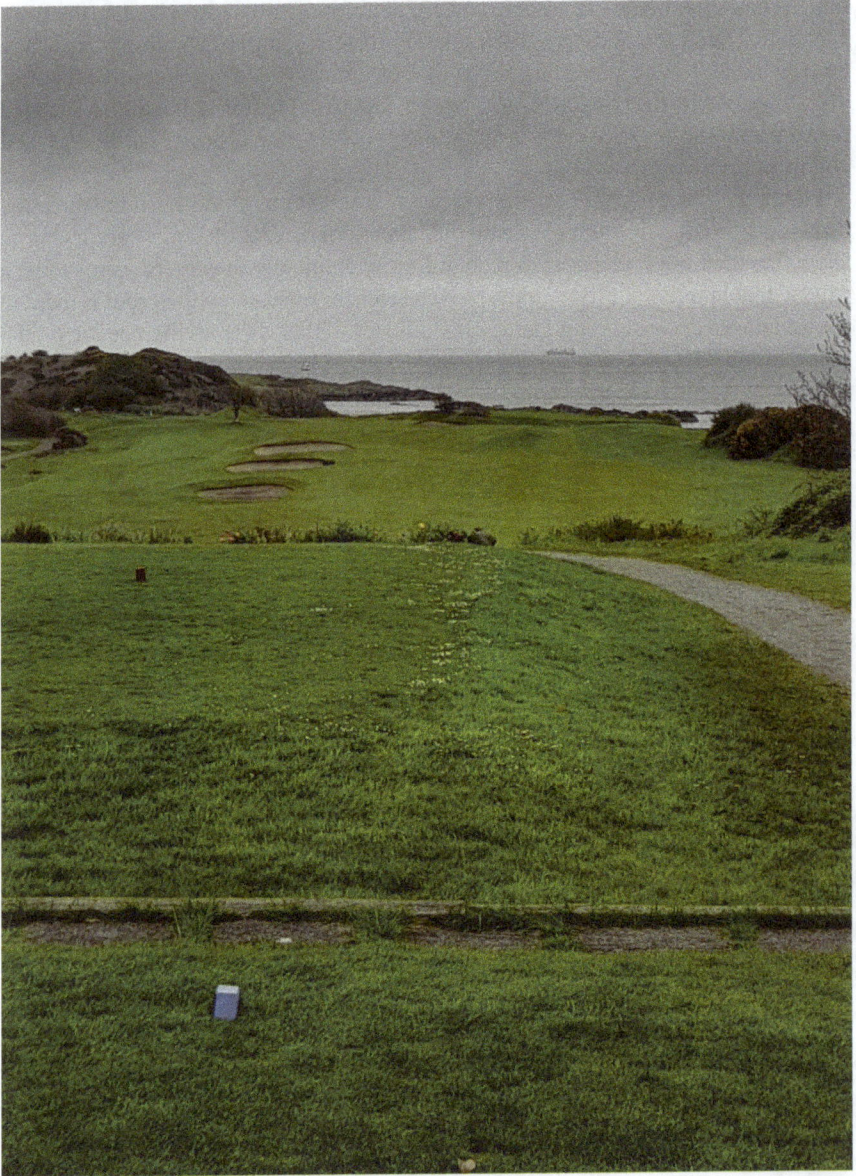

Figure 12.1 A photograph of a golf fairway looking down from the 'Tee.' There are sand bunkers on the left, long deep grass on the right. This represents a pictorial image of a gap:

'teardrop,' possibly representing a commemoration of/for the thousands of immigrants forced to sail to America and Australia in the 19th/20th centuries at times of struggle and famine. It was, in my imagination, also about the fishermen lost at sea from this important fishing town. The 'gap' here is the narrow lough entrance which leads to the Atlantic Ocean and the 'core' is the future unknown.

Figure 12.2 The fid is a tall wooden sculpture about 40–50 feet tall situated on a pier. It is centre position. Looking from the pier towards the ocean. It looks like a large tear drop with a sharp point at the top. It is a tool used by fishermen.

When we search for the core of the matter, things, self and identity, whatever, the journey has many elements and stages in our endeavours. The core may manifest itself in many ways. Last year I developed this through the concepts of the 'lost and stolen heart.' The core, as formulated in those theoretical postulations was manifested at times in therapeutic settings when my heart was touched to the core, which could not only be described/defined under conventional psychodynamic language and concepts. At those times I had little or no control and was led by a power which, as yet, I do not fully understand.

Increasingly, over the years, I began to notice many areas where the identity of a field of theory and practice was created and maintained through opposition, even though both sides held similar core values. Many start from the same starting point, that is, Freudian, Jungian and Kleinian. Indeed, S.H. Foulkes, the originator of group analysis, started as a Freudian psychoanalyst. Some hold to the original script, others adding and developing; diverging and separating. For such developments to occur it brings in its wake splits and chasms, gaps of a greater or lesser proportion. When I trained as an art therapist there were two schools of training which, although they had central core values, splits emerged between 'art therapy' and 'art psychotherapy.' Also, in the field of therapeutic communities, although there were central core values that united them, there were a great many splits and gaps, creating further tension and separation.

This brings me back to the concept of the core. In therapeutic sessions, when my heart had been touched, it transcended intellect into physical experiences that were either solely mine, a reaction to the patient or group or a direct emotional connection, etc. Such physical sensations as pain in my heart area, warm feelings at times of joy, hairs on the back of my neck standing up, somatic reactions when parts of my body unconsciously resonated with the patient or group, feelings of tenderness and calmness when in harmony with the patients/groups. In all of these experiences, the gap is either filled, entered, crossed over or loses its purpose. The core is accessed, entered, pulls one in or emerges, with or without intellectual permission.

When I spoke about a caution against a scientific approach, I was proposing that if one goes down a scientific road of enquiry it takes us further from what I believe to be the heart as the core point of reference. It would also take us away from what many believe psychotherapy to be: a form of art and psychodrama/drama. What would be the scientific purpose of explaining away compassion, empathy, affection, joy, sadness, tenderness and certainly not love.

Spaces and Emptiness

The previous commentary highlighted aspects of the 'gap' and which elements were engendered to fill them. If we take this from another angle, that is, by setting aside the road and the mountains of our opening picture of Mamore Gap, we are presented with a 'V' shape section of air. As such we are drawn to look more at air and space as emptiness. The following fragment stretches our imagination:

> Empty space, said the driver. There's a funny thing to think about. The back of the van is full of empty space. I brought it from my town. But I've opened the door several times since I left. So, is it still empty space from my town or is it now several new empty spaces? This is the sort of thing one thinks about sometimes. If the back of my van were full of chairs the question wouldn't arise. One

assumes that the space between the chairs remains the same all through the trip. Empty space however, is something else.

(Hoban, 1973, p. 153)

This echoed a number of the points I raised in my chapter on 'The Fullness of Emptiness' (McNeilly, 2006b, pp. 201–222). That chapter was an exploration into the deeper strata of emptiness which contained fuller elements. In looking at this with these new objectives in mind we move into a set of journeys beyond the inclusive concept of the 'gap.' In my illustration of Mamore Gap, the 'V'-shaped sky is the central point (core) of our vision, but the overall definition of its name includes the road, the mountains, as well as the sheep, cows, streams and foliage. In the same way, the Fid image draws us out to the Atlantic Ocean but incorporates the sculpture, harbour, fishing nets, boats and the 'ghosts' of immigrants and fisherman lost at sea.

So, if we draw parallels with our work in psychotherapy such complex pictures will arise, which will set our course moving us one way then the other. The patient, or the group, will bring their stories of their lives. One minute our focus will be on specific points which led them to our door. Then as the stories unfold the spaces and gaps will start to be seen. These then take us in and out, back and forth in time (a meandering process). The spaces will be filled or avoided accordingly but what is important is the 'consideration of the whole.'

The Space of Prolonged Absence

Some of the major points of consideration in therapy revolve around the ongoing gaps between therapists, patients and groups, such as, holiday periods. Patrick Kavanagh, in his autobiography *The Green Fool*, reminisces about his mother, which captures beautifully intimate dialogue along with the complex 'in-betweens' of said and unsaid thoughts and emotions, that is, 'the chinks between her cracked speech':

> She sat facing me and held my hands. Her face was green and haggard, she was dying of cancer of the stomach – 'Oh! Patrick', she said with all the pathos and sympathy of a sick woman, 'if you could get to high school, you'd leave them all behind'. She spoke her heart to mine for a half hour. I cannot remember the actual words she said. She spoke brokenly, appealing, wistfully. She believed in me.
>
> I was not deeply moved at the time, but I had an instinctive feeling that in the chinks between her cracked speech there was the intuitive wisdom of a woman.
> (Kavanagh, 1938/1975/1977, p. 85)

Kavanagh wrote these words in psychotherapy in the 1930s and even though there is a great beauty in his prose, it was at a time when Irish men, predominantly, were supposedly removed from their feelings. How true this is I do not know.

A pessimistic view is that life is the space, or gap, between birth and death. A colloquial phrase is 'life's a bitch and then you die.' Birth opens up gaps and spaces, death closes them down. There is a great deal written about the gaps and spaces in treatment programmes, that is, therapist's holidays, pregnancies, illness. One of the more recent areas of interest has been the prolonged period of struggles with the COVID-19 pandemic in which the majority of therapist/patient/group contacts have either been through telephone and video conferencing, for example, Zoom, Skype, arrangements. I can only imagine what this has been like, that is, whether it has been successful or not and the particular elements that heralded seen and unforeseen problems. In a way it is presence (via video conferencing) and absence (no actual contact) combined. I have been able to present seminars via Zoom which, although having some benefit, was not the same as personally sitting in group or individual supervision. A somewhat sterile affair. The electronic space is filling the air waves with a semblance of feelings, emotions and spontaneity. One wonders if research will be undertaken to evaluate what has happened during this period of therapeutic starvation, that is, rates of self damage, regression, suicide and psychological improvement. It may be worth considering the variants between more formal psychodynamic/analytic and other interpersonal models, with attention to therapeutic love and heartfullness. For example, in a more formal analytic situation, the therapist has been seeing the patient for a considerable length of time. At one point, the patient speaks about missing the therapist:

It was like when I was at boarding school. I missed them, my family, the warmth and smell of them, being touched, and in my home. I miss being with you!.

Therapist's response:

I remember when you told me before how you started to starve yourself at boarding school and you couldn't touch your mother. Are you angry that we can't touch?

Although trying to fill the therapeutic space via video conferencing when this therapeutic method is in place, the computer screen may seem averse to facilitating the emotional interactions. There may be a danger that the computer screen could cement a distance if a psychoanalytic stance is maintained and the therapist may not even be aware of it if there is not some degree of warmth coming from the therapist. This could lead to failure. In this instance, stated above, the therapist did not respond or acknowledge the patient saying she had missed him. Of course, this is just one response but if it is balanced with more personal and emotive comments/ attitude things may even out. On the other hand, if the principles of therapeutic love and heartfullness come to the fore an alternative response from the therapist could be:

I remember how you were when we first met, it was as if there was an impenetrable screen between us but now, we have a different screen. We both have a right to be frustrated and angry, hopefully not to the point of your not eating again. I also miss meeting with you in real time.

Such a response helps to symbolically dissolve the computer screen.

In closing this chapter, I hope that I have gone some way in opening up the contrast between scientific ventures in order to gain credibility and the more abstract and personal/emotive aspects that move us towards the search into gaps and spaces. To follow the artistic creations of the patient with a search through scientific ventures into the brain and neurological functioning is on par with seeing the mind as synonymous with the brain. The soul, the uniqueness of the person and those with them, be it therapists or others, is reduced to mathematical equations. Man as a mystery is lost.[1]

This closure moves us towards new explorations of thoughts, comments, phrases and powerful, apparently meaningless exchanges within the rich and fertile ground of psychotherapy. I give the last word to E Graham Howe:

The therapeutic relationship is not only 'face to face' and 'heart-to-heart'. It is also 'SPACE-TO-SPACE.'

(Howe, 2005, p. 60)

Note

1 Further commentary on the soul is expressed in the closing epilogue.

Chapter 13

The Thoughts I Threw Away

Your heart metabolises love the same way as your stomach metabolises food.

The above quote was something I said many years ago to a patient who struggled with her anorexic symptoms while at the same time being afraid of her loving feelings for her child. It seemed to come to me 'out of the blue' as we moved between matters of the heart and stomach, that is, her difficulty also in feeding her child. The impact that this had on the patient led to a lessening of the patient's symptoms. This was one among many phrases which seemed to build up internally for me as a type of bank deposit to be accessed later when appropriate.

When such moments emerge if we try to use these words and phrases in later transactions, we in part, put a lid on the future 'oil rich' emergences. Throwaway comments may be said to be without meaning and purpose but I feel that they are of great value. It was a happy coincidental accident that a friend alerted me to the following translation of a German story she had made:

> a man walks down the streets with his little bag and collects the thoughts that fall from people's heads. These thoughts are considered by them to be superfluous to requirement. He takes the bag of thoughts home and plants them in his garden. Beautiful flowers grow, but with an ephemeral existence. So, he goes out again to collect what people consider to be worthless.
>
> (Feth, 1996)[1]

The Origins

Over the years, I heard many colleagues, students and patients say the most beautiful and wonderful things, which became relegated to secondary or non-existent positions. For therapists and trainees they would, instead of holding the intrinsic meaning of the spontaneous, try to find and describe their therapeutic endeavours in accepted theoretical jargon. As such, these rich thoughts, language and imagery were thrown away, rarely to be valued and therefore forgotten. When something is thrown away, it implies that it was either of no use or had served its purpose and

DOI: 10.4324/9781003536857-16

is superfluous. For some it is difficult to throw anything away as it will 'come in handy someday.' For some it is valuable whereas it is clutter for others.

As we develop this line of thought it moves us to think about those things that have worth or value that are thrown away which the owner either values or not. In England there is a television programme called 'The Antiques Roadshow.' It is not uncommon for someone to say that they brought the item for 10 pounds in a charity shop and the expert then values it for thousands. So, waste turns into value, like the alchemy of lead being turned into gold.

Unlike the owner giving/throwing something away, valuables can be lost or stolen, leaving a space/gap. Some may deal with this better if the stolen object has only monetary worth. The gap is soon covered over leaving scar tissue which fades in time. If something has more of a personal/emotional importance, the gap may never be gotten over, or at least, it takes a lot longer. A parallel is easy to identify for the many patients in therapy, and others generally, who struggle with emotional scar tissue. In Chapter 2 I spoke about the light stealing my words. In a way I played a part in throwing these words away. These were words that held value for me and I had not realised the power of sunlight to steal my words. So, our line of enquiry now moves us to look at things that *have* value and are thrown away, at times without even realising it. This will also consider what remains after throwing away and what is the outcome when it reaches something or someone else.

In 1999 I was watching a television programme on Duke Ellington's life and music. One of the central revelations in the programme was that many of his works were never written down, played once and then forgotten. In one scene it shows him composing the work alone on the piano. Then he brings his musicians in, plays and hums his and their parts, then they play it live before the audience (probably after some practice) then it's finished, gone and not played again. Duke tells us in the interview that composing and writing it is but one part, but the real food that we get is when it is played. He feeds off the musicians and the audience. Then the meal is over and he moves on.

On further reflection I could see that some of these thoughts were connected to psychotherapeutic theoretical areas. In a similar way to Duke Ellington the composition and music of the words in psychotherapy had been played – and then they were gone, as with my developing ideas around thoughts being discarded. Then I thought, let's try and catch them again and make more sense. However, there is a cautious counterpoint in that possibly there is a good reason for them to be brought to the surface and then thrown away (forgotten) and not turned into tricks of the trade, becoming useless and sterile, that is, 'there was a man who didn't taste chicken as a child because of deprivation. When he grew up, he gave his children chicken but didn't have any himself' (I first heard this from my group analyst Robin Skynner). When I have replayed and used such statements, I often pause and think 'did I say this before?' The original beauty and magical impact are no longer there. Although I love the Van Morrison album 'Astral Weeks' (Morrison, 1968) each time I play it, there will never be a first time of hearing it again.

The title of this chapter emerged from a group experience I was conducting which led me to write a paper called 'The Paradox of a Fart.' In that session the members seemed to be oscillating between humorous comments on bodily functions (especially farting) and other more serious matters which were paradoxical, that is, once something was achieved then it disappeared so, 'what was the point.' It was at this point I said that "a fart was also a paradox," that is, 'once you heard its presence then it was gone. What remained was smell, embarrassment, lingering associations, relief.' The humour on the fart and other bodily functions was therefore a presentation of a lighter side of the difficulty in grasping and understanding deeper more serious paradoxes.

Staying in line with the pointlessness comments mentioned in the paradox group session, there was another time that led to an important phrase. In that instance the dynamics were connected to feeding imagery, that is, not being given things as a child, actual and psychological feeding. This translated to the present day difficulties of getting and sustaining sustenance from relationships, so it was pointless to try. I said that "the point of the breast is the nipple and if there is no nipple, then you can't get the milk." The group used this well to look at the absence of a symbolic nipple, not only in group, but also the areas of life they struggled with. In another group session one woman informed everyone in an extremely pleased way that she was pregnant. Much of the dialogue in the session was about their difficulty in finding meaning. It was not until the closing stages of the session that she beamed, pushed out her breasts (clothed) and shook them around saying that this was a bonus – getting large breasts. I said that "the meaning of your breasts getting bigger and the satisfaction you feel may not just be about getting ready for feeding" (she had previously spoken about what her small breasts had meant to her). I'd also stated that "the road to meaning is full of potholes" as is also the road of multiple meanings within breast symbolism. Could we equate this with the saying 'the road to hell is full of good intentions?'

Therapeutic Gaze

The 'therapeutic gaze' is a term I coined but I don't know if other theoreticians have coined it. It emerged in some of my work with individual patients. In the therapeutic setting I recall two women who needed the reassurance of being looked at. For both of them it was the gaze (my looking at them) that held, for one: security, for the other, intrusion. At these times they were in my eyes and I in theirs. In order for the therapist and patient to co-exist in the gaze, it offers stability and an opening up by the patients, giving permission, or not, for entry. The phrase 'a window to the soul' (1611, proverbs 30:17) has biblical origins, which I'm sure many writers and others will have made use of. One woman in my groups spoke of not being able to look at people. I said that "unless you look at people it would be difficult for you to know if you are being seen." For many people, the look is not a therapeutic gaze but an intrusion, a paranoiac fear of destruction.

It is also seen by some therapists as not desirable to look at one's patient, clearly a method used in classical psychoanalysis.

In one of my student groups, we were struggling with disclosure issues. One member was able to disclose more personal details. Another struggled until she disclosed her feelings of ugliness about a part of her life. Eventually the dialogue turned to giving birth. The woman who disclosed had created a sense of satisfaction through the beauty of trust, whereas with the others feelings of undisclosed ugliness were painful. The trusting woman told the group that the child who is born via caesarean is beautiful, whereas with natural birth the child is ugly. Although I can't recall my exact interpretation I suggested that with some disclosures there is a feeling that to do so, will bring forth ugliness. However, with a feeling of safety/ trust, opening up can bring aspects of beauty, satisfaction and pleasure. Returning to natural or caesarean birth this will demand greater or lesser levels of touch. I imagine that the mother will be in a heightened, open, vulnerable and agonising position. She will experience the surrounding touch of those helping her to give birth. At the same time her inner world (actually and symbolically) is accessible, further I said that: "I imagine this as I have only viewed child birth on television but have heard many accounts of giving birth from female patients."

"I was touched" – "it's a touching moment" – "a lover's first touch" – "he's touched (in the head)." In a group session, the dynamics of touch were foremost. At one point I said: "to be touched is either like a hammer to the head or a feather to the heart!" In another individual session I said: "love can make your heart skip a beat and can also tear it apart." With both of these spontaneous statements I was pulling together the powerful impact upon people within the gestures and emotions of that which touches, along with such elements moving to the heart and creating a fluttering feeling, often beyond comprehension.

In another group session, we were talking about various demanding situations. This ranged from people's demands on others as well as demands being made upon them. This had a predominantly 'taking' image and therefore perceived as negative. What was difficult to see was a positive dimension, that is, if you were being demanded from, then people were seeing something positive within you which was trying to be reached. Also, if one was demanding of others it also involved a giving over of oneself to another.

In many of my group and individual sessions there is often the search for and an idea that unconditional love exists. Such a concept exists in 'Person Centred Therapy' and other forms of counselling. What exactly does this mean? A phrase which is in vogue is 'quality time,' again what does this mean? I questioned the existence of such a thing as 'unconditional love.' It seems to imply that love exists in a vacuum. I said "that for anything to grow and develop it has to do so in a culture and this depends also upon conditions surrounding the culture." The dialogue within this session which was looking for unconditional scenarios was equally involved with the dynamics of being a victim and victimisation. At one point I asked "is there such a thing as an unconditional victim?" I was unclear why I asked this but

I think it was connected to the idea that a victim, or victimisation, exists in a vacuum waiting to be enacted by another or the perpetrator enacts a situation which forces someone to fill a vacuum of suffering. I was questioned on what I meant by this and, although I couldn't be clear, I said: "have you heard of unconditional surrender?" Unconsciously I was drawing the connections between the victim and the politics of surrender although this was not developed at the time of this session. Upon reflection, after reading this many years later, I am still not clear about its meaning, and it is something I hold in reserve for another day.

There are also many well-known sayings which we can draw upon. In a group session a woman spoke about her attempts to smash her new conservatory. This was linked to a conflict with her husband who told her she was getting precious about something. My immediate association was "those who live in glass houses shouldn't throw stones." Why did I associate with this? What emerged in the session was her urge to externalise internal damage and if she could smash up her conservatory this would show her husband the extent of her rage. By turning the conservatory into shattered, broken glass, this would equal the extent of her inner broken fragments coming into the world. His simple statement: "you're being precious" (this was connected to her reaction to his wanting her to throw away precious keepsakes), missed all of this, minimising and negating her. With further exploration, the notion of smashing the conservatory was linked to the creation of preciousness; something which should be approached with care, respect or reverence and not to be touched and if so, there is a violent reaction. With this in play it was clear that at certain points, there were defensive positions which periodically others got through when the defence doesn't hold.

Creating a Structure for Throwaway Thoughts

Up to this point I have spoken primarily about the origins of my interest in thoughts being discarded. Much of this has been evidenced through what emerged spontaneously. These throwaway thoughts could be described as 'fragments.' However, these 'fragments' proved to be more important than was originally thought, as they either heralded valuable outcomes, that is, what happened next after what was said and its relevance for key points of change. Such changes could be transitory or would have had more lasting effects. We also need to consider what was happening before these inspirational moments which led to that which emerged. The basic premise of "it came out of the blue," as stated earlier, seems to imply that it was floating around in the sky or the ether and landed without permission or control on the recipient's runway. However, a contrasting view may move us back to the psychoanalytic perspective of the rumblings in the resonant unconscious. Equally, this implies a similar message that something has triggered a deep internal recess. Of course, there may be times when the verbal 'outpouring' could be as a result of both sources, 'out of the blue' and 'unconscious,' coming together which could be seen as: a conjunction of things happening in the outside world; synchronistically colliding with deep conscious and even deeper unconscious particles. Looking at it from another angle, in keeping with my findings on therapeutic love and heartfullness, when a particular line or phrase emerges, as I have illustrated and to which I have postulated that it has not materialised in a vacuum, I believe it to be that the heart is the original source. For example, in a group session the spontaneous dialogue may be moving along a particular theme with each member contributing from their own life experiences. Some may not be as verbal but yet they are involved in their own way. The group may well proceed harmoniously and at different points the smooth flowing dialogue turns to disagreement and dispute, throwing things into disarray. Then something may happen, such as an interpretation from the conductor or a similar intervention from a group member, alters the course of the session, lessening the group tension leading it back to a point of harmony.

If we look at this from the therapeutic love framework, the starting and continuing stages of smooth dialogue create an environment of mutuality, with the group's heart creating a flow of dialogue and emotions akin to a symbolic blood flow. Then when things move to more conflictual dynamics the symbolic heart rate increases through the dialogue and other nonverbal expressions. Then, just at certain crescendo points the heart (this time I mean the actual heart) with its deep emotional capacity and wisdom makes an appearance through either a statement or phrase, that is, those which I have labelled as potential thoughts to be thrown away or built upon. I recall a member of one of my groups said: "Wow! Where did that come from Gerry?" when I said something that seemed quite ridiculous and at the end of the session she said: "I see where you're coming from now, but it's still weird!"

There will be similar things at play in individual therapies but the transactions occur linearly between two people. The physical intensity is channelled through them sitting between 3 and 6 feet apart. The arrangement is also a vertical transaction between conscious and unconscious, and a horizontal arrangement, face to face. Nevertheless, I believe, it is still driven by the heart.

How Loud Is a Thought?

Thinking is a silent, internal process making its appearance through the medium of language, building bridges in communication. Yet! In the process of prayer, contemplation, meditation there are beliefs, particularly through prayer, that 'greater' powers are hearing us. It is quietly so loud that the Gods can hear us. Therefore, this internally quiet process of thought carries a powerful message of cutting through the Earthly World, thus giving a direct majestic link to greater powers. However, in day to day living and psychotherapy generally, the internal silent thinking, which for the thinker has varying levels of volume, has to cross the divide. As we follow this developmental line in the ongoing discourse and dialogue of inner silent thoughts to the formation of speech and hearing, those thoughts, some of which have been deemed fodder to be thrown away, they will be created and heard differently. Those deemed to be of potentially greater significance will be heard as if they have acquired increased decibels. Let me illustrate this. Before one of my group sessions, I had a dream in which I was discussing various points of abstraction in my private and work life. At the end of the dream, either my colleague or I said: "abstraction will lead to clarity!" just before waking. Returning to the session, the group were struggling with the conflict between being 'proud of oneself' and being 'full of oneself.' The former was a statement of positive affirmation, the latter a phrase of boasting. My dream came back to me as the session progressed. The group oscillated between these phrases and how they were experienced in their personal lives as well as their interpersonal relations in the group, that is, those who were proud of their developments and those who were irritatingly bragging, boasting, devaluing others. As things progressed the groups verbal volume increased and gradually they were reaching points of unity, that is, those who had difficulty in being proud were afraid of others critical impressions of them. Those who were boastful struggled with emptiness and worthlessness. At one point I intuitively shared my 'close of dream' sentence 'abstraction will lead to clarity.' I said that this seemed to mirror the group's struggles which were being worked through, that is, there were many abstractions to be considered within positivity and negativity. A further theoretical formulation could be postulated

> Abstraction = stretching out thoughts/ideas → greater clarity → multiple points of clarity.

The converse of such a group session is when groups are in a more fragile state. Individuals are withdrawn from one another and are disturbed in their 'fragmented separateness,' concretising the fragmentation and solidifying abstraction. The group may therefore be equated with a recurring dream instead of a section of waking reality. As the group is formed each week for their session it is as if they move into a dream world from the external waking life.

Patients Phrases

As stated earlier, there have been many times when a patient says something or reaches new levels of insight that encapsulate a moment in time. Sayings and phrases will have covert and overt meanings whereas others are beyond comprehension. Some will also have particular intents, that is, when a patient says: "I don't want to go there." At other times there are well known sayings like:

- The grass is greener on the other side = wishful expectations being elsewhere.
- You can't have your cake and eat it = expecting too much.

Such phrases often rely on the use of analogy and metaphor. In my experience I have found that the over-use of metaphor/analogies can represent a method/way of defending against the disclosure of more intimate details. One phrase I have used to deal with this is: "you're trying to put us off the scent, a bit like escaping through water to stop the dogs following."

In one of my groups one or more members kept asking questions to other members: "How are you in yourself?" This was meant with friendly good intent but developed into a repetitive introduction. It sounded like a superficial enquiry in the hope of a 'deeper self' response. Nearly always the response was: "I can't complain! No one listens if I do!" This doesn't allow for the positive properties of complaining – it's letting off steam and little to do with a response. Often in both individual and group therapy people have described how they interact with close family and friends with such phrases as: "It's anything for an easy life," "I'm trying to please" or "We try to get along." Such phrases could also be statements of appeasement, possibly a way of flattening or converting anger and other dynamical forces. If we question these in situ it will assist in not allowing these to be used as 'throwaway thoughts' and dialogue.

The phrase: 'tied up' is fairly common as is 'tied down.' Someone may not be contactable and are said to be 'tied up.' Being 'tied down' often reflects being psychologically restricted or/and oppressed. Both terms will also have literal meanings for those patients who have suffered actual traumatic abuse. When patients speak about high levels of emotional struggle and confusing thoughts, they may use the phrase: 'I feel tied up in knots,' sometimes located in the stomach region. A lesser conflictual saying: 'I can't see the wood for the trees' gives a similar picture. When such sayings and phrases emerge in therapy settings they can be missed or ignored as just superfluous links in language occupying the spaces between really important things to be reached. In a group session the 'tied up' theme emerged. Indeed, much of this was how I felt tied in a number of ways through the session. Although this theme was common to everyone in the group it was dominated by two members. Sharon, over many weeks and months spoke and raged about her unhappy childhood and how she was mistreated by all whom she came into contact with. The more we all tried to help, clarify, identify and agree with, the more Sharon maintained her intransigence. So, everyone was 'tied up' in meaningless repetition and the bonds and knots tightened. Rachael, in a not so entrenched way, spoke about being tied to her father. Her father has lived his life through 'doing for' and 'giving to' Rachael. Even though Rachael complains the group makes many suggestions for change, she remains tied. For both of them this is clearly a very difficult set of dynamics begging to be changed with the counter of the fear of change being maintained. Equally, it was a struggle for the whole group. The 'being tied' complex of words could have been potentially lost or thrown away. At the close of this session, I built on this and I said: "although you are trying, and in part succeeding to help one another, to untie 'the knots' and disentangle things, it really comes down to each person to see how they can do this."

"Put a lid on it!" is another relatively common phrase, which may be used when someone doesn't want to continue with hearing another. It is a terminating phrase. The coffin lid being put on is a stark image. In a group session this term was being resonated to in terms of people needing to find resolutions or ways of stopping repetitive, negative thoughts and actions. At one point Alison spoke about her fear of opening up being like 'Pandora's box.' My immediate thought was 'we wouldn't have heard of Pandora's box if it hadn't been opened.' In the Greek myth, Pandora was forbidden to open it but curiosity got the better of her, thus releasing all the ills that beset man, leaving only hope within, as far as I have understood it. This is so apt within the therapeutic arena, when the ills have been opened up, released and unresolved, hope remains. Hope needs the shackles that tie it down to be undone. This led to a much freer exploration in the group on the release of painful memories and relationship problems which rendered them feeling a little crazy at times and the reactions of trying to put a lid on that which is released/freed in order to understand what has escaped.

Before proceeding with more detailed accounts of thoughts, sayings and phrases let me share some brief snapshots of relevant dialogue:

> Some thoughts are thrown away at the beginning of therapeutic sessions such as when there is a manic release, a high rush of opening up. In my response, I have said such things as: "What's the rush? We have plenty of time. This is like a galloping horse! There is often the wish to run while crawling."

As I was leading one of my groups from the waiting room to the group room Cynthia said:

> We should be given tea and biscuits.

> *Peter:*   "We won't be given that, it's not allowed."

Both sentences are open to be thrown away. However, when we sat down, I came back to this and I said:

> That's what you get when you give blood!

This unconsciously picked up on the groups concerns and developing dialogue on injury, accidents and giving/receiving blood. At one point, Alison pulled out an appointment card she'd received inviting her to give blood. So! The initial statements before going into the group room could have been left outside but were incorporated into the session.

Another variant of discarding is that of moving it, temporarily, to another space, that is, a left luggage department; putting something on hold; mislaying; putting a reserve on it. Phrases like: 'I'll come back to this'; 'for the time being,' that is, it will do me temporarily and then I'll change or discard it. Of course, such temporary arrangements may well become permanent. With all of these scenarios there is an acceptance of something deemed to be transitory with the intention of attending to it later.

In another group session Harry spoke about his concerns for his daughter's life of addiction. As the group was offering their views about his situation he seemed to have had enough and said: "I will put it on the back burner," that is, he would come back at a later point as he couldn't go further with talking about his wayward daughter. In closing I said: "If you put worry on the back burner does that mean that you get stewed anxiety?" This was another abstract thought which I chose to put into the groups cooking pot instead of leaving it unsaid and lost.

The Expansiveness of the Group

So far the illustrations I have presented have focused primarily on things that individuals, including myself, have said or done. In individual therapy, it is easier to focus on specific thoughts in contrast to the multiple possibilities within groups. In the immediate action of the group as it expands through dialogue, the group analyst is working on many levels and sometimes the 'throw away' comments are missed as a result of the groups concern for other matters. Often it is the 'off the cuff' comment which comes in handy in order to put into simple language what may be a complex dynamic. This is not so much a 'throw away' comment but more a 'throw in.' It has the intention of unblocking something or to illuminate a process in the 'group as a whole.' If successful it can create movement, curiosity and push the group back into analytic communication. For example:

The group had reached a point where they faded into both silence and to a lesser degree, glancing out the window, and then back to the floor. This went on for about ten minutes and then I said:

> It's like the floor has become a large magnet and is in control of your separate communications. Periodically some of you have fleeting eye contact or escape to looking out of the window.

I did not have to challenge this as a defensive avoidance and they quickly moved into a lively dialogue in examining the things they were contemplating within the silence and the flight out of the window.

In many group sessions particular patterns will emerge in relation to those who speak and those who remain silent, or individuals who take the lead and others who follow. For example, in one group this became evident with one side of the group maintaining a verbal half circle while the other side looked on silently. Some showed interest while others were removed and bored. This continued for weeks and months. At different times I summoned up various lines: "It's like a set of scales, talkers one side, non-talkers the other" or "This is a bit like a play with the talking on stage, performing, and the audience watching. However, everyone's participating in one way or another." By inputting it in this way it helped to remove the implication that they were doing something wrong.

In another session John was speaking about his struggles with his 16-year-old daughter going out to a dance.

I said: "It will be difficult to accept her as a woman if you can't let the girl go."

He looked puzzled. Quickly the women in the group came in excitedly about their similar struggles with their sons. This brought into relief the fears of their children's growing sexuality. At one point I said

Intercourse is not only about physical sex.

Once again John is puzzled and the women took off which developed into sharing their interpersonal struggles. Further I say:

This seems to be linked to struggles between pessimism and optimism. In the enactment of optimism this is a form of social intercourse and desires for the future.

In the closing part of the session things turned back to the pessimism surrounding illness and the fear of death. Once again, a 'throw in' comment from me:

It's difficult to see anything optimistic about death, but with each death experience these are developmental stages in growing up.

Dave had the last word:

You're on good form tonight, Gerry!

The session ended with rapturous laughter. My interventions worked but there were times when they didn't. When this happens it can be for a number of reasons. It may be that the 'thought' did not fit to the group or individual, or it was totally wrong. At other times it sounded too esoteric and grandiose. The group at such times responds with something like:

"Gerry's off again!" This is not bad as I've been 'brought down a peg' and the group descends into warm laughter. A case in point was when Jenny was speaking about feelings of nothingness and the events in her life when this emerged. I tried to elaborate the other side – somethingness. I spoke of both of these positions being interrelated and how we looked for something in others to fill our own nothingness (emptiness). They looked blankly at me. I paused and said:

Well! That fell on stony ground. I suppose it means something, but not here.

Once again, the group laughter said a lot about how therapeutic love is shown and expressed by their tolerating my flamboyant comments.

Expletives

Where would we be without expletives? There are many terms to describe them, such as swearing, foul language and dirty-mouthed. However, when these are used there will be many meanings and views on their acceptability or not, whether in therapy or life in general. For some in therapy this is helpful by providing space to verbalise thoughts and feelings which are difficult to express in any other way, so this serves a protective purpose for self and others. For others the use of, and being the recipient of the expletive, is an assault on the senses and morality. In a way these expletives are thoughts that are 'thrown away.' For example, in one group session, Clive was in full flow with foul language and at this stage, due to his having started recently in the group, others were permissive. His main bone of contention was his struggles with his boss at work. At one point he asked me: "Is it okay that I'm swearing?" I did not respond one way or the other. Eventually the others gained courage to say that he, Clive, alone was not the sole author of obscenities and gently steered him towards more appropriate language and also their own associations.

The Therapist Swears

A gasp went around the room when I use the word 'fuck.'

Mary: "You're not allowed to swear, you're a therapist!"

Like many people I can use bad language at times. I have rarely used it within the therapeutic setting. For me these have not been phrases/thoughts to be thrown away but have been 'thrown in' to make a point. When I am told that I am not allowed to swear each patient saying this is faced with their image of me and how I have temporarily resigned my role as a therapist, whereas others have valued it as me being human and on a similar level to them. Granted, returning to 'things coming out of the blue' as I began this chapter with, it can send shockwaves throughout the group, either making things better or worse, but one never knows until it is said. There is a constructive intent which may initially be perceived as attacking or shocking, but does not have this intent.

In one group session, two members were dominant throughout. Sarah had initiated things following the previous week, when she began to understand that vulnerability is a strength, not a weakness. In this process she had been feeling more connected to Harry, the other group member. However, this moved into their joint problems with their mothers, which went on for about 30 minutes, with the others being almost spellbound. Then I said:

It may be difficult to just tell someone to fuck off.

Shockwaves ensued with all of them saying: "Gerry you can't say that," "I've never heard you swear," "that's funny!" and "where did that come from?" After a few minutes I expanded for both Sarah and Harry. They wanted to tell their mothers to fuck off but this would be seen as improper. I suggested that to tell someone to fuck off, granted there was an element of anger, was also a statement arising from frustration. It was a direct statement which could stop the frustration. Hence, a new start can then be developed.

The Strokes I Threw Away

The above variation brings to the fore aspects of art therapy, that is, the strokes of the brush, pencil and crayon; the stroke of the hand over clay; and the stroke of creating and discarding.

The majority of what I have presented will be at play in both individual and group analytic art therapy. The emergence of thoughts with potential to be discarded, thrown away, can be evidenced in nonverbal ways and through the concrete art materials. When the artistic creations are being made, this involves forming strokes and stroking out elements that either fit or not. This may be specific if it is a conscious/intended creation. If it is more abstract and spontaneous, with no fixed intent, the formation permits freer 'stroking in' or 'stroking out.' Like primarily verbal therapies a whole range of dynamical elements will be at play. As the concrete image is formed, particular symbols, colours and spaces may be seen as superfluous and are rubbed out = thrown away. The creator may miss the value of these which are then subsequently lost. Another aspect can be seen if the creator is disappointed or unhappy with the picture and throws it away or by painting over it, creating something new and leaving it covered with formless colour. Even when someone moves from the blank page to construction, this could also be seen as throwing the blank page away. This may be seen as positive in the move from emptiness to fullness but it may also be a way of not exploring the blank page, and allowing self and others entry, a bit like a smokescreen.

Things can also become more literal. Concrete images, whether partial or fully complete, can take on a life of their own, that is, an embodied image. This is in keeping with Schaverien's views although hers are more erudite than mine (Schaverien, 1992, pp. 79–102). On the positive side, the image can embody an achievement or a part of one's life becoming joyous and successful. It is then kept intact, like a great work of art. However, if it exhibits and embodies negative, unhappy, destructive components, it may be cut or torn up and in its most raw manifestation – set on fire = cathartic release. Regarding the use of clay, this will be a more tactile expression. Try as hard as one can to discard the concrete clay image it returns to its base property – clay. As one can imagine such elements will need to be handled with great care. An ultimate destructive rare situation can arise with attempted and actual suicide. Then, not only the concrete image and thoughts are thrown away, but the person's life. This comment applies across the therapeutic board.

In a similar way to primarily verbal groups all of the constituent's will be present in the art group. Some variations may be of people diminishing their art work in contrast to their peers: "Your picture is beautiful, I can't paint." Group members throwing away the value of spontaneous creations: "I was just doodling it doesn't mean anything!" People throwing away their own unique creative struggle when they copy others art works, or short circuit struggles with deeper unformed thoughts and feelings by repeated use of writing words.

Final Thoughts on This Chapter

Words that are thrown on a page will find their own way. Books cannot be written until the first words are thrown down like a 'gauntlet.' The art of 'throwing' pottery depends on 'sheer feel' and 'muscle memory,' which is also employed in the world of golf and possibly the majority of sports. When thoughts spontaneously emerge, it is possible that a psychic key and lock system has been activated. Something has triggered the thoughts, and then a word, phrase or concept has thrown life into it. When such processes occur between people, a dynamic spark has been struck. How often has Martin Luther King Jr's "dream" speech been used by others with great impact.

Throw away words?

Note

1 No direct English translation.

Chapter 14

Outside the Consulting Room

Intuition – The Language of the Heart

Is 'therapeutic love' different from compassion, caring, empathy, sympathy, benevolent understanding? Every therapist, as far as I understand it requires all of the above, and more. However, I believe it is possible to experience such emotions/frames of mind without an affectual, palpable attachment, as occurs with therapeutic love and heartfullness. Therapeutic love is both visible and invisible. By this I mean that once the heart's power and influence come into play one can see a great deal more of the emotional experiences of all parties, yet there is a great deal more unseen. Psychoanalysts and psychotherapists who would not entertain the notion of therapeutic love will, in all certainty, experience empathy, compassion, pleasure, humour etc., but may intellectually translate these into analytic material, waiting to be interpreted. Therefore, a primary difference is that 'therapeutic love' creates and fosters a direct/immediate link/route between the heart as a dominant force and the mind, while the formal psychodynamic models have a more intellectual route. With more formal models and psychotherapeutic perspectives, particular feelings, such as compassion, caring and sympathy, can be experienced at a distance through the intellect.

With these points in mind the specific dimensions of invisibility/visibility are quite difficult to grasp and define. This can be considered when the patient is telling their life stories and the therapist is listening, translating and responding or not. As each emotional plane becomes manifest during the session, one can see physical expressions of the patient through such things as rate of speech; emotional cathexis; physical manifestations through laughter and tears; outbursts, which at times can be physical; and unconscious somatic expressions such as breathing difficulties, headaches and dryness of the mouth as just a few examples. From the therapist's side, this is more passive with a visible stillness apart from his/her mouth opening to convey what is felt to be necessary – or not. Equally the therapist may also have physical reactions as stated for the patient both on a conscious and unconscious level, part of which may also be invisible. Turning to invisibility dimensions both parties, patient/therapist, have to experience their inner worlds and how the complexities of their inner experiences are either held within and for what purpose,

DOI: 10.4324/9781003536857-17

while the process of movement into the external spaces between them is developed. On its simplest level, the patient has a dialogue with their inner world and conveys it to the therapist, or remains silent, the therapist responds or not.

When we compare psychoanalysis and psychodynamic therapy with the concept of 'therapeutic love and heartfullness' a different picture emerges. True, similar processes are at play between both the therapist and the patient. One cannot initially have visibility to each other's internal world. Then, when particular events and/or emotions emerge it is the heart which stirs and creates a bridge in the strength of its presence. Distance is negated and direct affect occurs with both being joined at the heart.

It is within this dimension, that intuition and instinct play their parts. With this in mind one can see the complexities of the therapeutic encounters within the enclosed spaces of the consulting room. A major leap is then required in moving outside the frame of the session, both psychologically, and at times concretely, demands much from all invested parties. In beginning to address 'that which is external' to the therapy, the less definable, unpredictable and controllable factors now come into play.

There are many things that are involved beyond the actual therapeutic venture. I dare to suggest that many therapeutic professionals would agree with me that possibly even larger contributing factors are those challenges beyond the consulting room. The management and handling of such extracurricular can be extremely important, which will either make or break the therapy; the patient; the therapist. Many of such scenarios have to be given a great deal of thought and care. Much of this is also processed and dealt with through instinct and intuition, as stated earlier. There are a wide range of events and experiences which I have encountered over many years.

I am reminded of an event in which I acted through putting things in motion outside the session. I had been seeing Victoria for individual psychotherapy for approximately two years. There had been a number of crises during this period. I shall not go into details of what led up to, or constituted this particular crisis, which I am about to elaborate. There had been a number of life events which exacerbated her existing state of anxiety and depression following particularly moving sessions which I felt had held a great deal of significance for her. She 'went missing' and I was contacted by relatives, friends and other professionals expressing their concern. She did not respond to any of my phone calls and eventually our 'crisis intervention team' and the police were brought into action. Eventually Victoria telephoned me from her home apologising for missing her appointment and was oblivious to the extensive concern generated. As we were speaking, I assumed from a room removed from the front door, there was loud banging. I heard the policeman's voice shouting for her to open the door. Straight away her anxiety rose saying:

It's the police Gerry, what do they want?

I told her they had been looking for her. While everyone had been running around fearing the worst, she had decided to go away to a hotel in order to have space to think. Many people will do this without any scenarios of police hunts happening but obviously those close to Victoria felt they had cause for concern. As we were speaking on the phone with the police shouting through the letter box opening, I then had to act like a crisis negotiator between Victoria and the police, so as they wouldn't break her door down. I was able to do this by agreeing to come to her house straight away to be with her while the police interviewed her. The 'therapeutic frame' which we had of only meeting in the consulting room no longer applied. Subliminally this event may well have activated a therapeutic love component of a child gone missing being found by the police alive and being reunited with its parents. This would not be alleviated through waiting for the next therapeutic session being convened. Were there other synchronistic forces at play which made her phone me minutes before the police arrived?

Synchronicity has been written about extensively in psychotherapeutic literature, for example, Jung is well known for this, that is, collected works (Jung, 1969, pp. 417–531). In contrast to Jung's views, I was drawn to the novelist Russel Hoban. In his book, 'The Lion of Boaz-Jachin and Jachin-Boaz' (Hoban, 1973) Hoban paints a beautiful picture of synchronicity in which an estranged father and son are reunited by bringing to life the lion, at a time when there were no lions, with both father and son creating pictorial images from two distant points. I cannot do justice to synopsising the book. However, the synchronistic vein, as it appears to me, was central to all of his books that I read.

Some years later a female patient raised considerable concerns. Cynthia was going through a particularly traumatic period in her life and had reached a crescendo of despair in her therapy with me. At the closing moments of a session she said something which, although not overly concerning as it was dressed up with reassuring facial expressions, raised my concern that she may attempt self damage or suicide. I struggled with Cynthia's one parting sentence, for confidentiality's sake I will not quote it. It was as if her heart was speaking to mine which motivated me to act as I did. There was something about this sentence which I was intuiting as a warning message. As I worked in close proximity, the same building, as our crisis intervention team, I sought their advice. There were practical risks in contacting her based upon her wish for certain people not to know that she was in therapy which would be compromised through direct personal intervention from professional agencies. My concerns were deemed valid and that emergency action was required and the crisis team went to her home. They arrived at a point when she was just preparing to overdose on medication. This was clearly fortuitous in that it stopped a serious attempt at suicide to which, some time later, Cynthia was very grateful. However, the immediate 'fallout' of this had strong repercussions as it disrupted her family life further, causing a great deal of conflict to develop. There was also a strong negative reaction to me which took many months to work through and resolve. I was blamed for making things worse. However, if I had not acted as I did would she have killed herself? No one knows, but as I had strong evidence from her past, I felt that she may have gone through with it. I think that also a part of her was wanting me to know and act by the way she had phrased the sentence which evoked my concern in the first place.

A new thought emerges from these reflections. Certainly, my knowledge of the patient played a part in this but there were other previous times when she had said things which brought my concern but not to the same extent. In this case it was my intuition that said this particular sentence was different. Does this then lead to the question: 'is intuition a language of the heart as stated at the opening of this chapter?' I have written in more detail about intuition in a previous publication where I was hypothesizing that 'intuition is wisdom without words' (McNeilly, 2006b, p. 154). This is not so far removed from seeing intuition also as a language of the heart (McNeilly, 2006b, pp. 153–160). This is akin to my defining resonance as the 'Language of the Dynamic Silence' (McNeilly, 2006b, p. 38). My heart was opened up through a disguised message which resonated to deep pain and despair with her heart which was silently crying out through a disguised sentence. Would I act differently now, knowing the many later months of turmoil and attack I had to work through with her? I would! Therapeutic love is also about a willingness to immerse oneself in such difficult and demanding transactions when one has to act in this way outside the consulting room. There are particularly difficult clinical conditions which demand greater external demands and dynamics such as:

Dissociative Identity Disorder (DID) – That Which I Do Not Wish to Write About

I have spent the majority of my working life with people with extremely complex psychological conditions. It is not my intention to go into detail on those people with D.I.D but I want to emphasise that to be involved with this client group one cannot maintain a strict psychodynamic psychotherapy discipline in respect to methodology. Simply, I want to share some brief snapshots of my work with such patients. For those readers not accustomed with this diagnosis it has replaced the old term of 'multiple personality disorder.' It is an extremely controversial diagnosis, although clearly defined in the DSM 5™. Some dismiss the diagnosis while referring to it as a 'false memory syndrome.' The phrase in italics above relates to my resistance to writing about this difficult condition as it meant that I would have to remember and re-experience varying levels of trauma for the patients and myself.

I had been seeing Gloria for about a year and one day when I was with another patient, I heard shouting, screaming and banging outside my room. I was interrupted by my secretary who needed me to attend to Gloria who had come for her session and was creating havoc. She was running wild in an upstairs room banging the walls with her head and fists and there was a real risk of hurting herself or falling out of an upstairs window. Like earlier, with Cynthia, I once more had to become a crisis negotiator, but as well as verbally I had to physically restrain Gloria. I had to hold her in such a way as it would not be too restrictive, steering clear of body areas which could evoke traumatic memories. At the same time I was speaking with her different dissociative personality identities. This physical demand was extremely taxing and her strength far exceeded her small body weight.

This went on for in excess of one hour until an ambulance arrived to take her to a general and then a psychiatric hospital. I was also tasked with having to accompany her and carry on with my role as a negotiator with other doctors and nurses who knew nothing about this diagnosis. Once again, the unexpected shift from being her psychotherapist to moving into being an actual practical container was called for. This, I believe, is another variant of therapeutic love. I had to act without a great deal of analytic thought as my 'Charge' was in danger.

Paula also has D.I.D. In the early stages of her therapy a sequence of crisis events occurred over a two-month period, culminating in her being attacked by a stranger when she was experiencing one of her child identities, resulting in extreme dissociation. This then brought into relief heightened level of anxieties emerging with allied professionals, particularly Social Services and her children's school. This heralded the professionals fear, raising the possibility of her children being removed due to her being seen as an unfit mother.

Although this did not carry the same demands as I encountered with Gloria, it was similar in that I had to deal with, and allay, other professional's concerns as they had no comprehension of such a complex condition. As well as increasing my sessions with Paula I eventually had to attend a formal Social Services review. Unexpectedly I was being seen as 'the expert,' similar to an 'expert witness' in a court case. Due to the high level of concern I felt I was being bullied into giving a 'definitive' statement that nothing further would go wrong. It was also difficult to convey what was 'right' with Paula that had helped her deal with a very traumatic past and lifestyle which had played its part in forming the dissociative identities. Once again, the question of therapeutic love emerges. It is true that much is required in working analytically during the sessions in the process of trying to achieve optimal levels of personality integration. At the same time I had to deal with unforeseen events and critical incidents which necessitated acting outside the consulting room. Another analogy of 'running by the seat of one's pants' comes to mind. Here one is constantly changing positions and internal/external perspectives. It is not an easy task to 'move with' the patient through multiple personality presentations to unforeseen events, then bringing these back for further exploration. With less complex patients, although complex in their own right for different reasons, the therapist is not pressed in the same external reality way. The person with D.I.D has to deal with an ever-present state of flux which, on the whole, is unpredictable. Of the five separate D.I.D patients I have seen, that once they became aware of their condition, they were able to develop lifestyles which accommodated such unpredictability. Nevertheless, they were at times ruled by their switching personalities, sometimes with severe and serious consequences. These switches brought with them full or partial amnesia and time loss. This also brought major challenges, not least whether I believed in the authenticity of their diagnosis. I did believe their diagnosis to be genuine. To be believed is important for all psychotherapeutic alliances. If it is not present the therapist may not be convinced or committed to helping the patient. Trust has to be imbued but trust may have little to do with what can be proven true or not. Would we trust someone who says: trust me!?

As stated earlier it is not my intention to expand in any detail on this complex diagnosis. My intention has been more to draw attention/focus upon the relationship between myself and the patient in regards to how this fits with the concepts of therapeutic love. During therapeutic sessions one is dealing with fracture and fragments as the patient unfolds and unravels their life stories. Depending on the severity of the original trauma experience and its eventual symptomatic formation, at times numerous personalities, the therapist equally has to move with and through this labyrinth. There were many times when I felt as if I was fracturing and fragmenting. The patient has to live with this 24/7 whereas I lived it one to three hours a week, although seeping through to the rest of my life.

Such scenarios are something of a headache for psychotherapists working along the lines of conventional transference/countertransference methodology. With D.I.D the therapist has to be prepared to be constantly on the move between one presentation and the next. Therapeutic love with the D.I.D person is not so different to those with other severe personality disorders who will present their own challenges. In a strange way one could say that the 'personality disorders' are a 'multiple framework,' having at least ten subcategories, as noted in the DSM 5™ with further lesser derivatives and cross overs. The true D.I.D could be seen as multiple separates rolled into one person. The therapeutic work with D.I.D becomes much more intensified at times when further action is required, such as with Cynthia, Paula and Gloria. When things in their therapy became calmer and more accessible it was enough to identify and empathise with their emotional states where my heart was dominant, as I have alluded to earlier. With D.I.D the emotional states need active response and guidance. At one point Gloria told me that I should get paid for group therapy in seeing her. My experience as a group analyst almost confirmed this and came to my assistance at difficult times.

Levels of Concern

As I began to formulate my thoughts upon wide and far reaching points of reference I realised that these ranged over a 'complex level of difficulties' which demanded varying levels of response. As such these put increasing demands on the working relationship within the face-to-face therapeutic sessions. One could assume that having to attend to external factors would have damaged the therapeutic relationship, but I found to the contrary. On the whole, experiencing and going through these challenges, strengthened much of the work. I even saw these as essential elements of the psychotherapeutic ventures. Of course, many psychotherapies are simply conducted within the confines of a regular weekly arrangement, as one sees in private therapy, in which both, or more, parties meet and then go their separate ways. There may indeed be points of crisis in which the therapist provides phone contact or additional sessions and within this context the therapist can maintain a relatively private distance, allowing the therapeutic frame to hold. However, with the more complex and severe clinical diagnosis, further disturbing demands may erode and undermine the frame. Much depends on the therapist's ability to deal with these developments, their flexibility and how such things are brought back to the sessions and made use of. For example, a crisis that emerges through a suicidal enactment, along with a hospital admission, is a case in point. At such times does the therapist visit the patient in the Hospital or not as one of the external challenges.

When the same or similar challenges emerge within the National Health Service departments, the picture can be more expansive and/or extreme. Patients in these settings, particularly those with more complex diagnosis such as personality disorders, often see psychotherapy as the main or key package of care within a multi-system approach. This increases the number of other agencies, such as general practitioners, psychiatrists, social services, hospital admissions, medication and crisis intervention teams. So, here one can see that there is much to be considered 'outside the consulting room.'

Level 1

If things are held within the simple arrangement of level 1, where the patient/group attends their session and then goes home, there may be little recourse for concern on external matters, apart from the odd General Practitioner involvement, phone consultation, or an extra session. Some crisis can also be contained within a simple level 1 but how this is managed depends on the working relationship between patients and therapists.

General Points of Consideration

Setting aside those therapies within private practice I have noted over many years particular areas outside the consulting room that need to be kept in mind when establishing a psychotherapeutic package. Each of the following areas needs careful management so as to ensure that the therapy runs as smoothly as possible, and each requires a great deal of mutuality between therapist, patient and others. Here are some points of note:

- Written correspondence, that is, professional assessment reports.
- Personal liaison with medical practitioners.
- Links to psychiatric hospitals.
- Multiple professional agencies working alongside.
- Home visits.
- Working with relatives of the nominated patient.
- Supervision – This is necessary on all levels.

All of the above, will be relatively easy to deal with for the greater percentage of time but there are times when things can go wrong, leading to:

Level 2: More Difficult

As stated above some critical events can be dealt with more easily and defused. But if the crisis is more extreme and potentially dangerous, this will demand greater involvement with a number of agencies, that is, an attempted suicide following a regressive period. This may necessitate hospital admission, some continuing contact with the therapist, re-engagements with psychotherapy afterwards or moving to an alternative therapy.

In the case of groups, a more difficult scenario is when groups form alliances outside. This can be through pairing or even whole group formations. This will happen for many reasons and consequently undermines and potentially fragments the group. This can become malignant and if not resolved can lead to destruction of the group.

Impact on Others

Happily, for me there have been relatively few negative impacts on others connected to those who have been in therapy with me. However, it is not uncommon for patient's partners, relatives, friends to be impacted one way or another, that is, the husband says "I want my old wife back!" or, as one patients partner wrote to me and said: "Thank you so much for helping Mary. You should know how much this has helped me and our children!" or when a patient gets better and then their spouse deteriorates, as some illustrations.

Pregnancy

Many patients will struggle to get pregnant; become pregnant; struggle with fears and look towards abortion; unexpected pregnancies for whatever reason. Although this is created 'outside the consulting room' that in the nine-month gestation period many things will come into play in the balance and transitions from outside to inside. This is a complex area whether in individual or group therapy. There have been many pregnancies during my career which have carried significant levels of importance, that is, groups claiming the newly born as a 'group baby'; mothers bringing their new born to the group sessions or to celebrate the birth with the group or me; in individual therapy when one patient almost went into the early stages of labour in a session; those patients who wanted to continue with their therapy up to the last minute and getting back, sometimes as soon as days and weeks following delivery. So, the interchange between inner and outer has many levels of significance.

Chance Encounters

Although this area of concern is within level 2, sometimes an unexpected meeting outside is simpler and more conducive to the ongoing therapy. Much depends on the actual therapy and at what stage it happens. There can be negative outcomes if the therapy is at a level of impasse. It may also offer a link with external reality which gives pleasure and warmth in the therapeutic relationship. Some of my personal illustrations were when I unexpectantly met my patients in bars, restaurants, my golf club, in a swimming pool, on holiday in Thailand (that's some coincidence), a train station, in shops and supermarkets, seeing me playing music at a concert. I recall a chance meeting with two patients together, a mother and daughter, at a large music venue. The interesting thing was that both had been my individual patients at different times. On another occasion two men, Mike and John, were speaking in a group session. Mike owned a garage/car sales and John saw no harm in my cutting a financial deal with Mike on a car. "What's wrong with putting business Mike's way?" He could not see the relevance of this in the group:

John: "What happens in the world outside has nothing to do with the group!"
Mike: "I don't agree with you John!"

I had told the group that, by chance, I had gone to Mike's garage when I was look-ing to buy a new car and had met Mike there. We agreed that I would not pursue the matter but it was nice to see he was doing so well.

John to me: "You should have been able to separate social pleasure from business!"

He implied that I had a problem.

Mike: "It could have caused us both problems!"

Meeting in Patient's Homes

There have been a few times when I have had to go to patient's homes, whether it was to deal with an unexpected event, or conducting a period of therapy. I have spoken about this in more detail earlier when my patient was confined to bed with a broken back. Such incidents are more difficult to deal with as they raise issues around technique and method. Another demand on the therapeutic frame having to be broken was that on two occasions I had to help a patient leave the locked build-ing we were meeting in through a window as the emergency alarm raged.

Major Incident

There are times when things emerge in sessions which promotes the patient to physically move 'outside the consulting room.' This may happen if something is so difficult to deal with, whether emotionally or physically, the patient tunes out emo-tionally or actually leaves the room. There are times when something occurs which is out of control of the therapist or patient/group. An extreme situation was when we had to tell the group someone they knew had been murdered which had, under-standably, an extremely powerful impact with 'that out there being that in here.' Such a powerful dynamic occurring 'outside the consulting room' takes a consider-able inordinate period of time to be processed and integrated and gives credence to how psychotherapy is anything but direct face to face contact in a small, confined space of time. On reflection one positive element in this is that it was not an art group which would surely have brought powerful images immediately to the fore leading to extreme emotional exposure in too short a time. Certainly, art groups, as well as primarily verbal groups, create imagery in sessions dealing with severe trauma, self damage and suicide.

Level 3: World Influences

All psychotherapy occurs within the world we live in even though it exists as confidential and private arrangements. Sometimes the world and its political manifestations imposes or breaks through into the consulting room. The survival of psychotherapy departments in the NHS has been depended on political circumstances. I have been involved, at times alongside my patients, with fights against closure of my department. On one occasion this reached a 'Question' in the British Houses of Parliament when our concern on potential closure was discussed. On the grander scale of things the 'world conflicts' such as the Gulf and Bosnian Wars have created many scenarios ranging from painful associations to dealing with actual death of friends and loved ones. There were times when I got it wrong during the Bosnian War. The group was dealing with a number of painful struggles at home but the main dialogue revolved around the Bosnian conflict which I questioned as an avoidance. It would have been more helpful to address what connected them. With the fallout of the 'Twin Towers' in New York, possibly there has been hundreds, if not thousands of drawings/paintings of the towers crumbling in art therapy sessions. Maybe the COVID-19 symbol has entered art therapy rooms. Who can have missed that little red/black spiked bouncing ball on our television screens?

Impact on Therapists

Do you leave it behind after work? This is the type of question I, and other therapists, will be asked at one time or another. Although I have proffered glib, well thought out responses, the simple fact is that 'It' never left me as I would travel home on the train or car cogitating as I went with many outcomes, some more resolved than others. Forty years later particular events have remained unresolved. As the chapter's title suggests, this happens 'outside the consulting room,' making its way back to the consulting room. I came across a few beautiful comments written by Marion Millner in 1934 and republished in 1986, which succinctly describes such processes:

> Once on a night journey in a train when I could not sleep for the crowd of day impressions which ran through my head, I happened to 'feel myself' down in my heart and immediately my mind was stilled that in a few moments I fell

into peaceful sleep. But it surprised me to think that I lived for twenty five years without ever discovering that such an internal placing of awareness was possible.

(Millner, 1986, p. 69)

Experiencing the present with the whole of my body instead of with the pin point of my intellect led me to all sorts of new knowledge and new contentment. I began to guess what it might mean to live from the heart instead of the head, and I began to feel movements of the heart which told me surely what I wanted than any making of lists.

(Millner, 1986, p. 178)

From a dream:
   Then I said, 'the self in all these things does not know, it just is. I will sink down into my heart and just be.'

(Millner, 1986, p. 185)

It was also around Millner's time when Ferenczi was developing his own adaptation to psychoanalysis which brought into relief love in therapy. Thompson speaks of Ferenczi's technique.

The analyst may demonstrate a reluctance to provide the necessary adaptation to analysands needs by, for example, being unavailable for extra analytic sessions or not responding to phone calls between sessions. The conclusion drawn by the analysand in this scenario is that the analyst is not able to provide the holding environment required for the regression to dependence to proceed further.

(Thompson, 1943, pp. 64–66)

So, this shows historically early considerations which are similar to my own formulations beyond the therapeutic session.

The following illustrations are brief snapshots related to external factors.

External Influences

1   In a group session, that on entering the room, a burglar alarm was raging in the vicinity for over an hour of the groups time. As the session progressed the dialogue revolved around the times when they had broken down through their illness. Simone had raised her current fears on her more general battles to eradicate woodworm from her house. The momentum of the dialogue intensified in speaking about their vulnerabilities and strengths. I said at one point: "Like this irritating burglar alarm, and symbolically like woodworm, once health has been broken into by illness, life becomes difficult."

2   In the therapeutic community where I worked, much depended on understanding and incorporating what goes on outside the therapy rooms and using this

within the overall community dynamics. On one occasion, there was a 'critical incident' that necessitated an armed police response. This was at a time when there were world events that necessitated such a response, possibly an over-reaction at the time. However, the bottom line was that instead of the patient intending a destructive action to the community residents it was based on a wish to be re-admitted. The world outside was dangerous and unloving and possibly he yearned for the love of the community.

3   The Power Cut

In an evening group session, after about 20–30 minutes the lights went out and total darkness ensued. The local neighbourhood was in darkness and we decided to sit it out until power was resumed, which took a further 20–30 minutes.

Initially no-one seemed bothered and there was humorous banter and play-ful comments. I felt that the silent anxiety and fear of the dark was not being voiced. They were being brave. As things developed there were accounts of factual elements not being accepted, that is, Tanya had been divorced for some time and could not accept the losses incurred. Harry was also battling with not being able to accept that his children who were now grown up and did not want contact with him. At one point following the 'non-acceptance' dia-logue I said: "I wonder if the dark felt comfortable or anxiety ridden?" there were a few grunts which were impossible to see from whom. Some acknowl-edged the discomfort others saw it as practical. Then just as I was voicing what I thought was an appropriate interpretation, the light came on and we all fell about laughing. This seemed to dispel the anxiety and even though they moved away from the more difficult dynamics which were evident in the dark-ness, it did not feel evasive.

4   Contacts and Relations Beyond the Patients/Groups Authority

When people enter individual therapy or join psychotherapy groups, there will be attempts and safeguards put in place to maintain the privacy and con-fidentiality of the arrangement. This can at times be difficult as a result of 'unforeseen' circumstances. In small village and town communities this can be especially problematic to manage so as to ensure that friends and relatives would not accidently come across one another in therapy. Safeguards are 'writ-ten in' prior to initial assessments. Fortunately, this has held firm on most occa-sions. One practical approach was that I asked new patients at assessment if they knew of anyone in therapy within my service, but not their names or fur-ther details. I also had a wall map of the local community and I placed pins on patient's addresses in order to indicate potential neighbours, so as I was able to facilitate the logistics.

An illustration of how this went wrong was that Clara joined a group where Hilary had current membership. They were distant neighbours and had sporadic practical community social involvement, but were not really friends. With dis-cussion they both felt that continuing in the same group would not be problem-atic (famous last words). Things went smoothly for a few months. This began to spiral down. This also brought into relief unresolved feelings in Hilary's life and her own relationships with the group. After many months Clara left the group and Hilary remained. Hilary had been able to process just what this unforeseen event had meant to her, Clara did not. By accidentally meeting Clara in the group Hilary had been obstructed in her use of the group. It took us many months to work through this period.

There is a variant of this when two, or more, group members form potentially harmful alliances within the group. The actual joining together of people in this way is unforeseen, but there will be something that draws them together initially and then making this into a concrete relationship outside. Although this will be seen to be happening at some point in the groups life there have been times when I heard, months, or years afterwards, that liaisons and friendships had formed after therapy, so therefore it is not always negative. I recall one group was split in which four of the members were constantly dissatisfied, unhappy that I and the group was not helpful or making them worse. The other four were enthusiastic and favourable about the group, feeling the others were attacking the group. Unbeknown to me the negative faction had formed their own subgroup outside in a local café, preparing a plan of attack in the following session. Although the group survived there were casualties. It was difficult to see if the seeds were sown inside or outside the consulting room.

There are also times when the interchange between outside and inside the group becomes more complex with a range of warring factors: in a group session Steve told the group that he'd been drinking alcohol before the group. This was followed by Michelle being somewhat loud and forceful with Karen in trying to get close to her. It transpired that Michelle had also been drinking just before the group. So, at this early stage the group was dominated by fast and conflicting dialogue which threatened the group with a potential stoppage of the session as alcohol was not acceptable before the session. As the session progressed I was silently, with an internal desperateness, trying to make sense of it all, along with some verbal interactions aimed at bringing the internal/external splits together. Then I decided to claim my authority in a more direct way. I told Michelle and Steve that I would normally tell people to leave the session but I felt we should hold the group together even though I wanted to throw them out. If this happened again, I would eject them, and their therapy would likely be curtailed. Sadly, I think that this did not work as the session continued on the fumes of alcohol, with extreme, exaggerated, tearful 'drink talk,' with confessions of secrets and desires for false intimacy. Symbolically, the group's wall/boundary became permeable. I think that by my not taking up my authority and throwing the drinkers out was a mistake which took many months to work through, which had both favourable and unfavourable outcomes. If I had thrown Michelle and Steve out, they would probably have gone to the 'pub' across the road and become 'drinking buddies.' The following diagram illustrates this:

Interacting Challenges[1]

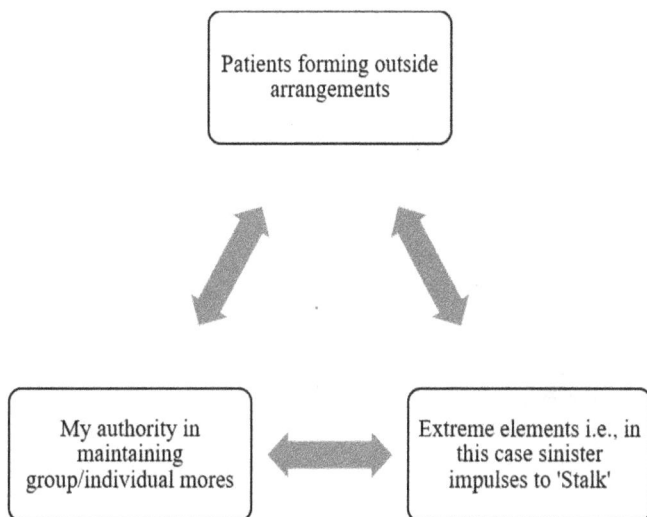

Not all things that occur outside the consulting room are so difficult or controversial. In one of my groups, there was a desire that they, apart from two members, meet together outside socially on other occasions, maybe for a drink or a meal. However, Belinda felt otherwise. She imagined that they would not be able to function as a group because we were here for a different purpose. There was some merit in this, but also in the others' desire to strengthen their personal relationships as the group had been a positive part of their lives. Jamie spoke about a previous period, a year or so ago, that the group had gone for a drink without me. It could not be enjoyed as they all felt they really should not have been there, but it also helped one quieter and shyer member to come out of her shell. However, this did not transit back into the group with a move back to her original position.

There has also been times when I would mentally and physically move out of the group premises, or individual therapies, depending on the situation. These were times when, due to practical reasons, I could not use rooms to see people, so I met with them outside. Now we were 'truly outside,' that is, in the garden. Although there was some benefit in continuance of the session, this never really worked well. With individual patients I never met with them beyond their sessions, although for some we had a coffee following our final meeting. For others, after considerable lengths of time, they made contact with me after completion of therapy and we'd meet in a café. Such meetings were for short periods of time and mainly catching up on a more social/surface dialogue.

Although for some there was unresolved separation dynamics, on the whole these meetings were about a continuance of the therapies influence into the patient's life developments. With one of my long-standing groups, we had a meal together after our last session. The current membership had been together for between two and seven years. One member even brought her partner to the meal. There was talk of them continuing without me but they realised that they would be building on their friendships as compared to meeting as patients. I also felt that I was letting go of friends and I felt the parting in my heart. Was I over-involved? Possibly, but 'so what'? I liked and loved them in a therapeutic way as they did with me.

Legal Matters – Court Cases – Confidentiality

As stated at the beginning of the chapter confidentiality and privacy are of the greatest importance in our work. However, at times confusion arises in just what each of these words mean. Many of the 'directives' established to define and uphold such principles are created and developed 'outside the consulting room' and then filter through to the therapy in action. I shall also speak of the times when privacy and confidentiality were seriously compromised and critically threatened, no more so when the external reaches of the law came, culminating in Crown Court cases. More of that later.

A few years before I retired, I wrote a 'Paper' which was presented as a seminar in my place of work. This was geared to an array of psychiatric professions: psychotherapists, psychiatrists, psychologists, nurses, occupational therapists, art therapists. The papers title was 'Confidentiality: Old Standards – New Development.' In what I call 'the old days' the word 'confidential' was not so separated from 'private.' It was between me and the patient with a 'needs to know' principle, that is, the Medical General Practitioner or relevant others at times of crisis. Psychotherapeutic notes of sessions were not included for others to see and could be drawn from if the therapist thought fit. With developing years this began to be eroded which I noticed at the turn of the last century – my work environs mirrored other external colleagues from other geographical Counties. As the paper dominated system became increasingly computerised, the potential for confidentiality was being breeched. It was certainly a time to see that outside the consulting room risks were gaining in strength. We were moving from a 'needs to know' to 'knowing at the press of a computer key.' There was a drive to having greater access to clinical notes on multiple levels and the stories we told our patients earlier about 'what you tell me stays with me' could no longer apply, even though across the psychiatric board, many patients felt the first principle still applied. There were many new methods and systems which triaged the patient along with structures intended to make access to services easier, but I felt it made things worse (on the whole) as they became more complex, structured, diagnostic, prescriptive. There were many hoops to jump through for patients and staff along with an erosion of guiding principles inherent in each separate professional discipline to formulate things clinically from their perspective. Increasing political and financial constraints added further to this dominance of medical administrators and red tape procedures. When patients face us for the first time, they will be of the opinion that they are speaking in the strictest confidence, only to find out later on that others within the psychiatric network could become involved or even have access to their notes if problems arose. Possibly, like a policeman, we should have 'read them their rights.'

Moving back to the word confidential, which is linked to such words as confide, or confidence, warrants a degree of trust and a willingness to be honest. To have confidence in the 'Professional' demands a degree of 'blind trust' from the beginning. If this is missing, or not established from assessment into treatment, therapeutic ventures will be hard fought. If things go well then greater degrees of confidence in the therapy will evolve. Returning to the word private that although it has similar connotations to confidential it is less administratively restrictive. Secrets need sensitive handling in therapy and the principles of confidentiality should not push people to disclosure with a remit of assumed privacy by the patient, only to find that it potentially could be shattered later.

During my work practice, there were times (approx. 2000–2011) when directives were handed down from senior management to be followed to the rule. There was complete clinical agreement across the professional groupings that this could be detrimental if adopted, but it was. At such times there seemed to be little communication between managers and clinicians. This was, in essence, the 'Old fighting the New.' This increased bureaucratic regime, which handed down directives to follow, I believe contributed to professionals being more and more guarded in their practice, watching their back and in fear of litigation. In many ways it took the heart out of 'up and coming' bright and promising practitioners, which in turn diminished a greater creative work force. Hence, the patients at times were short changed. Of course, there was great and good work going on but these are my impressions from one point or perspective.

One illustration of an over-riding of bureaucratic process above the clinical was related to a young woman who was in individual therapy with me. This was in the early stages of her therapy which increased our concern. She told me that she had received a questionnaire in the post from my employing 'Trust.' Unbeknown to me and my colleagues the Trust were engaged in a research project, approaching patients at random. The letter went to the patient's parental home and as she had not wanted her parents to know she was in therapy, so this created problems. It fed into her paranoid tendencies. Another patient's assessment letter from me ended up at British Gas because a wrong digit had been pressed on the fax machine. One could say that confidentiality is a holy thing if religiously inclined or, it is a state of privilege. But possibly these concepts are missed within bureaucratic formulations.

A great deal more could be said about confidentiality but I feel I have meandered on the subject long enough. The main purpose in this exploration has been to highlight the elements and ingredients of confidentiality by giving attention to its major importance when considering key factors outside the consulting room. If this is faulty the therapy will be potentially faulty. In the beginning patients and therapists are strangers and have to learn to trust one another.

Court Cases

As stated earlier, I would come back to legal matters. In bringing this chapter to a close I come to one of the most challenging set of experiences. The legal implications in therapy are extensive which on one hand can be dealt with easily, that is, writing reports or liaising with solicitors and other legal bodies regarding dynamic formulation and diagnosis, whereas on the other hand more serious events occur: it can feel like a mine field. The area of legal proceedings against a therapist will not be addressed here as I have never been in that position and can offer nothing in respect to this. I want to focus upon a particular event. For both legal and clinical confidentiality I will not speak about the actual cases but will only say that the prosecution went in favour of my patient. I will focus on the impact of the case on the patient's 'well-being' and on the therapy itself, myself included. When this event happened it was so evident that 'outside the consulting room' took prominence and I had to continually have one step in the consulting room and the other in Crown Court.

I have spoken in detail about Colleen previously but here I want to focus on the court case which materialised about 18–24 months following the start of her therapy. As I write this I remember that there were one or two more similar cases at this time but they were more straight forward. The police hunt for my notes was on but these officers were thoughtful in building the case. Right from the start of proceedings Colleen wanted me to play an active part and generally speaking our sessions together continued without too much disruption apart from the times when there would be things that needed attending in preparation for the 'Case.' This extended over an 18–24-month period. So, from the beginning of therapy to the end was about four years, with a third being linked to the 'Case.'

The matter of my confidential notes was a central issue. It entailed Colleen and myself reading through all of my notes, including other allied professionals, both in my 'rooms' and in the 'Court rooms.' It was during these times that my 'Trust's' solicitors and barrister would also read these. The central point on which the 'Case' was resting seemed to have been the importance of my notes. The 'Crown's' solicitors and ours, which also included another barrister for Colleen, were going back and forth. The Crown barristers wanted the lot, I/we offered 'thought through' replies to their questions. Eventually, the Judge made his decision that he would read all the notes and then make a decision after a recess. How on earth he came to his decision after two to three hours, as it was three years of comprehensive notes, I don't know. I was so impressed with our barrister who carefully went through my notes and painted the most evocative and empathic synopsis of the notes which showed Colleen as having had painful and traumatic life experiences and showed Colleen's strength and motivation to deal with 'what life threw at her.' I was certainly anxious that my notes were upheld sensitively and anxiously awaited the Judge's verdict. He ruled that my notes would not be disclosed apart from my initial assessment notes and two clinical letters, which he praised as well as acknowledging the pressure I had been under which should not have been necessary. Following the court case our legal department was setting up a policy that such notes should not be released without due diligence.

For Colleen this period was extremely taxing, culminating in three court appearances. Probably for the greater part of this time, we were dealing with recall of early events, some re-experiencing of affect, new points of crisis that mirrored such events and dealing with new issues. The fact that I was with her during the sessions, dealing with further points of crisis outside our session times and being with her in the 'real' world, helped her to feel that she could go through with it all. She also had to deal with seeing and having distant contact with those people linked to the original trauma.

After it was all over we had to assimilate the whole experience for both of us. It had been a victory for her, although some things did not go her way. In resuming therapy after the 'Case' things seemed to get back on course and she was integrating much of her early years via the 'Case' and into the future until the time came for my retirement.

I would rather not have had to deal with this, and other similar cases, but I had no choice. The world entered the therapy room and brought us both out, only to return stronger for both of us. This, I believe, gives credence to the need for psychotherapists et al to not only consider what happens 'outside the consulting room,' but seeing that there are times when one has to step outside, literally, to take up a whole range of challenges.

Setting aside the specific and specialised areas I have covered so far in this chapter there are many more general events and situations that occur outside the consulting room. These range from simple phone calls with relatives and other professionals; requests for letters of opinion; compiling clinical correspondence; media enquiries as some examples. Each of the above will carry their own specifics that have been illustrated throughout this book.

Hopefully I have shown that to be a psychotherapist in the ever changing National Health Service, and also in private practice, is much more than listening to a patient and interpreting. I am not saying that those therapists and psychoanalysts who adhere to a more stricter discipline does 'only' this – they do much more. Sometimes, I think that in their use of the conventional therapeutic language and mechanisms, they may be unaware that they are governed by matters of the heart, which I have stated are at play in therapeutic love and which has allowed me to respond to matters outside the consulting room more readily. I trust that this has been clear with the foregoing commentary.

Note

1   As with the complex range of warring factors noted, stalking was a conflictual dynamic at the time. I have not elaborated on this as it is too sensitive an element which would threaten anonymity if used.

Chapter 15

The Lighter Side

Humour

The drawing (Figure 15.1) came to me when I was thinking about how to convey the process of the way humour relates to heartfullness and therapeutic love and can be missed in the serious venture of psychotherapy. Like the man fishing above, the therapist casts his line into the river of silence as he waits for the patient (the fish) to bite. When hooked pain may well be involved. I have been told that fish do not feel pain when hooked, but I doubt it. In this search to 'catch' the fish the man is oblivious, or does not see the fish jumping in the air, laughing. Maybe humour is the fish that got away.

The idea of psychotherapy having a lighter side may be difficult to accept, particularly in the more intense and analytic approaches, or with the more complex and disturbed groupings. Dealing with such areas is rarely a 'barrel full of laughs.' However, in all of my years of practice, there were light moments in the majority of my client groups where we could go beyond the pathos into easy interaction, fun, hopeful expectations and links to the wondrous events in their worlds, which made the heavier 'stuff' more tolerable. Of course, in the normal course of events, people do not approach 'in depth' psychotherapy for a light experience or a good laugh. Nevertheless, humour will seep through in all of this at one time or another and in different forms. In my experience there seems to have been more potential for humour to emerge in group therapy and group training events, than in individual work.

Although I said earlier that it was hard to envisage a lighter side, there are many forms of therapy and counselling that has lighter components built in, such things as: positivity, mindfulness, kindness, fun, care and guidance. However, this does not imply that they are 'not serious' in their own right. Looking back to my time in the therapeutic community a lighter side was essential in order to deal with the much heavier manifestations in the lives of people with severe personality disorders and other complex conditions. Such communities were built upon either five day or residential contacts over considerable lengths of time. In addition to both small and large psychotherapy groups dealing analytically, they were within a framework of creative, psycho-dramatic, social and occupational activities, which lightened the intensity of what occurred in the more formal therapy groups. I was involved in gardening,

DOI: 10.4324/9781003536857-18

Figure 15.1 A man is fishing in a river, his left side in profile. A fish is jumping behind him conveying the written message "you can't catch me!" and this is connected to a similar position in therapy when lightness and humour are missed in its seriousness.

cooking, music, magazine productions and sports. On one sports day I recall we had a 'wheelbarrow race' and I was partnered with a patient. As the race was preparing to get underway, Colin began telling me about the stars and the cosmos in which he'd had a career. Eventually, as we were on the starting mark I said: "Colin, your job at the minute is to be a wheelbarrow!" He took this in good heart.

I recall another event in which it was decided to surprise the sleeping patients, in the residential community on a Saint's Day. This community had employed 'Social Therapists' who mostly came from Sweden and the culture on this day in Sweden was rising before dawn and bringing cakes to parents. The Swedish therapists adapted this for the patients, sang and I played flute. The residents were not only shocked out of their sleep, but some were also caught in rooms they shouldn't have been in. This led to serious discussions later.

On another occasion, there was a time that the community decided to give the art room a full clean, which also meant washing the walls. Everyone got stuck in and as it was a summer's day, I took off my shirt, I had a vest below. After we finished, I looked for my shirt but it was nowhere to be found. Eventually it was located torn in shreds as someone thought it was a rag for the wall washing. There was a great deal of laughter at my expense. One of the patients loaned me a shirt as I had to go to present a lecture at the University later in the day.

So, one can see lightness and humour in this small sample of things which shows its importance. There are hundreds more vignettes which give credence to lighter and humorous ingredients being essential, at times more so, in psychotherapy. Hopefully we will move to seeing that even in giving respect to the seriousness of psychotherapy this does not preclude laughter and at times hinges upon it. For me laughter and humour are just as serious as expressions of pain and suffering.

A more general trend, certainly before I retired in 2011, was that for psychotherapists/counsellors, humour was viewed as defensive, negative, evasion of more important material. On one level, this was true but for me meaningful humour should be welcomed as compared to interpreting it as a defence. It is knowing the difference between its validity and its defensive properties that is important.

Humour in the Literature

I was able to locate some very interesting commentary that paralleled my own findings. Here are a few of these.

In the preface of Herbert Strean's edited book – 'The Use of Humour in Psychotherapy' he says:

> Although laughing and crying are two basic, inborn emotional reactions, psychoanalysts and psychotherapists have been much more interested in the phenomenon of crying than laughing. In contrast to the many clinical papers in the professional literature that deal with the patient's inability to cry and mourn, there are few that discuss the dynamics of the patient's inability to laugh. Most professional commentators on the subject (laughter) have pointed to this behaviour as a means of acting out, a way of resisting, a sign of a regressive transference, a maladaptive response, and frequently a disguised form of hostility.
>
> (Strean, 1994, p. xi)

And further:

> "Sigmund Freud was an active joke teller and used this within many interactions with patients and non-patients. Furthermore, he carefully subjected the many facets of jokes, humour and wit to psychoanalytic investigation. He demonstrated, for example, that humour reflects a part of the superego that looks upon the ego with the warmth and understanding of an empathetic parent." – "Despite Freud's affirmative orientation to humour and his freedom to appreciate it – it has taken mental health professionals six decades to permit the masters perspective on humour to take the effect it might have in our work with patients…"
>
> (Strean, 1994, p. xii)

Strean's edited book, comprising of 25 authors, covers a lot of ground addressing humour from a wide range of perspectives.

Murray Cox develops this further, looking at Humour as indicative of accepting the 'whole' person, which parallels Strean's position:

> Nevertheless, if the patient is to be received as a whole person, rather than an 'utterer of symptoms', then to be 'taken seriously' implies that his laughter and humour is as much part of his presentation as his formal 'complaint'. It therefore follows that the therapist's appropriate response is not always that of sombre, solemnity; indeed, shared laughter may facilitate disclosure much more rapidly than an emotionally neutral response.
>
> (Cox, 1978, p. 10)

Further:

> Every experienced therapist knows that the manic defence is a reality. Trivial giggling, incongruous gaiety, may be and often are ego defence mechanisms. Nevertheless, to belittle all humour and genuine shared laughter is to trivialise what can be one of the deepest human experiences. When laughter is not a defence it may be an enriching reinforcement of corporate solidarity. The ability to laugh at himself is, paradoxically, an indication that a man is able to take himself seriously. Similarly, a group that dares to accept laughter, will also be able to tolerate tears.
>
> (Cox, 1978, p. 61)

In his four Centenary Addresses in 1956 Ernst Jones gives us a humorous response to a patient:

> Some fifty years ago (1906) I had occasion to treat a neurotic patient who had been in the habit of consulting a neurologist who was then perhaps the most distinguished one in England. He advised the patient to take a trip to the West Indies. On his return in an unaltered state, he was told to take a trip to the East Indies. When this also proved to no avail the neurologist despairingly advised a trip around the world. That was when the patient came to me.
>
> (Jones, 1956, p. 70)

So, what could this be? An untreatable patient; an inadequate neurologist? A playing for time; or Ernst Jones vs. the World? With the remaining text I shall meander through a number of illustrations which have been taken from a range of settings. Returning to my 'fish' illustration at the beginning, the points of fun and humour that emerged in these sessions did so mostly at unexpected, spontaneous moments, just like the fish, laughing at our solemn therapeutic dialogue attempts, breaking through and begging to be caught. Something, conscious or otherwise, stirred the humorous fish, rearranging what was to follow in its wake.

Humour in the Assessment and Early Stages

As I suggested earlier, the first meeting with the patient carries an extreme level of importance. Usually the patient will be highly anxious and/or afraid. It may be their first time in such a setting whereas for us it may amount to hundreds of times. So, to come in with light hearted and humorous comments may be disrespectful, inappropriate, or even wrong. On the other hand, a well-timed quip, joke, spontaneous funny parallel to the patient's disclosures may calm the waters of anxiety and fear, thus de-stigmatising the patient's condition. Of the many initial assessments I have undertaken, a few stand out:

A lady in her middle years arrived for her first meeting with me. She had come with her dog and asked if she could bring the dog into the meeting. She said that it would sit quietly. This was a 'first' for me and I thought, why not? All went well for about ten to 15 minutes until the dog's ears pricked up, responding to another dog just outside the building. There then developed a four-way dialogue, in that we humans had a turn, then the dogs had their own language dialogue – we ended up in tears of laughter and eventually completed the meeting.

On another occasion in the early stages of individual therapy Mary spent a lot of time bombarding me with questions. She was outraged that I rarely answered her questions. In response to my asking her questions she said: "You wouldn't need to ask me questions about my past if you'd read my earlier notes!" (from other professionals). I simply responded: "I tell you what, next week I will get your notes and put them on your chair. I will have the session with your notes. You can take the week off!" She went into fits of laughter and she could see that in a way her questions were a way of avoiding the start of our relationship and possibly I was the same.

Returning to the first assessment meetings Samantha went into some detail about how she felt split in two; being two separate people, that is, in one of her dreams one part of herself is lying on a couch trying to sleep and the other part is standing anxiously guarding the front door. She felt that this summed up how she is generally. At one point I suggested that, like a best friend, one part was looking after the other. She went on to speak about her eating problems in which she doubles up on quantities for consumption. I said: "Well you have got to feed your best friend, haven't you!" She flashed a beaming smile and there was a clear rescinding of her anxiety.

On Groups

I could no more kiss my father as I could Gerry.

Celine said this quite spontaneously in a group as she was in full flow which could be conventionally linked to issues around transference. The comment brought immediate laughter and I then had to sit through a range of humorous comments about me. Celine felt unguarded as the comment emerged without thought. However, she opened the door for others to follow suit, even though she withdrew a bit in her embarrassment and for a time placing her hand over her mouth.

On reflection that when lighter commentary and humour materialises in individual therapy it will be a more direct connection which seems to be centred upon the patient/therapist bond. Whereas in groups, although having similar properties to the individual arrangement, it will take a wider consideration. When points of humour emerge they will often be at either a point when the group is stuck or struggling, or when dialogue is freer and more relaxed. Although there may not be a purposeful intent, such releases can have a cathartic effect, assisting the group to develop further. Granted, as stated earlier, there will have been times when particularly difficult and complex dynamics are raging and humour, light heartedness, emerges defensively. At such times one's experience guides us to detect these events. At these times what is presented as funny, mischievous, teasing does not feel to be in tune. As people flow in this way it feels tight, incongruous, has an underlying irritation.

Trainee psychotherapists and counsellors are expected to undergo their own therapy or be part of an experiential group in order to qualify. I have conducted many such groups in my time. Although there are similarities between trainee and treatment groups there are also differences, that is, the trainee has to experience it within a total teaching framework and I also have to keep in mind the teaching and academic components. With the following illustrations it has been constructed in a way to protect anonymity.

In one session they (trainees) had been, in a similar way to a treatment group, opening up a lot of very personal details and struggling with looking at their relationships with one another, along with the pressures they were under in the commitments to training. It felt collectively that things were sinking deeper and deeper after 50–60 minutes. I then said: "It looks like people are being put off the training minute by minute!" I wasn't sure how I said this but immediately there was a ripple of laughter around the room. A bit like saying: "3 years training in one session." It felt as if the serious intensity was forced into the aim of sorting so much out before the end of the session. The group became freer and the sinking feelings evaporated. On reflection, I'm not sure what type of humorous intervention this was but part of my conscious intent was to cut through what was moving towards an impasse. Analytic interpretations from me at this time would not have moved things and would have been appealing to the patient side of the students as compared to addressing the students learning. In essence I think that humour used in this way could be described as a 'cut and thrust' way (probably not the best metaphor). One could simply say it was a comic statement but for the comedy to be effective in such serious circumstances it had to have quite a strong unconscious drive, and in this drive there must be a purpose in using it in order to do some level of good and assist change. Otherwise it may be desperate, aggressive, flippant and disregarding of the real pain and suffering that people go through in such situations.

In another group session, this involved members elaborating on parts of themselves which could be identified as personal/idiosyncratic mannerisms, foibles and gestures. These were at times playfully resonated to:

Claire was sharing how much she feels she had changed in 12 years.

Jackie to Claire: "That's because you're old!" Everyone breaks into laughter. This was a joking response to Claire continuously speaking about her age, the senior citizen who should be followed because of her life experience. The laughter was gentle and conveyed caringly.

In another therapy group, it was one patient's leaving session. The group was sharing the good feelings about what this woman had contributed to the group. At one point Tony said that she had helped him and had offered a 'professional objective' and thoughtful contribution. I gave it a few seconds and then I simply said "professional" and looked directly at Tony. There was an immediate wave of laughter, including Tony, and this was seen as a recognition of his need to seek help from people to give him advice and professional input, which he often struggled with me about. He then started to tread water and explain why he had said it and so he was getting himself more and more into a mess and I said simply that "you are digging a hole even deeper trying to get out." He was able to take this in a fairly light-hearted way.

In a student group, they had moved into dialogue revolving around dying, death, forms of burial, cremation, etc. Not surprisingly this turned to gallows humour and the macabre. With the growing intensity of the dialogue content, so too did the jokes and humorous responses. This then moved them to more details about friends and family losses. This took into account stories revolving around rituals and death ceremonies. At this point it felt more like a treatment group. I was even caught up in it when I had a fleeting image of coffins being buried vertically as the Irish writer Flan O'Brien had purported should happen, which made it easier to get to heaven and took up less ground space. Sadly I cannot recall in which of his books he wrote about this. By this point nearly everyone had spoken of the ways their relatives had 'moved on' (died). On reflection, I think that it was the freedom of movement earlier in the session into a manic type dialogue and to not feel self-conscious or that they were doing something wrong by using this humour, which anchored the group.

In another student group there was a silence for about 15 minutes which seemed to be a follow on from some changes in the academic expectations which they were not prepared for which had been upsetting. One woman said "It's quite a heavy atmosphere, we all feel heavy" I said: "I don't!" It felt like I had touched a nerve. Further I said: "I wasn't feeling heavy so it must have been something you brought in." This immediately caused a round of laughter. This seemed to resonate with the phrase: 'bringing shit in on the soles of one's shoes.' This was the trigger which disrupted the tiredness/heaviness.

So far the trainee/student groups I have referred to are those occurring in Britain. Generally speaking, there are similar dynamics and structures in other countries that I have worked in, but there are elements which I have experienced as different.

In one group that I was conducting in St Petersburg, Russia, on the second day of the 'coup' in 1991, there were interesting points of note. One of my first impressions was that humour presented itself very quickly (within minutes) and continued unabated and incessantly in training sessions. This, without a doubt to me, was a cultural method of defence, which at times seemed to be a necessary tool to be used. At such times interpretation had little effect. Possibly it was also a way of guarding against invasion by the West. Another strand was the use of metaphor, which in itself was interesting when copious metaphoric similes were offered, it added further to an escape route. Getting to the 'heart of the matter' was a daunting task. To put this into context, I recall one of the early statements from a group member in one of the first sessions was that:

> if Yeltsin was not successful in getting Gorbachev back from the gang of six, (I believe it might have been five who kidnapped him), then they were afraid of what would happen to them because they, the authorities, would know that they were mixing with Westerners.

This not only brought up anxiety for them but certainly made me and my colleagues anxious. If Yeltsin was not successful in fighting the coup antagonists then we may end up badly, that is, imprisoned or possibly even killed. Fairly quickly after these statements were made this group went into manic reactions and formations around humour and the use of metaphor. Attempts at interpretation to help explore and expand the meaning of these things were moderately accommodated and often rejected and fought against. There were times when there was fragmentation and the group would move into 'in-house' humour relevant only to that group which defied interpretation and in other sessions getting into extreme use of metaphoric language.

In contrast to this, humour has come up in some of the work I have done in Portugal, although generally speaking, the Portuguese students have not used the same level of metaphor. Although the issues of time keeping were quite important in the Russian setting, it was even more so in Portugal, that is, lateness was an occupational hazard and therefore humorous statements revolved around this: if you say you are going to have a session at 10 am then expect people by 10.30 and they might not turn up or stay. Humour in these settings was much more guarded and covert in earlier years. They found it hard to accommodate the idea that humour might generate some sense of motivation and inspiration. They would laugh timidly but it would not get much further. Therefore, it was difficult to use humour in these settings at the time. In a way they needed to be dependently taught and fed and attempts to question this were fought against. As time developed over the years, things loosened up, and both timekeeping and humour were much easier to be experienced and dealt with.

Moving back to points of humour in relation to therapeutic groups, here are a few more illustrations. Bearing in mind my opening comments on the humorous fish, the fish symbol emerged in a session. They had been struggling with particular events and it felt to me that the more they tried the more elusive meaning and understanding became. I simply said: "it's hard to catch a fish with your hands." The mood lightened with their associating to the metaphor with lots of jokes and stories about fish. I did not elaborate immediately but later went on to say "if you try and catch a fish with your hands it can easily jump away as compared to using a net for the fish to jump into." They all began laughing and as this was Kerri's final session after three years, I said to her "Well, that's one thing you will probably miss; my crazy comments." "Yes!" she said and began recalling such things I and others had said which she would remember with great fondness in the future.

At times it may feel somewhat incongruous if the therapist uses humour when for the greater part of their time they function with aloofness, distance, silence. However, there are many other gestures and mannerisms, such as facial expressions, for example, puzzlement, curiosity, smiles, frowns and disinterest. These in turn may be seen to be an oscillation in the therapist's dual presence: serious solemnity and humour/light heartedness. For example, in one group session they were discussing my predominant silence. They felt I should say more; Claire felt I was impish in the way I smiled; she thought I had pointy ears under my long hair. This was in contrast to how some of them saw me as critical.

In one group session three of the women were talking about past relationships with men and lovers. This revolved around extreme switches of mood. Martina jokingly said: "That's hormone problems!" they all began laughing at this. I said : "If a man said that would they get off so lightly?" there was more laughter and a lively dialogue on monthly hormone cycles as well as 'ribbing' me for being a man and I didn't have to worry about this. Belinda said: "Men, the only thing they have to worry about are 'eruptions'" (this should have been erections) – more laughter. As there were no other men in this group such dialogue, both funny and serious, was more in operation. Often, even though they knew very well that I was a man, they incorporated me into the feminine identity. At various times throughout my career, I was symbolically seen to have feminine credentials, for example, the midwife, mother, grandmother and honorary woman.

Another group started the session talking about a television video, some of them had seen it previously. Victoria highlighted the battle she had with her son, prohibiting him from access to the film as it was sexually above his age. The others resonated to this which evolved into dialogue on discipline and maintaining parental boundaries for their children. Gradually they moved back to the video and how it brought up embarrassment and enjoyment in equal measures. There was an association to the scene in 'When Harry Met Sally' (Reiner, 1989) and the actress (Meg Ryan) was faking an orgasm at the restaurant table. How free it was. This in turn moved them to look at their own inhibitions and sexual pleasures. They looked at old and new terminology: 'gay' used to be about happiness; a 'boner' is now an erection; 'bonking' was the old term for sexual intercourse. Valerie: "my mother thinks a bonk is a bang on the head." We fall about laughing. Deirdre: "my daughter is 11 and we were having dinner last week, my mother was also there. My daughter asked me: mammy, what's oral sex? Once again, we all laugh. She tells her daughter she'll tell her later (maybe five years later)". This then allowed them to speak on the need for honesty with children. This dialogue takes an unexpected turn with Samantha breaking down in floods of tears because of a dream she'd had of her mother dying. The others are very supportive and this heralds a deep and moving dialogue on love and lost love in their parent's death or fading years. The group's dialogue about sex is alive and changing, while there is loss and mourning in the mix. This also reflected the 'group as a whole' position, as the group was moving toward total closure in four months' time. The recognition of the coming loss of the group brings with it a desire to get as much life out of it as possible. Hopefully this illustration shows how both humour and the openings of serious and solemn dimensions go hand in hand.

On Mishearing

When considering the gap between being the thoughtful, predominantly silent therapist and the bringer of light heartedness and humour, sometimes this can bring mishearing. This is not only confined to the therapist and there will be many reasons that individual and group patients will hear accurately or mishear. On the wave of productive dialogue in a group, with the group analyst listening and watching, that if he/she brings in a humorous, ironic, provocative, mischievous comment, it will not necessarily be heard by everyone in the same way. The true intent may take a time to filter through so as he is not only seen as a fool.

In one group session I had been attempting to expand some meaning on the term 'licking one's wounds,' a term which indicates 'self-soothing.' I said: "one of the differences between licking your own wounds rather than letting someone else do it, is that you end up with a tired tongue." There wasn't a direct response but after five minutes Linda said: "Gerry, that's a very violent and terrible thing to say." Everyone, including myself, was puzzled by this. Further she said: "putting your tongue out is a vile image!" Gerry: "Linda, I said tired" she laughed uproariously and said: "I thought you said tearing!" Everyone else heard 'tired.' I came back and suggested there may have been a link between 'tearing' and 'tired' as we had been speaking about broken relationships as these could be described as a mixture of tired and torn. Linda gave another angle to it as she had recently been to a play, 'Andromitis' in which a number of people had their tongues torn out.

In another group session the dialogue revolved around having children or not, and whether this involved natural maternal feelings or something that had to be learned. At one point I said that "not having children left them with an 'empty womb.'" Although most of them heard this accurately Henrietta said: "Gerry, what's an empty room got to do with this?" There was an eruption of laughter with the others clarifying things to Henrietta, who also saw the funny side of this. This chance mishearing was extremely important as it heralded a humorous moment which then allowed the group to move on to a much deeper level, talking extensively about empty wombs and empty rooms.

Slow Open Groups

As I have pointed out in my various group illustrations the term 'slow open' is one that is applied to group analytic groups as originated by S.H. Foulkes (Foulkes & Anthony, 1957/1984, pp. 65, 67, 161). The majority of the groups that I have conducted would be within this category. Basically, such groups will have a life span of many years with a fixed day and time, usually once or twice a week. Being 'open' this means that the membership changes according to the progress of each patient and the process of personal change is seen to be 'slow'; some taking many years to complete their therapy.

With this in mind humour and light heartedness in a group that has been together for a number of years can have a much firmer and genuine foothold than in more fleeting and transient groups. Light heartedness feels genuine, warm and pleasurable in groups who like one another and who have weathered turbulent times. Such groups have a more solid base of appreciation of one another. As well as enjoying the playful and funny experiences humour tends not to be used arrogantly with sarcasm or belittling. Equally, stronger groups have the ability to challenge one another if there are defensive uses of humour without recourse to criticising maladaptive use of humour.

In one of my groups I was able to see particular light and humorous elements. This group was due to finish in six months coinciding with my retirement. The membership of this group was between one and seven years for each individual. At the beginning of one session they were joking: "Will you take us on a cruise when you retire Gerry?" They had been speaking about this before I entered the room. Alison: "Gerry, we could sunbathe on deck and you can serve us cocktails. You can get us drunk and then if we need, you can give us therapy when we're sober!" We laughed a lot and there were more fast flowing comments on what it would be like on the cruise. Me: "I thought I was retiring and not carrying on serving you all while sunbathing, getting drunk and having a good time, and I have to keep working." I suppose that this was one way of starting to talk about pending closure. They then went onto speak of deeper meaningful day to day struggles outside. This also included the points of personal changes they had made. Humour returned towards the end of the session. Alison: "Gerry, I'm still waiting for my laminated certificate!", this was a recurring semi-serious wish that I treat their finishing like a graduation ceremony.

Some weeks later the dialogue turned to play. Granted, over the years this group membership, and previous patients would use humorous interactions which was one way of their playing with one another or conveying how they saw me or engaged with me accordingly.

In this session Bridget spoke of being anxious about mixing with other mothers at her children's playground. She didn't like waiting as the mothers gathered, not really knowing what to do. I asked: "What would it be like if you asked the other mothers to play 'tig' (a game of touching and running to escape)?" They all laughed here. Pauline: "It's hard not to play in a playground!" They moved away from this after a few openings about their own 'schoolyard' days. However, the one thing that emerged from schoolyard resonances was that of bullying and their recalling bullying events as well as some who had been bullies. This developed into equating with similar adult experiences which was not unlike the game of 'tig' in which they had been touched by others and had run away in order to survive.

Some weeks later Alison took up a central position. She had been the longest serving member. At times her insights were staggering along with her care and love for the others, including myself. I had figured highly in her life and at this stage she was free to challenge me with a humorous twist in the tail. She spoke about a number of internal dilemmas she had gone through and was now seeing these as necessary stages, although painful at the time. She joked with me about her dilemma of two weeks earlier: "It's your fault for keeping me here, the times I wanted to leave!" Some months later their concerns about the group's closure were voiced again. Alison had a dream in which she had rented me a room in her house, which I believe was a bedroom. I had made her sign a contract that we would not talk outside the group. I had given her a shirt to iron, and I had a wardrobe of colourful Hawaiian shirts. Everyone began freely associating and joking about the bedroom and the shirts.

It was not only humour being used to deal with the groups closure, as well as concerns for me. Marie, who tended at times to be the joking motivator who would say things to me teasingly, had a deep empathy for others behind the jovial mask. At one point Marie helped to move Clarissa through her resistant and blocked feelings after many weeks of silent struggles. This opened up their battles with suicidal urges in the past and present. They also recalled a past member who had killed herself. Clarissa: "It was hard for Gerry then as he was being given a hard time when Cynthia died! But this group is better now." This then moved into their speaking of how much they liked the group and were glad it was not aggressive or too confrontative. In a later session, they had been dealing with high levels of emotion and the level of disclosure was expansive. In the last 15–20 minutes of the session, things became chaotic and manic, with fast and at times nonsensical comments. Marie, as was her want, became the dominant person at this stage, even though she knew that this was evasive, she carried on. She told us about a friend who worked in a chicken factory who decided on the sex of the chickens (for whatever reason). The infectious laughter took hold with many associations on chickens and other animals' sexuality. This seemed to mirror the earlier dialogue on their conflicts around sexuality. It was difficult to know what this was about and interpret it. In the closing comments I said: "This might make sense at some point later. For now, let's not worry about interpreting. It's the joy of talking nonsense."

These few brief accounts show how, in a group sessions, light hearted and humorous comments/dialogue came to the group's assistance. These were stepping stones from one group position to the next. As such they were pivotal elements in the dynamical flow of the group. These same foci occur in all groups, but in this context, they have emerged in particular ways as healthy contributions from a group that is in tune with one another over prolonged periods of time. Words like catalysts, congruous, resonant and harmonic, among others, could be applied to such group phases. It is also interesting that the words 'light hearted' implies a relaxed more care-free attitude. We can also take it more literally as the heart becoming light, free of worry and intensity.

It was in my training group at the Institute of Group Analysis that I heard the phrase 'don't ruin a good story for the sake of the truth' from my group analyst, Robin Skynner (as I commented upon earlier). Indeed, for those familiar with Robin, either personally or through his writing, knows how inspiring he was. By his saying this to me he was challenging my way of avoiding some things and I was able to accept this. It was interesting that I came across a paper by Moeller, speaking about Adele Mittwoch, a training group analyst

> She (Adele) participated in an experimental group led by Robin Skynner. When the group had been going for about six months, Skynner said to a very beautiful woman psychologist "You're a very attractive woman, I could fall in love with you." That was all, but it was more than enough. The repercussions for the technique of treatment of such an intervention are considerable, because the balance of equal treatment is thrown out of kilter. However, this balance may in any case be an illusory misapprehension. The group analyst's garment is his psychic nakedness.
>
> (Moeller, 2002, pp. 493–494)

I did not understand this last sentence. In the cold light of day it is understandable that such an intervention would have repercussions (assumed punishment) as the way love is considered in the paper is via conventional analytic dogma, revolving around eroticism and group competing on these levels. Having known Robin, sitting in a group twice weekly for four years, there would possibly have been another vague or hidden meaning. The context of Robin's statement to the 'beautiful woman' is missing. Adele refers to the beauty of the woman but is her understanding/description the same as Robin's which would prompt the comments? Robin's lighter side is not accommodated.

Golf Illustration

I have digressed, meandered away from the simple comment of the 'ruining of a story' as stated earlier. Meandering back to the world of golf we can see similar commentary that goes on between golfers, almost as if it is a game within a game. For example, here is a snapshot of a fictional game, the interchanging dialogue is common in Ireland, intended to 'wind one another up' with playful banter, a form of teasing. I'm relatively convinced that such things are more universal: both players are on the tee of a par three hole with 185 yards to the green. There is a water pond in front of the players so they have to get over 120 yards to reach the dry land/green.

Player A – tees off (hits the ball) and it's not good. It flies and bounces over the water. Both players hold their breath as the ball skims the water and onto the green, moving towards the hole and both players cheer as, the ball drops into the hole. Both embrace and jump up and down, united in pleasure.

Player A: Turning to his partner/opponent he says:

Sorry about that, what luck, it's my first 'hole in one.'

Player B: "Don't let your mouth ruin a good shot."

This is a complimentary partner at this point, but underneath he is silently saying: "Keep your mouth shut you lucky bastard. I wish it had been my shot." However, there is no real malice in these thoughts.

On the next tee (the game is only getting started) player A once again has a stroke of good fortune, with his next shot going wild, hits a tree and ricochets onto a rock and lands 10 feet from the hole, in the face of mounting frustration of player B. Player A turns to player B with another grovelling apology and may now have registered player B's earlier unsaid expletives and then – 'kept his mouth shut.'

Player B's response to A is: "It's Golf Course knowledge" (you have a great experience of the course). This would appear to be a semi-sarcastic comment.

Sarcastic, the unspoken translation of 'course knowledge' is: you're really a great player; you know the golf course so well; you planned to hit that tree so as the trajectory of the ball would hit the rock and finally, you knew the slope of the green would take your ball to 10 feet from the hole.

So, these types of transactions and dialogues go on all the time on golf courses. Usually, such 'banter' (playful interactions) is gentle and developed with good will and humour. In reality during the American Masters Golf Tournament in 2020, Jon Rahm (No. 2/3 in the world), during the fun warm up game, skimmed a ball on purpose over the water. Everyone gasped as it rolled on over many slopes on the green and into the hole. Reality came knocking on my door some weeks later when one of my shots hit water and bounced on to the fairway. There was a collective cheer from adjoining groups of golfers and the shout of 'Barns Wallace.' He was one of the Dam Busters in the second World War bouncing bomb fame. With such an illustration this, I believe, shows how the love for the game of golf is as much a love for my opposition and partners in team golf. The in-house language, of which there is a great amount, allows us to connect on many levels.

Bearing in mind these comments: the following table will hopefully clarify the parallels within psychotherapy, light heartedness, humour and golf and its expansion into therapeutic love.

Key Points of Reference

One brief comment that I want to make in relation to how light-heartedness and humour makes their appearance is that these have to be driven from a spontaneous point of origin. Granted, there may be times, as I have stated, when a thought, impulse, impression is converted into a tool to help mobilise something, as when a group/individual patient is floundering or stuck, that is, my earlier comments about 'cutting and thrusting.' However, the quality of these spontaneous moments will be diminished if they become organised or contrived procedures, instead of letting each one have its life for a few brief moments and then what develops from this are the real nuggets of therapeutic gold. In Chapter 3, I drew attention to the American Research Institute: 'Heart Math,' where I spoke of their findings being similar to my own developments, although they were approaching 'heart feelings' from the initial physiological perspective, emanating from the heart and moving to identify feelings following the physiological route. For me it was physical sensations coming out of emotional factors. In the same frame of reference light-hearted and humorous elements should emerge spontaneously and lead to elaboration of and a greater personal insight and development, as compared to developing physical exercises to stimulate heart emotions (Table 15.1).

Table 15.1 Lighter Side Parallels with Psychotherapeutic Dimensions

The ruining of the story	The 'good story' of the patient's life is not 'ruined' with too much pathologising and good experiences are not diminished with too much or unnecessary interpretations/interventions
The application of humour	In developing therapeutic love it will be greatly enhanced by giving space for humour to be accepted, expressed and understood. The healing capacities of humour as an agent for change is diminished if treated only as conscious or unconscious obstacles and defences
Playful elements. These can be more readily incorporated into psychotherapeutic ventures. In classical psychodynamic principles, they can be accommodated and interpreted in many ways, e.g., defences, projections and countertransference However, if we look at these as heart driven manifestations being channelled within the therapeutic love framework they form as powerful healthy ingredients. This is developed/expanded in the neighbouring box	Playful dimensions within a therapeutic love framework. This allows both patients and therapists to interact in a more spontaneous, fluid manner. Fear of expression and mutual sharing shifts the stern faced therapist, from carefully considering the multiple levels of meaning to being more available to the patient. Such availability can allow the patient to feel more connected to the therapist. Regarding sarcasm, when working on this level it tends to be expressed more from its playful nature, whereas an analytic perspective may begin searching for aggressive or hateful foundations, i.e., sarcasm is the lowest form of wit

Chapter 16

Epilogue

Love problems are not situation specific. Love is not a specific encounter. A problem of 'not being loved' is more often than not a problem of not loving.

(Yalom, 1989, p. 377)

As I meandered through many texts on psychotherapy and its various schools and disciplines, I was struck by how little had been written by patients about their experiences of their therapy. A general tendency of these publications, as far as I perceived, was to present theoretical and clinical vignettes with material which would back up the theory. Of course, this is a fairly wild generalisation and there were some good presentations of what the patient experienced as the leading account on the therapies content and outcome. The quote above from Yalom is one of his many beautiful illustrations on therapeutic ventures, some of which I have used throughout the book. So, as I wind up this publication, I reflected on my own development. In my hundreds of initial assessments of psychotherapy candidates, particularly in my earlier years, I rarely asked a direct question about love. Yes! I asked how people felt about their parents, relatives, partners, children, not with the intention of an in-depth love perspective, but with the aim of seeing what was wrong or faults in relating. We would eventually, in most cases, come to love variations. In asking about feelings these had to be negotiated through thought in order to reach psychodynamic formulations, based primarily upon reaching meaning and understanding, not understandings about love as a direct physiological impact, that is, heartbroken feelings.

Hopefully with the publication of this book, it will move us into the future, offering new ways of considering existing theory and practice and possibly something new in its own right. At different points I have meandered back to much older theoretical writers and practitioners. In Chapter 4, I had suggested that love, of a non-erotic presentation, seemed to be given more credence at the end of the 19th and early 20th centuries. With this in mind I felt I could not finish and omit including the following quote from 1946 by Percival Symonds:

One may search through most of the popular texts of psychology without finding love even remotely considered, and yet the very fact that the word *love*

DOI: 10.4324/9781003536857-19

produces so pronounced an emotional reaction on most persons indicates its psychological significance in human affairs. Psychology has dealt adequately with the strong emotions but on the whole has ignored love. Its importance cannot be overvalued, and no topic in psychology has more profound implications.

(Symonds, 1946, p. 520)

This could have been written today.

References

Alexander, A., Einstein, S., & Grotjan, M. (Eds.) (1966). *Psychoanalytic Pioneers*. New York & London: Basic Books Inc.

Bion, W. R. (1961). *Experiences in Groups and Other Papers*. London: Tavistock/Routledge.

Bion, W. R. (1994). *Clinical Seminars and Other Papers*. London: Karnac Books Ltd.

Bohm, D. (1996). *On Dialogue*. Edited by Lee Nichol. London & New York: Routledge.

Browne, L. (2006). *The Emigrants Farewell*. London: Bloomsbury Publishing plc.

Buechler, S. (2004). *Clinical Values: Emotions That Guide Psychoanalytic Treatment*. Hilsdale, NJ: Analytic Press.

Byram-Karasu, T. (1992). *Wisdom in the Practice of Psychotherapy*. Basic Books, Division of Harper Collins Publishers.

Case, C. (1990). Heart Forms – The Image as Mediator. *Inscape*.

Collins. (Millennium Edition). *Collins English Dictionary*. Harper Collins Publisher.

Compact Oxford English Dictionary. (2008). Oxford University Press.

Cox, M. (1978). *Structuring the Therapeutic Process – Compromise with Chaos*. Oxford, New York, Toronto, Sydney, Paris & Frankfurt: Pergamon Press.

Estes, C. P. (1992). *Women Who Run with Wolves*. London, Sydney, Aukland & Johannesburg: Rider Publications.

Feth, M. (1996). *Der Gedankensammler (The Thought Collector)*. Guttenburg: Vezlager.

Foulkes, S. H. (1964). *Therapeutic Group Analysis*. London: George Allen and Unwin Ltd; further publications: Karnac Books.

Foulkes, S. H. (1990). *Selected Papers: Psychoanalysis and Group Analysis*. London: H Karnac Books Ltd.

Foulkes, S. H., & Anthony, E. J. (1957/1984). *Group Psychotherapy the Psychoanalytical Approach*. Maresfield & London: Karnac Books Ltd.

Fromm, E. (1949). *Man for Himself: An Enquiry into the Psychology of Ethics*. London: Routledge & Kegan Paul plc.

Fry, S. (2013). Television Documentary on Homosexuality. *Channel 4*.

Gabriel, P. (1986). Don't Give Up [Recorded by P. Gabriel].

Gilroy, A., & McNeilly, G. (2000). *The Changing Shape of Art Therapy*. London & Philadelphia, PA: Jessica Kingsley Publishers.

Godwin, G. (2001). *Heart (A Personal Journey through Its Myths and Meanings)*. New York: Harper Collins Publishers.

Goldberg, A. (1990). *The Realities of Transference – Progress in Self Psychology*. Hilsdale, NJ/London: The Analytic Press.

Grieg, A. (2007). *Preferred Lies – A Journey to the Heart of Golf!* London: Orion Publishing Group.

Groddeck, G. (1977/1988). *The Meaning of Illness: Selected Psychoanalytic Writings.* Maresfield Library, London: Hogarth Press & H. Karnac Books Ltd.

Guntrip, H. (1982). *Personality Structure and Human Interaction – The Developing Synthesis of Psycho Dynamic Theory.* J. D. Sutherland (Eds.). London: Hogarth Press and the Institute of Psychoanalysis.

Hadfield, J. A. (1962). *Childhood and Adolescence.* Baltimore, MD: Pelical Original Publication.

Halam, A. (2005). *Siberia.* London: Orion Children's Books, Orion Publishing.

Harrison, T. (2000). *Bion, Rickman, Foulkes & the Northfield Experiment.* London & New York: Jessica Kinglsey Publications.

Hoban, R. (1973). *The Lion of Boaz Jachin and Jachin Boaz.* London: Picador Books.

Hogan, S. (2001). *Healing Arts – The History of Art Therapy.* London & Philadelphia, PA: Jessica Kingsley Publishing.

Howe, E. G. (2005). *That We Might Never Meet Again.* London: Faber and Faber.

Irvine, A. (1914). *My Lady of the Chimney Corner.* London: Eveleigh Nash.

Jones, E. (1956). *Sigmund Freud – Four Centenary Addresses.* New York: Basic Books.

Jordan, J. V. (2000). *Odyssey in Psychotherapy.* In J. J. Shay, & J. Wheelis (Eds.) (pp. 164–165). New York: Ardent Media Inc.

Jung, C. G. (1969). *Collected Works Vol. 8.* London and Henley: Routledge and Kegan Paul.

Kavanagh, P. (1938/1975/1977). *The Green Fool.* Harmondsworth, London: Penguin Books.

Kerr, J. (1994). *A Most Dangerous Method.* London, Auckland, Melbourne, Singapore & Toronto: Reed Consumer Ltd.

King James Bible. (1611).

Kitzinger, S. (1988). *The Origins of Love and Hate.* London: Free Association Books.

Klein, M., Heimann, P., & Money-Kyrle, R. (1955). *New Directions in Psycho-Analysis.* London: Tavistock Publications Ltd.

Kohon, G. (1999). *The Dead Mother – The Work of Andre Green.* London: Routledge Publications.

Laing, R. D. (1965). *The Divided Self.* Harmondsworth: Penguin Books.

Laplanche, J., & Pontalis, J.-B. (1983). *The Language of Psychoanalysis.* London: Hogarth Press and The Institute of Psychoanalysis.

Lear, J. (1990/1998). *Love and Its Place in Nature – A Philosophical Interpretation of Freudian Psychoanalysis.* New Haven, CT & London: Yale and University Press.

MacLaverty, B. (2001). *The Anatomy School.* London, Sydney, New Zealand & South Africa: Random House.

May, R. (1972). *Power and Innocence – A Search for the Sources of Violence.* New York: W W Norton & Company Inc.

McCarty, R. (2015). *The Science of the Heart Vol. 2.* Boulder Creek, CA: HeartMath Institute.

McDougal, W. (1927). *Character and the Conduct of Life.* London: Methuen & Co. Ltd.

McNeilly, G. (1983/1984). Directive and Non-Directive Approaches in Art Therapy. *The Arts in Psychotherapy Journal, Inscape (Dec).*

McNeilly, G. (1987). Further Contributions to Group Analytic Art Therapy. *Inscape Journal, Summer 8-11.*

McNeilly, G. (1990). Group Analysis and Art Therapy: A Personal Perspective. *Group Analysis Vol. 23.*

McNeilly, G. (2006b). *Group Analytic Art Therapy.* London & Philadelphia, PA: Jessica Kingsley Publishers.

McNeilly, G. (2009). *Worlds Apart Colliding – The Picture in the Word.* Unpublished.

McNeilly, G. (2020). *Running between Raindrops and Trying to Keep Dry.* Unpublished.

Miller, G. (2007). A Wall of Ideas: "The Taboo on Tenderness". *Theory and Culture in New Literary History 38*(4), 667–681.

Millner, M. (1986). *A Life of One's Own.* London: Virago Press.

Mitchell, J. (1976). A Strange Boy [Recorded by J. Mitchell]. Electra/Asylum Records distributed by WEA Records Ltd.

Moeller, M. L. (2002). *Love in Group, Group Analysis 26th S H Foulkes Lecture Part 2.* Sage Publications Vol. 35 pp. 484–498.

Moon, B. (n.d.). *Art-Based Group Therapy. Theory and Practice. 1 st Edition 2010. 2nd Edition 2016.* Springfield, IL: C Thomas Ltd.

Morrison, P. (1986). A Change of Mind. Part 6: A Narrow Lane [Motion Picture]. Produced for Shadow Films.

Morrison, V. (1968). Astral Weeks [Recorded by V. Morrison]. New York.

Morrison, V. (1985). A Sense of Wonder [Recorded by V. Morrison]. On *A Sense of Wonder.* Mercury Records.

Murdoch, I. (1970). *The Sovereign of Good.* London: Routledge & Kegan Paul.

Oldfield, M. (1973). Tubular Bells [Recorded by M. Oldfield]. Oxfordshire.

O'Rourke, D. (2004). 'Galileo' songtitle on *Since Kyabram* CD ©Declan O'Rourke. Dublin: BMG Music Publishing Ltd.

O'Rourke, D. (2007). 'A SONG OF LOVE AND HATE' songtitle on *A Big Bad Beautiful World* CD ©Declan O'Rourke. BMG Music Publishing Ltd.

Park, D. (2014). *The Poets Wives.* London, New York & Sydney: Bloomsbury Publishing.

Pashinyan, N. (2018). Speech given via Armenian television broadcast, no reference to actual source. Armenia.

Pontalis, J. B. (2003). *Windows.* Lincoln: Board of Regents of the University of Nebraska Press.

Rank, O. (1960). *The Myth of the Birth of the Hero and Other Writings.* P. Freund (Ed.). New York: Random House Inc.

Reiner, R. (Director). (1989). *When Harry Met Sally* [Motion Picture]. USA.

Schamess, G. (1999). Therapeutic Love and Its Permutations. *Clinical Social Work Journal 27*(Spring), 9–26.

Schaverien, J. (1992). *'The Revealing Image': Analytical Art Psychotherapy Theory and Practice.* London, New York & Canada: Routledge.

Segal, H. (1964). Introduction to the Work of Melanie Klein. In M. R. Khan (Ed.), *The International Psycho-Analytical Library no. 19.* London: Hogarth Press 92.

Siegal, A. M. (1996). *Heinz Kohut and the Psychology of the Self.* London & New York: Routledge Publications.

Smail, D. (1984). *Illusion and Reality. The Meaning of Anxiety.* London & Melbourne: J M Dent & Sons Ltd.

Storr, A. (1960). *The Integrity of the Personality.* Harmondsworth, Middlesex, England: William Heinmenn Ltd.

Storr, A. (1989). *Solitude.* London: Flamingo, Fontana Books.

Strean, H. (1994). *The Use of Humour in Psychotherapy.* Northvale, NJ & London: Jason Aronson Inc.

Suttie, I. D. (1988). *The Origins of Love and Hate*. Harmondsworth, Middlesex, London – this reference London: Kegan Paul, Penguin Books, this reference taken from Free Association Books.

Symington, N. (1986). *The Analytic Experience – Lectures from the Tavistock*. London: Free Association Books.

Symington, N. (2008). Generosity of Heart: Source of Sanity. *British Journal of Psychotherapy* Vol. 24, issue 4, pp. 488–500.

Symonds, P. M. (1946). *The Dynamics of Human Adjustment*. New York: Appleton-Century-Crofts Inc.

Tabori, P. (1959). *The Natural Science of Stupidity*. Philadelphia, PA & New York: Chilton Company Book Division.

Thompson, C. (1943). The Technique of Sandor Ferenczi: A Comment. *International Journal of Psychoanalysis 24*, 64–66.

Thorne. B. (1990a). *Individual Therapy – A Handbook*. W. Dryden (Ed.). Milton Keynes & Philadelphia, PA: University Press.

Thorne, B. (1990b). *Infinitely Beloved: The Challenge of Divine Intimacy (Sarum Theological Lectures*. Darton: Langman & Todd.

Underhill, E. (1911/1948). *Mysticism – A Study in the Nature and Development of Mans Spiritual Consciousness*. London: Methuen & co.

Vaculik, C. L., & Nash, G. (2022). *Integrative Arts Psychotherapy*. London & New York: Routledge.

Webber, A. (2017). *Breakthrough Moments in Arts-Based Psychotherapy*. London: Karnac Books Ltd.

Winnicott, D. (1965). *The Maturational Processes and the Facilitating Environment*. Washington, DC: International Universities Press.

Wood, C. (2011). *Navigating Art Therapy – A Therapists Companion*. London & New York: Routledge Press.

Yalom, I. D. (1980). *Existential Psychotherapy*. New York: Basic Books Inc.

Yalom, I. D. (1989). *Loves Executioner – And Other Tales of Psychotherapy*. London: Bloomsbury Publications.

Yalom, I. D. (2011). *Staring at the Sun Overcoming the Dread of Death*. London: Piatkus Publications.

Index

Note: **Bold** page numbers refer to tables; *italic* page numbers refer to figures and page numbers followed by "n" denote endnotes.